European Economies Since the Second World War

European Economies Since the Second World War

Edited by

Bernard J. Foley

First published in Great Britain 1998 by
MACMILLAN PRESS LTD
Houndmills, Basingstoke, Hampshire RG21 6XS and London
Companies and representatives throughout the world

A catalogue record for this book is available from the British Library.

ISBN 978-0-333-65325-8 ISBN 978-1-349-26565-7 (eBook)
DOI 10.1007/978-1-349-26565-7

First published in the United States of America 1998 by
ST. MARTIN'S PRESS, INC.,
Scholarly and Reference Division,
175 Fifth Avenue, New York, N.Y. 10010

ISBN 978-0-333-65325-8

Library of Congress Cataloging-in-Publication Data
European economies since the Second World War / edited by Bernard J. Foley.
p. cm.
Includes bibliographical references and index.
ISBN 978-0-333-65325-8
1. Europe—Economic conditions—1945- —Case studies. I. Foley, Bernard J. II. Title: European economies since World War Two.
HC240.E83614 1998
330.94'055—DC21 98-3222
CIP

This book is printed on paper suitable for recycling and made from fully managed and sustained forest sources.

10 9 8 7 6 5 4 3 2 1
07 06 05 04 03 02 01 00 99 98

Contents

Acknowledgements vi
List of Figures and Tables vii
Notes on Contributors ix
Introduction xi

1 The British Economy: Missing Out or Catching Up? 1
N. F. R. Crafts
2 West Germany 25
W. Carlin
3 France: A Case of Eurosclerosis? 48
B. J. Foley
4 Italy: After the Rewards of Growth, the Penalty of Debt 75
R. Ranieri
5 The Benelux Countries 102
P. M. Solar and H. J. de Jong
6 The Iberian Economies: Divergence to Convergence? 124
D. Corkill
7 Scandinavia 148
H. Sjögren
8 The Visegrad Countries of Eastern Europe 177
N. J. Swain

Index 209

Acknowledgements

The publishers are grateful to the following for permission to reproduce copyright material.

Dr Angus Maddison for tables 3.3, 7.1 and 7.3

The Office for National Statistics for table 1.6 taken from *Economic Trends Annual Supplement*, Office for National Statistics, Crown copyright 1997

Institut National de La Statistique et des Études Économiques for table 3.12

Istituto Nazionale di Statistica for table 4.2

The Office for Official Publications of the European Communities and the Directorate General II of the European Commission for tables 3.13, 3.14, 3.5, 6.1, 6.2, 6.3 and 6.4

H. de Jong and A. Soete for table 5.2

The OECD for table 7.11

Macmillan Press for table 8.1 taken from M. Lavigne (1995) *The Economics of Transition* Macmillan

Cambridge University Press for table 8.7 taken from *M. Myant (1989) The Czechoslovak Economy 1948–88* CUP

Table 8.3 is reproduced from *The Economic History of Eastern Europe 1919–1975* edited by M.C. Kaser, by permission of the Oxford University Press.

Every effort has been made to trace all copyright holders but if any have been inadvertently overlooked, the publisher will be pleased to make the necessary arrangements at the earliest opportunity.

Figures and Tables

Figures

2.1 West German manufacturing: profit rate and growth of capital stock 36

Tables

1.1 Economic performance in selected years 2
1.2 Aspects of competitiveness 4
1.3 Relative productivity in manufacturing and marketed services 6
1.4 Snapshots of macroeconomic policy 11
1.5 Snapshots of microeconomic policy 12
1.6 Real output per person employed, Level and Growth rate 16
1.7 Growth of real GDP per person, Actual and adjusted for changes in inequality of incomes 1973–92 20
2.1 Growth, unemployment and inflation in the post-war period 26
2.2 Export market and productivity performance in manufacturing, West Germany and the UK in the 1980s 32
3.1 Growth of GDP and GDP per capita, France 1938–94 52
3.2 Age of machine tools (1952) 54
3.3 Comparative levels of productivity (GDP per man hour 1913–92) 54
3.4 Annual average rate of growth of gross capital stock 55
3.5 Average tariff rates, EC(6) 56
3.6 Annual average rate of growth of output and exports 57
3.7 Shares of French trade with EC(6) countries 1949–68, EU(12) 1992 57
3.8 GDP growth and rate of unemployment in France and the EU(12) 59
3.9 Average rates of inflation, selected economies 60
3.10 Discretionary impact of fiscal policy 60
3.11 Sectoral distribution of employment and value added 1950–90 63
3.12 Manufacturing labour force by size of establishment 1962 65
3.13 General government expenditure 67
3.14 Non-Accelerating Inflation Rate of Unemployment (NAIRU) 70
4.1 Selected macro-indicators: Italy 1951–73 77
4.2 Share of the workforce employed by sector in selected years 78
4.3 Selected shares of the value of exports of goods by composition and destination 81
4.4 Percentage share of visible exports of selected mechanical goods going to the EEC 82

4.5 Selected structural indicators 1973–93 85
4.6 Selected macro-indicators: Italy 1973–95 86
4.7 Comparative performance indicators 1973–93 86
4.8 Movement in Italy's nominal and real effective exchange rates 1973–9 90
4.9 Shares of Italian visible exports by destination 1971–93 92
5.1 Major growth indicators: Belgium, the Netherlands and Northwest Europe 1938–94 103
5.2 Sectoral shares of employment: Belgium and the Netherlands 1937–87 105
6.1 Per capita income: Iberia 125
6.2 Average GDP growth rates 1960–95 132
6.3 Spain and Portugal: inflation and unemployment 137
6.4 Unit labour costs 141
7.1 Growth of per capita GDP: Denmark, Norway and Sweden vis-a-vis Western European average 150
7.2 Rate of unemployment in Denmark, Norway and Sweden 1960–94 152
7.3 Sectoral distribution of employment and value added 1950–90 155
7.4 Swedish outward and inward foreign direct investment 1961–90 158
7.5 Number of foreign establishments in Denmark and average number of employees 158
7.6 Foreign establishments in Denmark identified by host country 1991 159
7.7 Percentage distribution of business sector employment by enterprise size 1991 160
7.8 Expansion of the public sector in Scandinavia 1960–85 161
7.9 Annual percentage increase in productivity in the private sector 1960–88 162
7.10 Women in the total labour force 1950–90 169
7.11 Contractual and actual hours worked by full-time employees in manufacturing 1990 170
8.1 Growth rates in Central Eastern Europe 177
8.2 Gross industrial output in the early 1950s 182
8.3 Revisions in 1950 to First Five Year Plans 183
8.4 Indebtedness in Eastern Europe 1971–90 187
8.5 Selected economic indicators for the Visegrad Four 1989–95 192
8.6 Alternative methods of privatization 197
8.7 Annual average percentage growth rates of National Income and Total Factor Productivity in Czechoslovakia and Hungary 1961–84 203

Notes on Contributors

Wendy Carlin teaches in the Economics Department of University College London. She has published extensively on the post-war development of West Germany and more recently on the economics of reunification and the restructuring of the East German economy. Her current research interests include an international comparative study of corporate governance and economic performance and the economics of enterprise restructuring. She is co-author (with David Soskice) of *Macroeconomics and the Wage Bargain* (Oxford University Press).

David Corkhill is Reader in Iberian Studies at Manchester Metropolitan University. He has written mainly on Portugal's economy and politics. His new book, *The Europeanisation of a National Economy: the Portuguese Case,* will be published by Routledge in 1998.

Nicholas Crafts is Professor of Economic History at the London School of Economics. He has published extensively on the development of the British Economy. Among his most recent contributions are *British Relative Economic Decline 1870–1995* Social Market Foundation and *Economic Growth in Europe Since 1945,* edited with G. Toniolo, Cambridge University Press.

Bernard Foley teaches in the Department of Economic and Social History at the University of Liverpool. His publications include books and articles on urban and housing policy and developments in national and international capital markets. He is the co-editor of *Regenerating the Cities* (Manchester University Press) and author of *Capital Markets* (Macmillan).

Herman de Jong lectures in economic history in the Faculty of Economics at the University of Groningen and fellow of the N. W. Posthumus Institute for Economic and Social History. He has written on Dutch inland trade and transport in the nineteenth century and on the long-run performance of Dutch manufacturing in the twentieth century.

Ruggero Ranieri is currently Research Associate and Jean Monnet Lecturer in the Department of History at the University of Manchester. He has edited books and published articles on the history of Italy's industrial development and Italy's role in the process of European integration.

Hans Sjögren is Associate Professor in Economic History at Linköping University having previously been at Uppsala University. His research interests cover business history, financial systems and financial crises. His publications include books such as *Bank och Näringsliv* (*Banking and Industry*) and *Obligationsmarknaden* (*The Bond Market*) and several articles dealing with aspects of banking and financial distress.

Peter Solar teaches at Vesalius College at the Vrije Universiteit, Brussels. He has written extensively on a variety of subjects including the post-war performance of the Belgian economy.

Nigel Swain teaches in the Department of Economic and Social History at the University of Liverpool. His books include *Hungary: the Rise and Fall of Feasible Socialism* (Verso) and *Collective Farms which Work* (Cambridge University Press). He has also published a number of articles dealing with the problems of the Hungarian economy and the economies of Eastern Europe. He is particularly interested in the difficulties confronting the rural sector.

Introduction

This book is not concerned with the European Economy as a whole, hence there is little discussion of the range of supranational institutions which have developed in Europe since the 1950s. Here we are concerned with the post-war economic history of a number of European Economies. Such an enterprise poses several problems. In the first place there is the issue of which economies to consider: some take the view that every case deserves attention but, given limitations of space, this is not possible in this volume. Hence there is a problem of where to draw the line. We have dealt with it by excluding those small economies which cannot easily be fitted into a larger grouping – specifically economies such as Ireland, Austria and Greece.

In the current volume therefore we have taken the core large economies – West Germany, France, Italy and the UK – as important in their own right while extending our purview to encompass those smaller, peripheral economies we perceive as more or less cognate groups. Hence Scandinavia, Iberia, Benelux and the Visegrad states (Poland, Hungary, the Czech Republic and Slovakia) are regarded perhaps controversially as relatively coherent entities. There is nevertheless a rationale for treating them in this way. Scandinavia, for example, comprises a group of societies which are culturally similar and for a long time enjoyed an extraordinarily wide social democratic consensus about the subordination of the market economy to the imperatives of the welfare state. This was sufficiently distinctive as to give birth to the notion of a 'Swedish model' of political economy shared by Norway and Denmark to some degree.

Portugal and Spain by contrast featured two of the most durable personal dictatorships in Europe under Salazar and Franco respectively. Portugal never attempted to follow the path of autarky pursued by Franco's Spain between 1939 and 1959 and was indeed a founder member of the Organization for European Economic Cooperation (precursor to the OECD) in 1948 and of EFTA in 1960. Nevertheless, both regimes were characterized by a rejection of liberalism, suspicion of market capitalism and very heavy-handed, sometimes irrational, intervention in the economy by the authorities.

The Visegrad countries of course also endured dictatorship, but of the communist variety and largely imposed by their giant neighbour, the USSR. They were pushed into adopting the Stalinist model of central planning and had to cope with its priorities and idiosyncrasies for some four decades. Hence in both Iberia and Eastern Europe 'economic rationality' was subordinated to political forces in ways which were very different from mature capitalist societies. The inclusion of a chapter on the Visegrad Four may strike the reader as somewhat out of place as there is no discussion of the other economies of the former Soviet bloc. Nevertheless, we considered such an inclusion desirable as moves by Poland, Hungary and the Czech Republic toward the European mainstream via membership of the OECD and NATO as well as candidate membership of the EU, place them in a different category than Russia and its immediate satellites. In the latter cases, subordination to Russia was complete while many peoples in the former USSR, including the Russians themselves, have historically been ambivalent about the degree to which their country is truly European. Some analysis of Poland, Hungary and the former Czechoslovakia is warranted therefore, partly because their post-war history is less well known and partly because this history may mean that they will constitute 'problem children' within the EU in the near-term future. For these reasons students of European history will find Chapter 8 intrinsically interesting while it will yield insight into the problems these new democracies may pose for the European Union.

Having decided which economies to include, the second problem is how far should one stress the common features of economic performance? There is a template of sorts. The main themes which come through are: the exceptionally rapid growth of the post-war boom between 1945 and 1973; the significance of the liberalization of international trade in the 1960s; the slowing down of growth after 1974; the acceleration of inflation and rise in unemployment in the 1970s; and finally and very significantly, the shift from the state to the market allied to sweeping financial liberalization in the 1980s.

These constitute some of the main themes of the volume but there are significant variations: not every economy fits the template precisely. The UK, for example, appears to have 'missed out' on the early growth surge – the so-called Golden Age. Why this was the case and whether the UK has repaired the slippage as a result of Thatcherite policies (and if so, at what cost) is addressed in Chapter 1. Spain and Portugal were also underperformers in the decade of the 1950s, but whereas Spain's economy stagnated, Portugal's expanded at about 4 per cent per annum – respectable at first sight but not enough to close the gap with its more prosperous neighbours. The explanation for this seems to lie, as argued in Chapter 6, in the stifling political economy of both countries. After 1959, however, when greater openness and some elements of economic liberalization were allowed, both economies picked up speed dramatically. Indeed, the acceleration of growth in the latter part of the period was sufficiently high to lift them into the ranks of the fastest growers. How far the political reforms of the 1970s, reinforced by the continued shift to the market and EU membership in 1986, has helped or hindered continued convergence toward the affluent economies of northern Europe is also discussed from a critical perspective.

The experience of the underperformers contrasts with the core economies of what became the EEC in the late 1950s – West Germany, France, Italy and the Netherlands. In these economies the experience of growth and structural transformation throughout the 1950s and 1960s was, by historical standards, extraordinary. Abundant supplies of labour, structural shifts from agriculture and high rates of capital accumulation fed the recovery and growth process, but a great deal of evidence now points to the phenomenon of 'catch-up' as highly significant. Catch-up implies making up lost ground and in this case relates to the ability to close the substantial productivity gap which had emerged between the economies of Europe and that of the US as a result of the combined effects of the inter-war depression and the Second World War. Of course, recovery and growth were also helped by a benign international policy environment in which low inflation, stable exchange rates, pressure for the reduction and elimination of trade barriers, and the diffusion of technology figured strongly.

One obvious result of this process was that by the 1980s West Germany had been transformed into the economic superpower of the region, as Chapter 2 demonstrates. This remains the case in spite of the unexpectedly large costs of absorbing the former East Germany and the baleful effects of record unemployment on West Germany's hitherto resilient institutional structures. France and Italy also benefited from catch-up during the Golden Age, but in both cases from very early on there was a conscious realization that a great deal of backwardness characterized their respective economies, hence modernization was high on the political agenda. In both cases too the opening of their economies as a result of the Treaty of Rome in 1958 was a decisive influence. The successes and failures of modernization – in particular Italy's difficulties with the South – as well as the later problems which beset each economy as growth slowed down are the subject of Chapters 3 and 4. For the Benelux countries the picture is slightly more complicated in that Holland was a participant from early on in the growth surge whereas Belgium exhibited similar symptoms to the UK in the 1950s – slow growth and a defensive mind-set. By the 1960s, however, Belgium had joined the high-growth club. How and why that occurred are explored in detail in Chapter 5.

By contrast, catch-up plays a much smaller role for the economies of Scandinavia – particularly Sweden – which had enjoyed very high levels of productivity and income since before the war. These economies were aided by the degree of political consensus which they enjoyed as well as the active labour market policies which maintained the quality of human capital they were able to deploy. Even here, however, the consensual mode of decision taking which kept the lid on inflation via 'solidaristic' incomes policies and sustained employment in the 1970s came under severe pressure in the face of escalating public deficits in the 1980s. Thus in Denmark and Sweden at least, the old consensus no longer pertains while Norway's position has been sustained by the judicious exploitation of oil and gas, as demonstrated in Chapter 7.

The Visegrad countries experienced a period of rapid growth in the 1950s but as the years of extensive growth via the mobilization of underemployed resources gave way to the need for intensive growth, the grip of communist orthodoxy proved stifling. This produced an increasingly desperate search for appropriate planning/motivational mechanisms – none of which dealt with the root of the problem – the lack of a reasonably coherent structure of incentives to encourage greater productivity and the efficient allocation of resources. Their story is one of decline and disintegration, as shown in Chapter 8. The question of how successful the transition to market economies has been thus far is discussed from a sceptical perspective, particularly in relation to the competence and commitment of the political elites which have come to the fore.

If the economic experience of the Golden Age in Europe was not quite uniform, nor was the policy reaction to the slowdown after 1973: some governments tried to deal with the stagnation via expansionary policies only to experience accelerating inflation with little impact on unemployment. Others were less tolerant of inflation, but most of Europe faced increasingly problematical public sector deficits, volatile exchange rates, calls for protectionism and rising nominal interest rates – although given the heights to which inflation soared in the 1970s, negative real interest rates were experienced in several countries. The explanation for the slowdown is usually posed in terms of the shocks to the world economy from the oil crises of the 1970s, but there is some evidence that a slowdown would in any case have occurred. Profit rates were already under pressure and the continuing productivity gains from catch-up were unlikely to be available for much longer.

The inability of governments to reduce unemployment and to restore the status quo ante also brought into question the post-war consensus on the role of the state in the management of the economy. This was partly a victory of ideas for the politics of the New Right but it also reflected events in the world economy. In particular the 'Mitterrand experiment' between 1981 and 1983 in France can be viewed as a signal event – a clear demonstration that the state's capacity to go it alone, that is, to undertake independent expansionary economic policy in the context of a global recession, was limited in a world of open economies and highly mobile capital. The thrust of policy since then, in France as elsewhere in Europe, has been on maintaining strict monetary discipline, containing inflation and achieving budgetary consolidation.

Even if the worst of the inflationary 1970s and 1980s is now over, deep problems persist in many European economies, in the form of sluggish growth and severe unemployment (the latter contrasts markedly with the record of the US and more recently the UK). Political elites in Europe now accept that changes are required to make the economies of Europe more flexible while maintaining control of public spending, but implementing such change in the face of entrenched vested interests is a different matter. If, in addition, exchange rate flexibility and control of monetary policy are given up in the quest for European Monetary Union these structural problems may be exacerbated for some economies or sub-regions. There is a great deal of institutional inertia built into many European economies which is decidedly unhelpful in the face of growing competition from the countries of the Pacific Rim and a resurgent US. Indeed, this now constitutes a major challenge to the model of social partnership which some European countries wish to maintain and which the new Labour government in Britain seeks to emulate.

Bernard Foley
The University of Liverpool, 1997

1 The British Economy: Missing Out or Catching Up?

N. F. R. Crafts

INTRODUCTION

The central feature of the early post-war British economy is relative economic decline, that is, the overtaking of British income and productivity levels by other faster growing countries. In the 1980s, many people began to believe that this process had ceased or even been reversed by the dramatic changes of the Thatcher years. In this chapter three specific questions about growth are discussed:

- How bad was British growth performance in the early post-war period?
- Have the failings which led to relative economic decline through the 1960s and particularly the 1970s subsequently been redeemed?
- What are the policy lessons from the post-war experience of economic growth in Britain?

In addressing these issues, it will be useful to distinguish between three different levels of explanation for growth outcomes and prospects. First, we can look at proximate sources of growth, namely investment rates, skill formation, innovative activity, and so on, reflected in the growth of factor inputs and productivity. Second, we can explore the underlying reasons for the behaviour of these proximate variables in terms of actions by managers, workers and policy makers and the institutional arrangements under which these were taken. Third, we can consider the fundamentals which sustain these actions: here we need to examine the incentive structures facing decision makers in both government and the private sector grounded on the one hand in the pursuit of votes and on the other in market forces.

After 1979, the new framework of Thatcherism changed the balance of policy objectives toward giving higher priority to economic efficiency and growth with less emphasis on economic security and reducing income inequalities. In so doing the political authorities abandoned both the post-war settlement and the assumptions on which policy had been conducted by both parties since 1945. This gives rise to a further intriguing but highly contentious question:

Was the 'Thatcher Experiment' worth it?

To answer this it is necessary to look at the trade-offs between growth and other policy objectives, to assess the impact of policy changes on outcomes and to make value judgements about the weight to be given to different components of economic welfare. Not surprisingly, there is no consensus here, but explicit consideration of the issues involved will provide valuable insights into the political economy of the post-war period.

AN OVERVIEW OF ECONOMIC PERFORMANCE

Before proceeding to a detailed consideration of the questions posed above, it is important to establish the outlines of British economic performance. Table 1.1 reports some quantitative evidence with respect to key objectives of policy.

Table 1.1 *Economic performance in selected years*

	1950	*1973*	*1979*	*1994*
Real GDP/person	6847	11992	13087	16371
Unemployment	1.8	3.1	5.0	9.6
Inflation	4.5	7.6	16.5	4.5
Growth	na	2.5	1.5	1.5
Gini coefficient (1)	35.5	33.1	33.5	
(2)		25.5	24.8	33.7

Sources:
Real GDP/Person: measured in (purchasing power parity adjusted) international dollars of 1990, Maddison (1995).
Unemployment: OECD standardized measure (%),Layard, Nickell and Jackman (1994).
Inflation: last 5 years average for the GDP deflator (%), ONS (1996).
Growth: average annual growth rate of real GDP/person since previous benchmark year (%).
Gini coefficient: of inequality of income where (1) is based on Personal After Tax Income and (2) is based on Equivalent Disposable Household Income, Atkinson (1995). The final entry is for the latest available year, 1991 (not 1994).

Table 1.1 shows that incomes have risen throughout the post-war period such that by 1994 real GDP per person was about 2.4 times the 1950 level. At the same time, this has not been enough to prevent a big move down the international league table such that Britain fell from sixth in 1950 to eleventh in 1973, thirteenth in 1979 and seventeenth in 1994 (Crafts 1996). The growth rate of 2.5 per cent recorded between 1950 and 1973 was among the lowest in the OECD, but at 1.5 per cent this was about average for 1979–94. In the 1950s, relatively slow growth was viewed complacently by policy makers, no doubt partly because they judged economic performance by the standards of the inter-war period. By the 1960s, however, in the era of 'growthmanship', interventions to promote higher investment and faster growth proliferated. After the Golden Age of the early post-war period, European growth has slowed down markedly since the early 1970s, but by a good deal less in Britain than elsewhere.

During the long post-war boom, unemployment in Britain, as elsewhere in Europe, was remarkably low, although rising slowly as time went on. The early 1980s saw a steep rise in unemployment, but by the mid-1990s this had declined somewhat and unemployment rates were below those in most other large European economies and continuing on a downward path. Inflation outcomes were also basically similar to many other European countries, with the low inflation of the early decades giving way in the 1970s and early 1980s to the worst peacetime inflation ever recorded. After two severe recessions and several policy experiments, by the 1990s low inflation had been re-established. Control of inflation has generally been a good deal less successful than in Germany or Switzerland, however.

Where Britain stands out most from the general European experience is in terms of recent trends in income distribution. Of the 16 countries in a recent OECD study 'the UK exhibit[ed] by far the largest increase in income inequality in the 1980s' (Atkinson et al. 1995). Table 1.1 reports the Gini coefficient, a much-used summary statistic of income distribution, which takes the value 0 if there is perfect equality and 100 if income is concentrated in the hands of one household. The data are not available on a consistent basis throughout, but the general picture is clear enough: until around the end of the 1970s there was little change followed by a marked increase in inequality.

Recent years have seen a proliferation of reports on 'competitiveness', and since 1994 the British government has published an annual White Paper on the subject. The definition of national competitiveness that the British government uses follows the OECD and is as follows:

> the degree to which the country can, under free and fair market conditions, produce goods and services which meet the tests of international markets, while simultaneously maintaining and expanding the real incomes of its people over the long term.

The original Competitiveness White Paper goes on to point out that to be competitive in this sense requires continuing long-run productivity improvement and a performance in this respect that compares favourably with that of other countries (DTI 1994, p. 9). The Department of Trade and Industry's annual look at competitiveness emphasizes the supply side of the economy and a variety of diagnostics of the economy's capability for raising output per person relative to other countries in future. In effect, this is an analysis of the likelihood of escaping relative economic decline. Table 1.2 reports in a similar fashion for a longer time period.

The estimates of world market share in manufactured trade are of interest as a diagnostic of the type suggested by the competitiveness literature and econometric research does suggest that the decline in this statistic is closely related to relative British weakness in innovative activities and skill formation (Greenhalgh 1990; Oulton 1996). A parallel decline in another (imperfect) indicator of innovative activity, the share of foreign patents in the US is also shown in Table 1.2. In each case the period of rapid decline is during the Golden Age. The contrast with Germany, which early in this century had similar export market and patenting performance, is striking – in 1992 Germany still had an exports share of 19.6 per cent and a patent share of 15.5 per cent.

Table 1.2 *Aspects of competitiveness*

	1950 (%)	*1973* (%)	*1979* (%)	*1992* (%)
Share of world manufactured exports	25.4	9.1	9.1	7.9
Share of foreign patents in US	36.0	12.6	10.8	7.5
R&D/GDP	1.7	2.2	2.1	2.2
Investment/GDP	14.9	18.3	19.4	17.3
18-year-olds with >2 A levels	5	13	13	20
TFP growth in business sector	na	2.6	0.6	1.5

Sources:
Exports: Maizels (1963), CSO (1992), ONS (1996).
Patents: Pavitt and Soete (1982), OECD (1995).
Investment: OECD (1996a).
A levels: Department for Education and Employment (1995) and various predecessor publications.
R&D: United Nations (1964), OECD (1995).
TFP: OECD (1996b); estimates relate to 1960–73, 1973–9 and 1979–94 respectively.

Investment as a share of GDP was much higher post-war than in any previous period, but lagged behind most other countries. This was due partly to a lower level of residential construction, especially compared with countries with greater war damage to repair, but, even allowing for this, in the Golden Age leading European economies tended to invest a few percentage points more, and this is still the case recently. The differences are not large enough, however, to account for more than a small part of the British growth shortfall. By contrast, in the 1950s and 1960s, Britain spent much more on research and development than pre-war and as a proportion of GDP this was second only to the US among OECD countries. However, the problem here lay in the effectiveness of the spending rather than its magnitude. In the recent past, R&D spending has grown slowly relative to other countries.

In the last ten years or so, education and training have been generally regarded in public debate as Britain's Achilles' heel. Such claims need to be carefully qualified. The real weaknesses have probably been in vocational training and in the standards of literacy and numeracy of the lower half of the ability distribution. In particular, Britain appears to compare badly with Germany in this regard. In 1979, the first year for which a comparison is available, 23 per cent of the British labour force had intermediate qualifications compared with 61 per cent in Germany, and a similar gap still existed in 1988 (Steedman 1990). The qualifications gap was noticeable among workers of all ages (O'Mahony and Wagner 1994) and must therefore have been quite long-standing. By contrast, at the 'elite' end of educational provision, Britain's achievements compare well with its peer group and the output of persons with A levels and degree qualifications has expanded rapidly, particularly in recent years.

Table 1.2 also reports TFP growth in the business sector. The business sector is all of GDP except that produced by government, much of which comprises non-marketed services where productivity measurement is highly problematic. TFP stands for 'total factor productivity' and takes account of the use of both capital and labour, whereas the more familiar notion of labour productivity simply measures output per employee or per hour worked. TFP growth results from the more efficient use of inputs, reflecting, for example, reallocations of resources, better economic organization, longer production runs, and so on, and from the acquisition and effective use of new technological knowledge. TFP growth can generally be expected to be much lower in the government sector than in the business sector.

TFP growth is central to long-run increases in living standards and thus to competitiveness; long-run growth potential is proportional to TFP growth and for an economy like Britain, TFP growth of 1.5 per cent per year would imply long-run growth of output a little over 2 per cent. In the absence of TFP growth, higher investment in skills or machines tends to run into diminishing returns. Historically, however, TFP growth has partly reflected transitory components such as the rundown of low productivity traditional agriculture and the technological catching-up of leading economies by more backward ones as well as the underlying long-run rate of innovation which is the key factor in competitiveness.

Total Factor Productivity growth in the 1960s was considerably higher than recently, both in Britain and elsewhere in Europe. The 2.6 per cent per year TFP growth of 1960–73 reported in Table 1.2 was eleventh of 20 countries for which the OECD gives estimates, while the 1.5 per cent for 1979–94 is fifth of the same group of countries. The Golden Age in Europe was characterized by a very high transitory component of TFP growth based on catch-up, structural change and moves to mass production underwritten by trade liberalization and technology transfer. Britain had less to gain from these sources of growth than most other European countries given her relatively advanced starting point in 1950. How to interpret recent British TFP performance is fundamental to answering the second of the four questions posed in the introduction and it is considered in some depth later on.

Table 1.3 *Relative productivity in manufacturing and marketed services (UK = 100 in each year)*

	1950	*1973*	*1979*	*1995*
Manufacturing:				
France	90.4	130.6	149.1	122.1
Japan	45.2	90.5	113.8	104.4
US	245.7	186.6	179.9	143.5
West Germany	97.5	142.0	163.7	116.8
Marketed Services:				
France		132.3	143.2	136.0
US		156.9	150.3	137.8
West Germany		100.6	115.4	133.5

Sources:
For manufacturing, Pilat (1996), extended to 1950 and interpolated to 1979 using van Ark (1993), and for services, O'Mahony et al. (1996). Please note that the Pilat figures are comparisons between the other countries and the US and were originally expressed using the US as the base country. The final year for the services comparison is 1993, not 1995. Productivity is measured as value-added per hour worked.

The most dramatic aspect of British productivity change has been in manufacturing. This should not be overplayed, given that manufacturing only accounted for 35 per cent of total employment in 1950 and fell to 20 per cent in 1990, but it has been much analysed and plays a large part in most assessments of both policy and performance. Table 1.3 reports on hourly manufacturing labour productivity in other countries relative to the UK, making a comparison relative to whatever the UK level was in each year. All four other countries have made substantial inroads on the lead that the US had established by 1950 at the end of a period when that country had forged far ahead relatively free of the adverse impact of war and was blessed by a large domestic market and abundant natural resources in a disintegrating world economy.

Through to 1979, however, it is clear that other economies were much more successful than Britain at reducing the initial manufacturing productivity gap. Since that date, labour productivity growth in British manufacturing has revived and some of the ground lost earlier to France, Germany and Japan has been recovered. This owes a good deal to a shake-out of inefficient firms and the overstaffing which characterized much of British manufacturing in the 1960s and 1970s (Crafts 1991).

Table 1.3 also reports labour productivity comparisons for marketed services which now represent around 40 per cent of employment. Here the pattern appears to be rather different. Two related points stand out. First, at the end of the Golden Age, productivity gaps with Germany and the US in services were considerably less than in manufacturing, while by 1995 this was no longer the case. Second, as the table implies, the time series pattern of productivity growth in services does not exhibit a surge in the 1980s, and for 1979–89 was 2.4 per cent per year compared with 4.2 per cent in manufacturing (O'Mahony et al. 1996).

HOW BAD WAS BRITISH GROWTH PERFORMANCE FROM THE 1950s THROUGH THE 1970s?

Evaluations of growth performance require careful handling. It is necessary to assess what was feasible as well as to look at positions in an international growth league table. It is also important to investigate the constraints on growth and to consider the policy response to these problems. Finally, in judging policy, it must be remembered that there may be trade-offs between growth and other objectives and to recall that, at bottom, politicians deal in votes not growth rates. In other words, growth outcomes have to be normalized for exogenous differences in circumstances and it should be recognized that 'failure' may be either unavoidable or at least the result of rational decisions.

Proximate Sources of Growth

It must be accepted that the UK could not have been among the fastest growing countries during the Golden Age. At the outset there was less scope for rapid growth from catch-up and post-war reconstruction. Other European economies could gain from the shift of labour out of agriculture and into sectors with higher productivity, but this was not an option in Britain: only 5 per cent of the labour force was in agriculture compared with 22 per cent in West Germany, 28 per cent in France and 45 per cent in Italy (Maddison 1991). There is a strong inverse rank correlation among European countries between initial (1950) income level and subsequent growth. Nevertheless, the British growth rate of real GDP per person at 2.5 per cent per year over 1950–73 was about 0.6 percentage points below each of Denmark, Sweden and Switzerland, the other three European countries with similar or higher income levels. Similarly, a regression analysis of regional growth in Europe found that, given initial income levels and employment structure, real GDP per person in British regions grew 0.5 per cent per year slower than elsewhere in Europe (Crafts 1995).

Maddison (1996) provides a growth accounting exercise which probes deeper into the proximate sources of growth but is based on fairly strong assumptions which are not universally accepted. His comparison of Britain with France and West Germany suggests that TFP growth rather than investment was much the most important reason for slower British growth. A good part of the TFP growth shortfall is attributed by Maddison to opportunities for catch-up and structural change not available to Britain, but in each case there is an 'unexplained' gap of about 1 percentage point per year which represents either measurement error or a shortfall not attributable to a different initial economic structure. Broadberry (1996) plausibly argues that Maddison's procedure somewhat underestimates the contribution of structural change to slower TFP growth in Britain and his calculations indicate that the TFP growth shortfall was probably nearer to 0.7 per cent per year.

Beyond the Proximate Sources of Growth

Given that the UK underperformed in growth terms by somewhere between 0.5 and 1 per cent per year during the Golden Age, where did its disadvantages lie? Disappointing productivity performance has variously been ascribed to some or all of the following: poor management of firms, inadequate training of workers, unfortunate industrial relations, and misdirected policy interventions. These led both to misallocations of resources and to failure to exploit the opportunities offered by new technology. Although this list would command quite general agreement, the weighting of each of these elements is controversial and there is no easy way of quantifying their relative contributions.

While examples of spectacular management failure, such as that at British Leyland, in the late 1960s and early 1970s were atypical, the literature is generally quite critical of British management in this period. British management operated in a financial system which differed from the European norm. In particular, British firms were uniquely (in a European context) exposed to hostile take-overs while being more reliant on outside investors and less closely monitored by banks than was normal elsewhere in Europe. Compared with German managers, British managers throughout the post-war period have been much more likely to have qualifications in accountancy rather than engineering (Broadberry and Wagner 1996). It is clear that the educational background of British management was in the early post-war period substantially inferior to that of their American counterparts and direct comparisons suggested that American managed firms operating in Britain tended in all sectors to have a substantial productivity advantage over their British rivals (Dunning 1958). As the 1960s wore on, an increasing amount of top management time was directed towards acquisitions as a spectacular merger boom developed in which pursuit of size rather than efficiency or long-term strategy became the best way to survive (Singh 1975).

Inefficient use of labour was a common complaint against British industry and frequently attributed to management failure – for example, in 21 out of 23 cases reviewed by Pratten and Atkinson (1976) management weaknesses were identified as problematical. Account should, however, also be taken of industrial relations, in which Britain was also an outlier, the only case in Europe of powerful, long-established but decentralized trade unionism (Crouch 1993). Here was both an unfortunate historical legacy and a system which deteriorated further in post-war conditions as shop stewards increased in number to about 175 000 in 1968 and 300 000 in 1978. Their power also increased considerably over this period (Batstone 1988). Prais (1981) provided detailed case study evidence for the 1960s and 1970s which showed that in 6 out of 10 industries that he investigated (brewing, metal boxes, motor vehicles, newspapers, tobacco and tyres) increases in productivity had been retarded by problems of negotiating appropriate manning levels when technological improvements became available. Bean and Crafts (1996) found econometrically for a cross-section of manufacturing during 1954–79 that where (the peculiarly British) multiple unionism, as opposed to union presence per se, existed, this resulted in a reduction of between 0.75 and 1 percentage point per year in TFP growth.

Given the difficulties in measuring its impact, it is probable that shortfalls in training are reflected in lower measured TFP growth. There seems to be widespread agreement that vocational training in early post-war Britain left a lot to be desired. The traditional apprenticeship training mode declined in engineering – whereas 8.7 per cent of employees were apprentices in 1938, this fell to about 4.5 per cent in the 1950s and 1960s and then to 3.4 per cent in 1980 (Broadberry and Wagner 1996). Unlike countries such as Germany, Britain did not develop a set of institutions centred on internal labour markets and employers' organizations to correct market failures and to make it worth while for juveniles to train (Soskice 1994). In 1975, 27 000 persons obtained engineering qualifications at Craft and Technician levels compared with 103 000 in Germany (Steedman 1988). The British vocational qualifications and productivity gaps in manufacturing were correlated (O'Mahony and Wagner 1994) and an upper bound estimate of the adverse impact on productivity is about 0.4 percentage points per year.

Throughout the Golden Age there was a great deal of experimentation in economic policy making involving efforts to raise the growth rate. Surprisingly, to modern eyes, supplyside policy did not focus effectively on addressing market failures in human capital formation or the diffusion of technological knowledge. Instead, the thrust of policy was to subsidize physical capital, to nationalize and/or not to privatize, to finance prestige research projects in aerospace and nuclear power, to promote national champion firms and in addition to maintain a highly distortionary tax system. In addition, short-run macroeconomic considerations often took priority.

To some extent, similar policy errors were made throughout Europe, but overall the damage done in Britain was relatively high, as international comparisons have often shown. Thus Tanzi (1969) concluded that the British tax system was the least conducive to growth of any OECD country that he studied; Adams (1989) found that early entry into the European Community provided an antidote to misdirected industrial policies in France that was absent in Britain; Kormendi and Meguire (1985) showed econometrically that unpredictable macroeconomic policies hurt growth more in Britain than in any other major European economy, the share of investment in nationalized industries was unusually high and the return on it astonishingly low (Vickers and Yarrow 1988); while Ergas (1987) contrasted the success of German technology policy in speeding up diffusion with the failure of Britain's more grandiose ambitions.

Policy Objectives and Constraints

Decisions about the accumulation of human and physical capital and innovation are influenced by institutions and economic policies. Indeed, key institutional arrangements (for example, systems of industrial relations and of corporate governance) typically are the result of government action and reforms require intervention. Democratic governments tend to worry much more about the short term rather than the long-term effects of policy. Consistent with these remarks, Price and Sanders (1994) demonstrate econometrically that government popularity throughout the post-war period has depended significantly on short-term macroeconomic outcomes, with the voters punishing governments for increases in unemployment and higher rates of inflation.

Moreover, those who fear that they may lose from change may easily be a majority and create a bias in favour of the status quo, particularly since it is not usually possible for politicians credibly to promise to compensate losers from policy reforms which will be of overall benefit (Fernandez and Rodrik 1991). Alternatively, it may be that gains exceed losses from change, but the former are spread thinly while the latter are concentrated such that there are votes to be lost but none to be gained. Thus it may often be politically rational not to implement growth-promoting supply side reforms and this seems to be a recurrent theme in early post-war British economic history.

Macroeconomic policy took a high profile and the pursuit of macroeconomic objectives frequently took precedence over supply side considerations. As Table 1.4 reports, the policy framework was very different from that of the recent past. The prevailing economic orthodoxy was Keynesian and, from the early 1950s, active demand management policies were employed. It was widely believed that this could deliver low levels of unemployment and prevent a return to the slump conditions of the 1930s, and that voters would severely punish governments who failed in this respect. At the same time, policy makers were persistently worried that, in tight labour markets, the collective bargaining system would promote high wage inflation. The implication was a continuing series of efforts to arrive at agreements between the government and organized labour to achieve wage restraint in return for other policy commitments, culminating in the so-called 'Social Contract' of the mid-1970s. This had an important implication; namely that, throughout, reform of industrial relations was effectively a no-go area. The fate of the Heath government in 1974 seemed to underline this message in that its attempt at radical reform, via the Industrial Relations Act 1972, foundered in the face of union opposition. The defeat of the government in the wake of the miners' dispute of 1973 led to a reversal of the legislation by the following Labour administration.

Table 1.4 *Snapshots of macroeconomic policy*

	Regime	*Policy instruments*	*Objectives*
1950	Bretton Woods	Fiscal	Full employment
		Wage restraint	BP surplus
		1949 Devaluation	Price stability
1973	Discretionary	Fiscal	Full employment
	Demand Management	Monetary	Growth
		Incomes	Price stability
1979	Medium-Term	Monetary targets	Price stability
	Financial Strategy	PSBR targets	Disinflation
1994	Ken & Eddie	Interest rates	Inflation
		Inflation targets	Lower output gap

At the outset, Britain had faced formidable problems of reconstruction. In particular, war left a legacy of a horrendous balance of external payments and a large overhang of unspent money balances, the result of forced saving during war-time, which posed a massive threat to price stability. Eliminating these problems through market forces would have implied a rise of more than 100 per cent in the price level and a still greater nominal devaluation of the pound. Not surprisingly, this was deemed unacceptable, controls on prices, imports and consumption were retained into the 1950s and top priority was given to raising exports and enlisting the support of both sides of industry for this goal. All in all, this was not a situation conducive to good supply side policies (Crafts 1993).

During the 1950s and 1960s this war-time legacy faded away and policy was conducted in a relatively benign world environment. Nevertheless, Britain became somewhat notorious for its 'stop–go' policies and, as noted above, it may be that attempts at fine-tuning the economy actually had adverse effects on investment and growth. It became harder to combine low unemployment with price stability as trade union membership and militancy rose. Frustration with the discipline enforced by the commitment to a fixed exchange rate under the Bretton Woods system gave rise first to devaluation in 1967 and then the move to floating in 1972.

The aggregate supply shocks of the 1970s delivered a fatal blow to the Keynesian era and also exposed clearly once again the constraints that macroeconomic pressures put on supply side policy. When disinflation was introduced from 1975, incomes policy was centre-stage in an attempt to regain price stability without jeopardizing employment, and again the cooperation of trade unions was seen as the key to success. This led to attempts to develop active industrial policies, precluded reform of taxation and confirmed the status quo in industrial relations. As one recent commentary concluded,

> The recurring theme of this review of the 1974–79 government has been that of the damage done by its anxiety not to offend the trade union movement. (Brown 1991, p. 226)

In terms of microeconomic policies, these years also seem like a foreign country from today's vantage point and this is reflected, rather imperfectly, in Table 1.5. Interventions sought both to promote investment and growth and to redistribute income and eliminate poverty. The most intense developments of industrial policy took place in the 1940s and from the mid-1960s through the late 1970s. Continuing themes were an emphasis on subsidizing physical investment and, as elsewhere in Europe, the promotion of national champions, that is, domestic firms that it was hoped would be technological leaders and successful exporters.

Table 1.5 *Snapshots of microeconomic policy*

	1950	*1973*	*1979*	*1994*
Investment by nationalized industries (% total fixed capital formation)	16.8	14.0	15.8	5.0
Industrial subsidies (grant equivalent % GDP)	0.4	2.9	2.8	0.1
Unemployment benefit/wages %	0.19	0.31	0.31	0.16
Current government receipts (% GDP)	31.1	36.3	38.3	37.3
Top rate of income tax %	97.5	88.75	88.75	40.0

Sources:
Nationalized industries investment: ONS (1996).
Industrial subsidies: Wren (1996).
Unemployment benefit/wages: (for single person), Metcalf et al. (1980) and OECD (1996b).
Current government receipts: (approximately the share of taxes in GDP), Middleton (1997) and OECD (1996a).
Top tax rate: Crafts (1991).

The 1940s and 1970s both saw substantial nationalizations. The results ranged from disappointing to disastrous, reflecting a failure to specify clear objectives or to develop adequate methods of control, and the consequent waste of investment and excessive employment of labour. The electricity industry epitomizes these problems, being used to support a disastrous programme of investment in nuclear power, paying well over the odds for power stations to support inefficient British suppliers and far too much for domestic coal. Its reliance on this latter source of energy sustained the size of the mining industry and gave undue bargaining power to the National Union of Mineworkers (Newbery and Green 1996). The policy reappraisals of the 1960s emphasized the pursuit of economies of scale and encouraged mergers, and the 1970s added to this a selective programme of soft loans seeking to pick winners. Subsequent assessments of these policies have been highly critical and they seem unlikely to have promoted productivity growth (Hindley and Richardson 1983; Morris and Stout 1985).

With regard to taxation, Britain was about average for European countries in terms of total taxes as a share of GDP, but was notable for its extremely high marginal tax rates. Taxes were much higher than before the war and this was inevitable given the increases in government spending on the welfare state combined with high defence outlays. The structure of taxation was established in the 1940s and has to be understood in terms of the context of holding down consumption of the middle and upper classes to free resources for exports. Nevertheless, given the widespread political support for reducing income inequality in post-war Britain, once in place, this approach to taxation proved very difficult to reform.

HAS RELATIVE ECONOMIC DECLINE BEEN REVERSED SINCE 1979?

In looking at relative economic decline, it is trend rates of growth that are the key. This makes an answer to the question quite difficult for several reasons. First, some influences on growth are transitory in that they reflect the transition to a new equilibrium level of productivity rather than a permanent change in the growth rate; a shake-out of inefficient firms and employment practices might be an example. Second, conversely, some changes that may have long-run effects on growth rates take a long while to show up and may even have a negative short-run impact, for example, macroeconomic stabilization measures. Third, it is necessary to distinguish trends from short-term fluctuations in time series of real GDP and many years of data may be required to identify a modest improvement with statistical confidence.

Moreover, public debate on this issue tends to be clouded by the fact that people have in mind at least three different questions, namely: (i) Has growth performance improved relative to our peer group?; (ii) Are growth prospects now superior to those of rival countries? (iii) Have growth outcomes been better than would have resulted with unchanged economic policies? Clearly, recent Conservative governments would believe that the answer to all three questions is 'yes', while their critics would dispute at least one of these claims.

The New Policy Framework

Given that economic policy changed so dramatically under Thatcherism, these developments will be sketched first before turning to assessing the impact on growth. The separate, but related, question of assessing the costs relative to the benefits is deferred until the following section. The poor performance of the 1970s economy killed off the post-war consensus and, in particular, the incoming government saw itself as seeking to escape from the trade unions' veto on economic reform (Holmes 1985). Mrs Thatcher herself, if not the 'wets' in her Cabinet, seemed impervious to the conventional wisdom that the short-run macroeconomic costs of her policy experiment would cost her office before any long-run benefits to the supply side materialized.

Tables 1.4 and 1.5 contain summary details of macro- and microeconomic policies early in the Thatcher period and recently. In macroeconomic policy, the central feature was retreat from discretionary demand management, and it became clear that the dismal days of the 1970s had put paid to the Keynesian era. The Medium-Term Financial Strategy (MTFS) sought to put policy on the basis of a pre-announced set of monetary and PSBR targets with a view to restoring inflation to mid-1960s levels by the mid-1980s, and both fiscal and monetary adjustments now responded to changes in inflation rather than unemployment. The immediate implication of the MTFS was a tightening of policy which precipitated a severe recession and a big jump in the exchange rate (Britton 1991). Difficulties in the control and interpretation of monetary targets led by 1986 to the adoption of an informal exchange rate target and then, from 1990 to 1992, membership of the Exchange Rate Mechanism of the European Monetary System. Since 1992, inflation targets have been set and policy has featured interest rate adjustments discussed publicly with the Bank of England. Throughout the period, supply side policy has been seen as the key to sustainable reductions in unemployment.

Despite the radicalism of this approach, unemployment and inflation have been on average about the same relative to other countries as in the Golden Age. At the same time the economy has been subjected to two quite severe recessions interspersed by a strong boom in the late 1980s, fuelled by credit deregulation. The magnitude of the adverse shock in the early 1980s and the dramatic rise in unemployment that ensued was not anticipated by the government, but appears to have delivered a pronounced change in trade union bargaining power and the conduct of industrial relations leading to major improvements in the efficiency of labour use (Bean and Symons 1989).

While the electorate would normally have punished the government severely and the change in macroeconomic policy would have appeared foolhardy despite these beneficial supply side effects, the Falklands War rescued the government (Price and Sanders 1994). As the 1980s progressed, and high unemployment was supplemented by increased competition in the product market and piecemeal legislation implementing trade union reforms, the result was a 'transformation' in industrial relations with a reduction in trade union membership back to the 1960 level, a restoration of control of the union hierarchy over the shop steward, the demise of the closed shop and reductions in multiple unionism (Metcalf 1994).

Table 1.5 captures some of the changes in microeconomic policies. Among the key elements of the new supply side policy in the early 1980s were reductions in industrial subsidies and privatization, taxation and trade union reform, deregulation in financial markets and indexing of welfare benefits to prices rather than earnings. The overall burden of tax was not reduced but the balance was shifted somewhat from direct to indirect taxation, and whereas government outlays had risen from 32.2 per cent of GDP in 1960 to 44.8 per cent in 1974, they fell slightly from 44.8 per cent in 1980 to 42.1 per cent in 1990. By contrast, in the EC9 countries on average government outlays were 30.7 per cent of GDP in 1960, 42.0 per cent in 1974, 49.0 per cent in 1980 and 50.6 per cent in 1990 (Middleton 1997). The thrust of policy was now to raise incentives and market disciplines rather than to aim for government sponsorship of investment-led growth.

Initially the government paid relatively little attention to education and training other than to abolish most of the Industrial Training Boards set up under the 1964 Act and to sponsor programmes like the Youth Training Scheme as a way of disguising unemployment. From 1986 onwards, as criticism of inadequate labour force skills intensified, there have been major reforms both in education and training provision. These have included the introduction of the National Curriculum in 1988, a doubling in the proportion of 18-year-olds entering higher education between 1988 and 1993 and a new system of National Vocational Qualifications started in 1986 (Robinson 1994).

This radical realignment of policy was facilitated by the apparent failure of the earlier regime in the 1970s. To some extent and for similar reasons, parallel traits would develop elsewhere in Europe, but much more slowly and timidly. Most of the policy developments of the early 1980s had effectively been precluded by the earlier attempts at seeking a 'Social Contract' with organized labour, and it was the apparent bankruptcy of that approach under British conditions that informed Thatcherism. Nevertheless, given the short-run consequences and the continuing problem of status quo bias on the part of the electorate, ex ante the 'Thatcher Experiment' was an extraordinary gamble.

The Proximate Sources of Growth

By now Britain no longer had the excuse of less scope for catch-up than elsewhere in Europe where, in any case, rapid catch-up growth had ended. Nevertheless, the relative improvement in British growth performance had more to it than this and econometric analysis suggests that, over the cycle of 1979–89, the Golden Age shortfall in productivity growth disappeared (Bean and Crafts 1996).

It was noted earlier that Total Factor Productivity growth is the basic determinant of long-run growth and that disappointing TFP growth lay at the heart of the shortfall of the early post-war decades. At the same time, measured TFP growth can reflect a variety of transitory effects as well as underlying trends. The key issues in assessing the chances of ending relative economic decline are what has happened to TFP growth and how sustainable is recent performance.

Comparing 1979–94 with 1960–73, TFP growth in the business sector has fallen from 2.6 per cent per year to 1.5 per cent, having been as low as 0.6 per cent in 1973–9 (Table 1.2). In the most recent period the UK ranks fifth in the OECD league table compared with eleventh in the 1960s. Prima facie, this represents a marked improvement and a vindication of the Thatcher reforms. There are, however, two reasons to be cautious over the implications of these estimates. First, at least some of the productivity improvements represent the unrepeatable, one-off effects of changes in trade union bargaining power, the shake-out of inefficient firms and privatization. Second, the comparison of 1973–9 with what followed may exaggerate the impact of policy on TFP growth because it also reflects delays in perceiving and adjusting to the slowdown in growth following the Golden Age (Darby and Wren-Lewis 1991).

Table 1.6 *Real output per person employed, Level (1990 = 100) and Growth rate (% per year)*

Whole Economy:					
1979	83.5		1989	100.0	
1980	82.3	–1.4	1990	100.0	0.0
1981	84.2	2.3	1991	100.8	0.8
1982	87.4	3.8	1992	102.9	2.1
1983	91.1	4.2	1993	106.4	3.4
1984	90.9	–0.2	1994	110.0	3.4
1985	93.5	2.9	1995	111.9	1.7
Manufacturing:					
1979	65.8		1989	97.6	
1980	63.6	–3.3	1990	100.0	2.5
1981	65.5	3.0	1991	102.5	2.5
1982	69.4	6.0	1992	108.4	5.8
1983	74.5	7.3	1993	113.7	4.9
1984	78.4	5.2	1994	119.1	4.7
1985	81.0	3.3	1995	120.7	1.3

Source: ONS (1996).

Nevertheless, these fears can be allayed somewhat by the fact that the overall TFP growth of 1979–89 was maintained through 1989–94 at the same rate.

Moreover, as Table 1.6 reports, the growth of labour productivity in manufacturing has also been sustained fairly well. It is here that there would be most reason to believe that the productivity improvement of the 1980s was a belated catch-up in response to a new colder climate.

Beyond the Proximate Sources of Growth

Economic policy in the Golden Age was at best unimpressive and at worst seriously damaging to British growth potential. Since 1979, the record is much more mixed with clear successes and failures and some aspects which it is still too soon to judge. A strong theme was the attempt by the Conservatives to correct many of the policy errors now widely agreed to have been made in the earlier period. For example, British tax policy now looks fairly similar to that elsewhere in the OECD when measured in terms of the combined corporate and personal income tax wedge (OECD 1991, p. 106).

The clearest and most important success has come with the successful reform of industrial relations, as noted above. The evidence suggests that the earlier negative effects of traditional British industrial relations on productivity growth evaporated during the 1980s (Bean and Crafts 1996). The most obvious failure has been in terms of macroeconomic policy where Britain has continued to have a relatively poor record in stabilizing the economy. The Lawson boom and its aftermath should in particular be seen as a serious unforced error. Oulton (1995) stresses that over 1977–94 the UK had the second highest 'skewness' (short booms, long recessions) in quarterly growth rates among his sample of OECD countries and estimates that this may have had a significant cost in terms of trend growth through discouraging innovation and investment.

Although mishandled in some respects, on balance, privatization has also been a success in terms of its impact on productivity performance. Privatizations have included British Airways, British Telecom, British Gas, the electricity supply industry, the water industry, British Steel and British Rail. Whereas nationalized industries accounted for 37.6 per cent of industrial investment in 1981, it was only 5.6 per cent by 1991. Many of these activities have subsequently been subject to regulation in which the general mode has been price-capping between periodic reviews rather than rate of return. This was with the intention of giving greater incentives to reduce costs and to innovate. On the other hand, opportunities to restructure these industries to increase competition (and also information for regulators) to put downward pressure on costs were not always taken (for example, gas).

The short-run impact on productivity growth was favourable: Bishop and Thompson (1992, p. 1187) estimate that aggregate TFP in the nine industries they studied rose from an index of 79 in 1970 to 90 in 1980 and then to 114 by 1990, such that the rate of increase nearly doubled in the latter decade. A detailed study of the electricity industry concluded that the present value of the net benefits was £6.9 billion, equivalent to a cost saving of 5 per cent for ever, mostly through improved operating efficiency (Newbery and Pollitt 1996, p. 23). A calculation based on the data in Bishop and Kay (1988) suggests that while the nationalized industries of 1979 accounted for only 5.7 per cent of employment, they contributed 17 per cent of all labour productivity growth between 1979 and 1988.

European comparisons suggest that product market deregulation (including privatization) has been strongly correlated with better productivity performance over 1980–94 and that this may have given the UK a gain of around 0.6 percentage points per year in TFP growth relative to the average EU member state (Koedijk and Kremers 1996). The long-run implications are not quite so clear, however. For privatization, this depends heavily on how the regulatory regime evolves. The initial price caps have in some cases turned out to permit 'excessive' profits and have provoked considerable disquiet. The operation of the RPI – X rule in practice involves interpretation by individual regulators and is hardly free of 'regulatory risk' or the impact of populist politics, such that cost-reducing effort and investment may be inhibited by fears that the returns will effectively be taxed away ex post (Rees and Vickers 1995).

The most difficult aspect of policy to assess is the impact of the extensive changes in education and training on human capital formation and growth. The general trend has clearly been one of rapid growth of investments both by firms and by persons. Real expenditures on training by employers seem to have roughly trebled between 1971 and 1989 and the fraction of employees receiving job-related training in the last four weeks according to the Labour Force Survey rose from 8.5 per cent in 1984 to 14.3 per cent in 1990 and 14.4 per cent in 1994 (Bean and Crafts 1996). The take-up of opportunities provided by the state increased: whereas 47 per cent of 16-year-olds stayed on in full-time education in 1986, ten years later this had risen to 71 per cent, and the number of vocational qualifications obtained rose from 739 000 in 1990/1 to 912 000 in 1994/5 (Robinson 1996). O'Mahony and Wagner (1994, p. 25) estimate that between 1979 and 1989 there was a small improvement in the manufacturing productivity gap with Germany due to the British labour force skills deficit. Broadberry and Wagner (1996, p. 258) report that the proportion of managers who were graduates more than doubled between 1976 and 1986.

On the other hand, there has been much criticism of the reforms of vocational training and continued deficiencies of the state school system with regard to the education of the less able. Critics are sceptical of the quality of the new vocational qualifications and note that the whole expansion has been at the bottom end of the hierarchy (Robinson 1996). Sadly, there exists no reliable quantification of the benefits of the policy reforms and there are still suggestions that 'our training system remains a formula for national decline' (Layard, Mayhew and Owen 1994).

It is hard to be dogmatic about the answers to the questions posed at the beginning of this section. There does seem to have been some improvement in realized growth performance relative to other European countries, albeit largely because of slowdown elsewhere. It would also be hard to argue that a return to old-style supply side policies is called for and growth has surely improved relative to a counterfactual of carrying on regardless with the policy stance of the 1970s. It is, however, still unclear how much, if any, improvement in long-run trend growth has been achieved either absolutely or relative to the UK's peer group.

WAS THE 'THATCHER EXPERIMENT' WORTH IT?

The answer to this question depends on value judgements as well as assessment of the impact of the policy changes. The key question is whether any increase in the growth rate outweighs the rise in inequality which the new policy framework produced. There is, of course, no consensus on this issue. This section does no more than present an illustrative calculation to suggest that the impact of taking income inequality into account when assessing growth performance could be quite dramatic.

Table 1.1 reported a sharp increase in income inequality in the UK between 1979 and 1991. This may exaggerate the rise in inequality in long-term incomes since expenditure inequality only rose about half as fast (Goodman and Webb 1995), but international comparisons can only be made at present using income-based measures. The pursuit of faster growth through restructuring of the tax system had a big impact on income inequality through shifts from direct to indirect taxation and reductions in top marginal tax rates. Johnson and Webb (1993) estimate that this accounted for about half the rise in inequality in the 1980s.

Changes in earnings and employment can account for the bulk of the rest of the rise in inequality, and also reflects policy indirectly. Throughout the period, government attempted to reduce the equilibrium rate of unemployment by making the labour market more flexible such that, by the 1990s, the UK had the least regulated labour market in Europe (Koedijk and Kremers 1996). By 1995, OECD estimates indicate that the traditional pattern had been reversed and Britain had a lower NAIRU than the other major European economies, although German figures are strongly affected by the assimilation of East Germany, and the estimated NAIRU of 6.8 per cent was well above the 2.6 per cent for 1960–8 estimated by Layard, Nickell and Jackman (1994).

In the context of a history of relatively weak skill formation in Britain and a sharp decline in the demand for unskilled workers resulting from biases in technological change and pressures from international trade, a relatively low NAIRU could only materialize as a result of the opening up of much greater wage differentials in Britain than countries like Germany, the Netherlands or Sweden (Nickell and Bell 1996). This outcome was facilitated by the weakening of trade unions. At the same time, the deteriorating position of the unskilled tended to raise structural unemployment and more than offset the impact on NAIRU of lower real unemployment benefits and reduced trade union militancy.

The most commonly used statistic of income inequality is the Gini coefficient (G). In effect, this implies a rank-order (poorest to richest) weighting of incomes such that it reflects a common value judgement that a pound of income received by a poorer person raises economic welfare by more than a pound received by a richer person (Sen 1979). This is used by Atkinson et al. (1995) to calculate the 'equivalent' level of national income taking account of the 'cost' of inequality as (100 – G) per cent of national income. A natural further step is to compute growth rates of this 'equivalent income' per person.

Table 1.7 *Growth of real GDP per person, Actual and adjusted for changes in inequality of incomes 1973–92 (% per year)*

	Actual	*Inequality adjusted*
Norway	2.9	3.1
Japan	3.0	3.0
Italy	2.4	2.8
Belgium	1.9	2.5
Portugal	2.1	2.4
Germany	2.1	2.0
Canada	1.5	1.8
Australia	1.4	1.7
Finland	1.6	1.6
Netherlands	1.4	1.4
Sweden	1.2	1.3
US	1.4	1.1
UK	1.4	0.9

Source: Crafts (1996) where 'inequality adjusted income growth' is based on actual income multiplied by (100 – G).

Table 1.7 reports the results of this exercise for a sample of countries with readily available estimates of G. The resulting change in the UK growth rate is large and makes British performance look much less attractive; the UK goes to the bottom of the league table with this approach. It must be stressed, however, that calculations of this kind require strong value judgements and do no more than show that, if rising inequality is regarded as costly, recent changes have been large enough to impact strongly on any evaluation of the Conservatives' record in seeking to reverse relative economic decline.

POLICY LESSONS FROM BRITISH POST-WAR GROWTH

This section draws some conclusions by pulling together some policy lessons that have emerged in this survey of British post-war growth experience. The following five aspects all comprise parts of a 'sadder but wiser' view from the vantage point of the 1990s. They should act as an antidote to theories which imply that raising the growth rate is simple and that governments that failed to do so must have been seriously incompetent.

1. Trade-offs between policy objectives are important. For much of the post-war period there were obvious conflicts between short-run macroeconomic objectives and growth-promoting supply side reforms. In the recent past, given the institutional and policy legacy, growth and traditional distributional objectives have been, to some extent, in opposition to each other.

2. It is not surprising that governments frequently fail to adopt policy reforms that will improve productivity growth. Not only may these require sacrificing other policy objectives, at least in the short term, but also they may easily be vote-losing since it is not usually possible credibly to promise to compensate losers.

3. Post-war experience is strongly suggestive of policies to avoid. For example, subsidizing physical investment and promoting national champion firms were unsuccessful in the 1960s and 1970s for clear reasons, although both might seem plausible strategies based on certain strands in recent growth economics.

4. Economic history is less good at identifying helpful interventions. For example, there are good market failure reasons to suppose that government should stimulate human capital formation and that this could raise TFP growth. Unfortunately, measurement problems are severe in this area and we still lack the basic quantitative information necessary to design well targeted programmes.

5. It should be clear both that institutions affect the growth rate and that generally reforming institutions is politically difficult – the switching costs are high. Windows of opportunity may only open occasionally such that, if nations are held back by their past, it is institutions that are the most likely culprits. In the British case industrial relations are a better reason than outdated machinery to see early industrialization holding back the post-war economy.

REFERENCES

Adams, W. J. (1989) *Restructuring the French Economy*, Washington, DC: Brookings Institution.

Atkinson, A. B. (1995) *Incomes and the Welfare State*, Cambridge: Cambridge University Press.

Atkinson, A. B., Rainwater, L. and Smeeding, T. M. (1995) *Income Distribution in OECD Countries: Evidence from the Luxembourg Income Study*, OECD: Paris.

Batstone, E. (1988) *The Reform of Workplace Industrial Relations*, Oxford: Clarendon Press.

Bean, C. and Crafts, N. F. R. (1996) 'British Economic Growth since 1945: Relative Economic Decline ... and Renaissance?', in N. F. R. Crafts and G. Toniolo (eds), *Economic Growth in Europe Since 1945*, Cambridge: Cambridge University Press, pp. 131–72.

Bean, C. and Symons, J. (1989) 'Ten Years of Mrs T.', *NBER Macroeconomics Annual*, Vol. 3, pp. 13–61.

Bishop, M. and Kay, J. (1988) *Does Privatization Work? Lessons from the UK*, London: London Business School.

Bishop, M. and Thompson, D. (1992) 'Regulatory Reform and Productivity Growth in the UK's Public Utilities', *Applied Economics*, Vol. 24, pp. 1181–90.

Britton, A. J. C. (1991) *Macroeconomic Policy in Britain, 1974–1987*, Cambridge: Cambridge University Press.

Broadberry, S. N.(1996) 'How Did the United States and Germany Become Richer than Britain?' Paper prepared for conference on 'Historical Benchmark Comparisons of Output and Productivity', Leuven.

Broadberry, S. N. and Wagner, K. (1996) 'Human Capital and Productivity in Manufacturing during the Twentieth Century: Britain, Germany and the United States', in B. van Ark and N. F. R. Crafts (eds), *Quantitative Aspects of Post-war European Economic Growth*, Cambridge: Cambridge University Press, pp. 244–70.

Brown, W. (1991) 'Industrial relations', in M. J. Artis and D. Cobham, *Labour's Economic Policies, 1974–1979*, Manchester: Manchester University Press, pp. 213–28.

Central Statistical Office (1992) *Monthly Review of External Trade Statistics Annual Supplement*.

Crafts, N. F. R. (1991) 'Reversing Relative Economic Decline? The 1980s in Historical Perspective', *Oxford Review of Economic Policy*, Vol. 7(3), pp. 81–98.

Crafts, N. F. R. (1993) 'Adjusting from War to Peace in 1940s Britain', *Economic and Social Review*, Vol. 25, pp. 1–20.

Crafts, N. F. R. (1995) 'The Golden Age of Economic Growth in Post-war Europe: Why Did Northern Ireland Miss Out?', *Irish Economic and Social History*, Vol. 22, pp. 5–25.

Crafts, N. F. R. (1996) *Relative Economic Decline in Britain, 1870–1985: A Quantitative Perspective*, London: Social Market Foundation.

Crouch, C. (1993) *Industrial Relations and European State Traditions*, Oxford: Clarendon Press.

Darby, J. and Wren-Lewis, S. (1991) 'Trends in Labour Productivity in UK Manufacturing', *Oxford Economic Papers*, Vol. 43, pp. 424–42.

Department for Education and Employment (1995) *Education Statistics*.

Department of Trade and Industry (1994) *Competitiveness: Helping Business to Win* (Cmd. 2563), London: HMSO.

Dunning, J. H. (1958) *American Investment in British Manufacturing Industry*, London: Allen and Unwin.

Ergas, H. (1987) 'Does Technology Policy Matter?', in B. R. Guile and H. Brooks (eds), *Technology and Global Industry*, Washington DC: National Academy Press, pp. 191–245.

Fernandez, R. and Rodrik, D. (1991) 'Resistance to Reform: Status-Quo Bias in the Presence of Individual-Specific Uncertainty', *American Economic Review*, Vol. 81, pp. 1146–55.

Goodman, A. and Webb, S. (1995) 'The Distribution of UK Household Expenditure, 1979–92', *Fiscal Studies*, Vol. 16(3), pp. 55–80.

Greenhalgh, C. (1990) 'Innovation and Trade Performance in the United Kingdom', *Economic Journal*, Vol. 100, pp. 105–18.

Hindley, B. and Richardson, R. (1983) 'United Kingdom: an Experiment in Picking Winners – the Industrial Reorganisation Corporation', in B. Hindley (ed.), *State Investment Companies in Western Europe*, London: Macmillan, pp. 125–55.

Holmes, M. (1985) *The First Thatcher Government, 1979–1983*, Brighton: Wheatsheaf.

Johnson, P. and Webb, S. (1993) 'Explaining the Growth in UK Income Inequality, 1979–1988', *Economic Journal*, Vol. 103, pp. 429–35.
Koedijk, K. and Kremers, J. (1996) 'Market Opening, Regulation and Growth in Europe', *Economic Policy*, Vol. 23, pp. 445–67.
Kormendi, R. C. and Meguire, P. C. (1985) 'Macroeconomic Determinants of Growth', *Journal of Monetary Economics*, Vol. 16, pp. 141–63.
Layard, R., Mayhew, K. and Owen, G. (1994) *Britain's Training Deficit*, Aldershot: Avebury.
Layard, R., Nickell, S. and Jackman, R. (1994) *The Unemployment Crisis*, Oxford: Oxford University Press.
Maddison, A. (1991) *Dynamic Forces in Capitalist Development*, Oxford, Oxford University Press.
Maddison, A. (1995) *Monitoring the World Economy, 1820–1992*, Paris: OECD.
Maddison, A. (1996) 'Macroeconomic Accounts for European Countries', in B. van Ark and N. F. R. Crafts (eds), *Quantitative Aspects of Post-war European Economic Growth*, Cambridge: Cambridge University Press, pp. 27–83.
Maizels, A. (1963) *Industrial Growth and World Trade*, Cambridge: Cambridge University Press.
Metcalf, D. (1994) 'Transformation of British Industrial Relations? Institutions, Conduct and Outcomes, 1980–1990', in R. Barrell (ed.), *The UK Labour Market*, Cambridge: Cambridge University Press, pp. 126–57.
Metcalf, D., Nickell, S. and Floros, N. (1980) 'Still Searching for an Explanation of Unemployment in Interwar Britain', Centre for Labour Economics, London School of Economics, Discussion Paper No. 71.
Middleton, R. (1997) 'Britain's Economic Problem: Too Small a Public Sector?', in S. James and V. Preston (eds), *Old Politics, New Politics: British History, 1945–1995*, London: Macmillan.
Morris, D. and Stout, D. K. (1985) 'Industrial Policy', in D. J. Morris (ed.), *The Economic System in the UK*, Oxford: Oxford University Press, pp. 851–94.
Newbery, D. M. and Green, R. (1996) 'Regulation, Public Ownership and Privatisation of the English Electricity Industry', in R. J. Gilbert and E. P. Kahn (eds), *International Comparisons of Electricity Regulation*, Cambridge: Cambridge University Press, pp. 25–81.
Newbery, D. M. and Pollitt, M. G. (1996) 'The Restructuring and Privatisation of the CEGB: Was It Worth It?', University of Cambridge, DAE Working Paper No. 9607.
Nickell, S. and Bell, B. (1996) 'Changes in the Distribution of Wages and Unemployment in OECD Countries', *American Economic Review: Papers and Proceedings*, Vol. 86, pp. 302–8.
OECD (1991) *Taxing Profits in a Global Economy*, Paris: OECD.
OECD (1995) *Basic Science and Technology Statistics*, Paris: OECD.
OECD (1996a) *Historical Statistics, 1960–1994*, Paris: OECD.
OECD (1996b) *Employment Outlook*, Paris: OECD.
Office of National Statistics (1996) *Economic Trends Annual Supplement*.
O'Mahony, M., Oulton, N. and Voss, J. (1996) 'Productivity in Market Services: International Comparisons', *National Institute of Economic and Social Research*, Discussion Paper No. 105.
O'Mahony, M. and Wagner, K. (1994) *Changing Fortunes: An Industry Study of British and German Productivity Growth over Three Decades*, London: NIESR.
Oulton, N. (1995) 'Supply Side Reform and UK Economic Growth: What Happened to the Miracle?', *National Institute Economic Review*, No. 154, pp. 53–70.
Oulton, N. (1996) 'Workforce Skills and Export Competitiveness', in A. L. Booth and D. J. Snower (eds), *Acquiring Skills*, Cambridge: Cambridge University Press, pp. 201–30.

Pavitt, K. and Soete, L. (1982) 'International Differences in Economic Growth and the International Location of Innovation', in H. Giersch (ed.), *Emerging Technologies*, Tubin: Mohr, pp. 105–33.

Pilat, D. (1996) 'Labour Productivity Levels in OECD Countries', *OECD Working Paper* No. 169.

Prais, S. J. (1981) *Productivity and Industrial Structure*, Cambridge: Cambridge University Press.

Pratten, C. F. and Atkinson, A. G. (1976) 'The Use of Manpower in British Industry', *Department of Employment Gazette*, Vol. 84, pp. 571–6.

Price, S. and Sanders, D. (1994) 'Economic Competence, Rational Expectations and Government Popularity in Post-war Britain', *Manchester School*, Vol. 62, pp. 296–312.

Rees, R. and Vickers, J. (1995) 'RPI – X Price Cap Regulation', in M. Bishop, J. Kay and C. Mayer (eds), *The Regulatory Challenge*, Oxford: Oxford University Press, pp. 358–85.

Robinson, P. (1994) 'The Comparative Performance of the British Education and Training System', LSE Centre for Economic Performance, Discussion Paper No. 644.

Robinson, P. (1996) *Rhetoric and Reality: Britain's New Vocational Qualifications*, London: Centre for Economic Performance, LSE.

Sen, A. K. (1979) 'The Welfare Basis of Real Income Comparisons: A Survey', *Journal of Economic Literature*, Vol. 27, pp. 1–45.

Singh, A. (1975) 'Take-overs, Natural Selection and the Theory of the Firm: Evidence from the Post-war UK Experience', *Economic Journal*, Vol. 85, pp. 497–515.

Soskice, D. (1994) 'Reconciling Markets and Institutions: The German Apprenticeship System', in L. M. Lynch (ed.), *Training and the Private Sector: International Comparisons*, Chicago: University of Chicago Press, pp. 25–60.

Steedman, H. (1988) 'Vocational Training in France and Britain: Mechanical and Electrical Craftsmen', *National Institute Economic Review*, No. 126, pp. 57–70.

Steedman, H. (1990) 'Improvement in Workforce Qualifications: Britain and France, 1979–1988', *National Institute Economic Review*, No. 133, pp. 50–61.

Tanzi, V. (1969) *The Individual Income Tax and Economic Growth*, Baltimore: Johns Hopkins University Press.

United Nations (1964) *Some Factors in Economic Growth in Europe in the 1950s*, Geneva: UN/ECE.

van Ark, B. (1993) *International Comparisons of Output and Productivity*, Groningen Growth and Development Centre.

Vickers, J. and Yarrow, G. (1988) *Privatization: An Economic Analysis*, Cambridge, MA.: MIT Press.

Wren, C. (1996) 'Grant Equivalent Expenditure on Industrial Subsidies in the Post-war United Kingdom', *Oxford Bulletin of Economics and Statistics*, Vol. 58, pp. 317–53.

2 West Germany*

Wendy Carlin

INTRODUCTION

When the post-war era opened, the UK not Germany was Western Europe's largest economy in terms of both population and gross domestic product. Germany (the Federal Republic of Germany, or West Germany as it was until 1990) overtook the UK in population in 1952, but it was not until the mid-1960s that the economy was larger (Maddison 1991, Tables A.2 and B.4). Reunification between East and West Germany in 1990 took Germany from being about one-tenth larger in population than the UK, Italy or France, to being some 40 per cent larger. But reunification did not increase the size of the economy (GDP) to nearly this extent because of the poor condition of the East German economy.

A major focus of this chapter is on the causes and consequences of West Germany's increase in economic importance over the post-war period. The chapter begins with an assessment of West German economic performance in the post-war period. Growth gradually declined over three major phases – that of reconstruction from 1945 to 1961, of so-called Golden Age growth from 1961 to 1973 and in the years of slow growth from 1973 until reunification in 1990. Germany's first post-war recession did not occur until 1966/7 and it was very short-lived. But in common with the rest of the advanced economies, a characteristic feature of the period of slow growth after 1973 has been the recurrence of deep recessions. These followed each of the oil crises, in 1973 and 1979. With the recessions came persistent unemployment which had been largely absent since the inter-war period. Unemployment had fallen through the period of reconstruction and was absent in the Golden Age years. Since 1973, unemployment peaked at a higher rate in each recession and remained at a higher level in each recovery. In the post-1973 period, German unemployment was typically about the same level as in the US, below that of the other large European economies but higher than in Scandinavia and Japan.

The implications of reunification for Germany's economic prospects are then examined. Unification created euphoria and a short-lived boom in the West. However, the scale of the task of rebuilding and integrating the East German economy into that of West Germany after 50 years under central planning rapidly became apparent. Five per cent of German GDP is now being transferred each year to East Germany to finance consumption and investment in the region. Will East Germany move on to a self-sustaining growth path to catch up with the West, or will it become dependent on transfers from the West and exhibit the problems of the Italian Mezzogiorno (the south of Italy)?

The chapter then focuses on economic structure, institutions and policy and draws some connections between these and economic performance. A striking feature of the German economy over the post-war period is its relative stability. In contrast to the UK, for example, changes in Germany's performance in growth, inflation, unemployment and income distribution have been much more gradual. Macroeconomic policy has been pursued more consistently than elsewhere; structural change in the economy has occurred more slowly than in many other countries, and institutions such as unions, the training system and financial institutions have changed relatively little.

This is followed by a discussion of Germany's importance in the European economy in the post-war period. Particular attention is given to the 1980s and to Germany's role in the European Exchange Rate Mechanism.

WEST GERMAN ECONOMIC PERFORMANCE 1945–90

Whether West German growth from the late 1940s to the end of the 1950s can be called a 'miracle' is a semantic rather than an economic question. What can

Table 2.1 *Growth, unemployment and inflation in the post-war period*

	1950–61	*1961–73*	*1973–89*
A: Growth: average annual growth of real GDP (%)			
West Germany	7.7	4.4	2.1
Average of UK, France and Italy	4.6	4.5	2.4
B: Economy-wide productivity growth: average annual growth of real GDP per hour (%)			
West Germany	6.9	5.2	2.7
Average of UK, France and Italy	3.8	5.3	2.6
C: Unemployment: average annual rate (%)			
West Germany	4.6	0.8	5.0
Average of UK, France and Italy	3.8	3.2	7.9
D: Inflation rate: average annual growth of consumer price index (%)			
West Germany	1.9	3.5	3.6
Average of UK, France and Italy	4.2	4.9	10.6

Source: Calculated from Appendix Tables in Maddison (1991).

be said in economic terms, though, is that compared to other economies, West Germany's growth performance in these years was exceptional. Many attempts have been made in recent years to identify a common growth pattern amongst the advanced economies. The contribution of capital accumulation and the growth of the labour force cannot by themselves account for the Golden Age growth of the 1950s and 1960s. One way of doing so is to include a term for the growth arising from the opportunities for catching-up by the European and Japanese economies to the US. With these three factors, growth rates in the advanced countries are well accounted for. Germany is the exception – there is still a considerable amount of unexplained growth in the 1950s (see, for example, Dowrick and Nguyen 1989; van de Klundert and van Shaik 1993, Table 5). Table 2.1 provides a summary of West German post-war growth, unemployment and inflation performance as compared with the average of the other three large European economies.

POST-WAR RECONSTRUCTION: 1945–61

A crucial precondition for the establishment of a process of growth after the end of the war was clarity about the political and economic future of the country. 1947 was a major turning point for West Germany since it marked the division of Europe and the start of the Cold War. The US committed itself to the economic restoration of West Germany and its inclusion in the Western sphere of influence. The announcement of Marshall Aid in the same year was of great symbolic importance for the West German economy in cementing Germany's place within the West European economy and in the emerging international trade and exchange rate system.

In spite of the devastation of Germany's cities and transport system by the Allied bombing campaign in the last stages of the war, the picture of desolation and destruction misrepresented the underlying industrial capacity of the West German economy. The common perception that German industry was largely destroyed during the war is false. The extent of destruction was insufficient to offset the new capacity installed during the war years, with the result that West Germany entered the post-war era with a capital stock more than one-tenth larger than it was before the war: neither the UK, Italy nor France were so fortunate (Krengel 1958; Armstrong et al. 1991). The transport links taken out by strategic bombing were rapidly restored and, by 1948, it was not physical constraints which were hampering the pace of recovery. The big problem facing the West German economy was the lack of a coherent set of economic incentives which would induce firms to place goods on the market and workers to turn up to work for wages. Prices and wages were fixed at pre-war levels which bore no relation to the reality of very low output and a hugely expanded money supply. The economy operated through a complicated form of barter which, although inherently inefficient, enabled a recovery in production. But for forward-looking decision making, such as investment in fixed capital or the pursuit of markets abroad, it was necessary for there to be clarity over who owned industry and for price, wages and money to be in appropriate relationship to each other.

The Currency Reform of June 1948 appeared to observers to have unleashed a 'miracle' of economic activity, as all kinds of goods that had not been seen for years appeared on the shelves of shops and worker absenteeism vanished. The preconditions for the success of the currency reform were not only the strength of the productive base of the economy and the clearing of the physical bottlenecks in transport and raw materials, but also the business confidence engendered by the inclusion of the western zones in the Marshall Plan. Businesses were typically in the hands of the pre-war owners and the Currency Reform benefited the owners of real assets. Alongside the Currency Reform, the German economic authorities, under the leadership of Ludwig Erhard and against the advice of most Anglo-American experts, introduced a sweeping liberalization programme. The bulk of price controls were lifted as well as the major quantitative controls over the allocation of resources. In the language of the post-communist reforms in the late 1980s to early 1990s, this was a 'big bang' policy. The fundamental difference between the context in Eastern Europe and in post-war Germany was the supply side: in West Germany, a recovery of production had already taken place following the collapse at the end of the war and businesses had owners and managers in place. A rapid supply side response to the removal of distortions in the economy could have been expected.

Even under such favourable conditions, a further round of macroeconomic stabilization was implemented in 1949 as inflationary pressure re-emerged. The German authorities were advised to reintroduce price controls and the rationing of materials, but they refused to do so: credit conditions were tightened. This choice of tight macroeconomic policy was probably important for growth because it interrupted the attempts of German business to return to their traditional price-fixing arrangements. By refusing to commit themselves to full employment by maintaining demand at home, the German authorities forced firms to rebuild their markets abroad. This seems to have been an effective competition policy measure.

West Germany benefited from a number of one-off opportunities which contributed to the extraordinary growth phase in the wake of the Currency Reform. In particular, there was a highly elastic supply of labour available to the economy in those years. A total of 3.6 million refugees from East Germany entered West Germany between 1950 and 1962 (adding to the 2.5 million who arrived between 1946 and 1950). It appears that there was a considerable transfer of human capital from East to West Germany in this period, as engineers and other skilled workers who were trained in the East fled to the West. In common with a number of other continental European economies (but unlike the UK), Germany benefited from the reallocation of underemployed agricultural labour to the industrial sector. In addition, the availability of the well trained and mobile refugees boosted profitability and competitiveness, reinforcing an export-led growth process.

ADJUSTING TO LABOUR SHORTAGE: 1961–73

West Germany's period of supergrowth ended at the beginning of the 1960s. From 1960 until 1973, growth is explained by the growth of the capital stock and by the continued opportunities for catch-up to the US. There is no contribution from labour force growth. 1961 marks a clear break in West German post-war economic history. The building of the Berlin Wall brought with it a sharp change in labour supply conditions as the inflow of skilled workers from East Germany ceased. The extra boost to growth from which Germany benefited in the 1950s as it recovered from the war and was reintegrated into international trade, disappeared. From this time, Germany falls into line with the typical European pattern of growth (see, for example, van de Klundert and van Shaik 1993).

Common to many other European countries, growth in the 1960s was still very high by historical standards, with both high investment and catch-up effects playing an important role. In this period, Germany benefited from demand buoyancy as an external effect of the strong growth of its markets, especially in Europe. Modernization of the French and Italian economies called for new capital equipment and this was largely supplied by Germany. Until the late 1960s, the government did not use Keynesian policies to boost aggregate demand: it was not necessary. The unemployment rate averaged less than 1 per cent from 1961 to 1973 (see Table 2.1).

A striking feature of this period is the way in which rapid growth was combined with very low unemployment and low inflation. Germany's overseas payments position remained very strong throughout, confirming that low unemployment was not being maintained at the cost of deteriorating competitiveness. This combination of features suggests that the equilibrium rate of unemployment (also referred to as the natural rate or NAIRU) was very low. The shift to a very tight labour market tends to raise the bargaining power of workers relative to employers in wage negotiations. It appears that the German unions chose not to exploit their bargaining power to the full, apparently recognizing the benefits for their members of protecting competitiveness and investment. Further evidence for this interpretation comes from the fact that the unions supported the recruitment of foreign workers, just as in the 1950s they had supported trade liberalization. At the same time, the employers' associations became better organized and maintained the discipline of industry-based wage setting under conditions of a very strong demand for labour.

The environment for growth began to deteriorate throughout the advanced economies toward the end of the 1960s (see Flanagan et al. 1982; Marglin and

Schor 1990; Armstrong et al. 1991). There appears to have been a common experience of a build-up of distributional conflict over wages, the pace and organization of work and the level and financing of government expenditure. Wage explosions took place right across Europe in the late 1960s and produced increased inflationary pressure and declining profitability before 1973. Although growth rates did not fall until after 1973, the developments at the end of the 1960s served to weaken the conditions for catch-up and for investment.

Germany did not escape these developments. There was, however, a particular twist to the German case. In 1966/7, Germany had its first recession since the war in which output fell. From the perspective of the 1990s, it appears to have been mild and brief. However, it had an important effect on German economic policy making. The recession brought to an end the domination of Ludwig Erhard and the Christian Democrats over economic policy and saw the entry into government of the Social Democratic party. The Social Democrats introduced Keynesianism to Germany by committing the government to the same four macroeconomic outcomes as had been part of UK government objectives since the early 1950s: price stability, high employment, external balance and adequate growth. They organized the first incomes policy in Germany (a voluntary one) which was highly effective in restraining wage increases in the upswing from the recession. But it was the extent of wage restraint agreed to by the unions which unleashed a wave of unofficial strikes in Germany and brought with it a change in union strategy and the adoption of a more aggressive bargaining stance.

At the same time, one of the important post-war international institutions which had helped to lock countries such as Germany into an open world trading system, began to collapse. This was the Bretton Woods fixed exchange rate system in which the US dollar was the anchor currency. As US economic dominance diminished with the growth in strength of European and Japanese economies, the dollar's key currency role was undermined. The Deutschmark appreciated rapidly between 1969 and 1973, and this combined with the high nominal wage increases to produce a deterioration of German competitiveness: Germany's unit labour costs in dollar terms rose at the rapid rate of 8 per cent per year faster than in competing countries. German firms tried to protect their export markets by not passing on the bulk of these cost increases, with the result that their profitability was impaired substantially. This contributed to the weakness of investment in the early 1970s.

With the final demise of the fixed exchange rate system in early 1973 and the floating of the Deutschmark, the Bundesbank regained considerable authority in economic policy making. With floating exchange rates, it was possible for Germany and hence the Bundesbank to set its own monetary policy. The Bundesbank made it clear that the reflection of heightened distributional tension in higher inflation would not be tolerated. The Social Democrats' Keynesianism was muted by Bundesbank control of monetary policy, and the

Bundesbank sought to honour its constitutional obligation to maintain low inflation by adopting a tight non-accommodating monetary policy.

SLOW GROWTH 1973–90

Slow growth was common across the OECD in this period and the comparative econometric analysis shows that Germany's performance was average. A major factor responsible for the growth slowdown in the 1970s in Germany was the weakness of investment, and this is partly explained by the decline in profitability.

The Bundesbank sought to establish its authority in the aftermath of the first oil shock in 1973 by refusing to accommodate the increase in wage and price inflation that followed the sharp rise in oil prices. The result was a sharp recession in 1974/5. This enabled the Bundesbank to establish its credible commitment to low inflation. The Bundesbank's policy rule was clear: higher inflation would produce monetary tightening and exchange rate appreciation. This produced a moderation of wage bargaining behaviour as the powerful engineering union IG Metall recognized that the employment of its members would suffer if external competitiveness was weakened by an appreciation of the Deutschmark. This episode can be seen as partially but not entirely reversing the upward shift in union bargaining intensity which occurred in the early 1970s. While the sharp decline in the manufacturing profit share was stemmed and, for the business sector as a whole, the profit share had recovered to its 1973 level by 1979, a return to Golden Age values did not take place.

There is considerable debate about the underlying performance of the German economy in the 1980s regarding the extent of supply side rigidities and about the appropriateness of the setting of macroeconomic policy. There are two divergent views about the strength of the supply side. On the one hand, the assessment presented very clearly by Giersch et al. (1992) is that weak performance in investment and productivity growth in Germany reflected mounting institutional rigidities which hampered the economy's ability to adapt to structural change and to increasing international competition. Several legacies of the 1969–73 period were identified as blunting investment incentives: a weakening of the industrial relations consensus, an increase in the size of the welfare state and the extension of employment protection. The alternative view (see, for example, Katzenstein 1989) focuses on Germany's relatively strong performance in international markets over this period and attributes this to the capacity for adaptation inherent in the German institutional structure. For example, it was argued that improved employment security was consistent with continued strong performance because of the incentives it created for firms to move into the production of higher quality goods. This was possible because of the improvements in training negotiated between unions and employers, associations.

These alternative interpretations of the supply side produce quite different judgements about the role of macroeconomic policy in growth in the 1970s and 1980s. The proponents of the supply side weakness view argue that an activist fiscal policy during the 1970s and, in particular, Germany's leading role in the coordinated international expansions of 1978/9 worsened the conditions for growth. Once interventionist fiscal policy was abandoned and its operation brought into line with tight monetary policy in the early 1980s, macroeconomic policy ceased to hamper growth (Hellwig and Neumann 1985). Germany's persistent current account surplus in the 1980s is attributed to the lack of sufficient profitable investment opportunities at home to absorb business savings (Giersch et al. 1992, pp. 245–50).

Those supporting a positive interpretation of German supply side performance argue that the very restrictive monetary and fiscal policies pursued from the early 1980s were unnecessary, in the sense that they were not required to impose discipline on the unions. Germany, it is argued, could have operated at a higher level of activity, and by implication with higher growth, without an unsustainable deterioration in macroeconomic stability. From this perspective, the persistent current account surplus reflects the failure to run the economy at maximum sustainable output (Soskice 1990).

Table 2.2 *Export market and productivity performance in manufacturing, West Germany and the UK in the 1980s*

	West Germany		*UK*	
A. Productivity performance: average annual growth of hourly productivity (%)				
	1973–9	1979–89	1973–9	1979–89
Manufacturing	3.4	2.3	0.7	4.3
Mechanical Eng.	2.7	1.5	0.7	4.2
Motor vehicles	4.4	1.3	0.7	2.9
Office machinery	11.2	4.0	10.2	6.2
Chemicals	3.0	2.0	–0.5	5.2
B. Export market share performance: share of country in world exports (%)				
	1980	1990	1980	1990
Machinery & Transport Eqpt.	16.5	16.5	7.5	6.0
– vehicles	21.0	21.5	6.0	4.5
– office eqpt.	10.0	7.0	6.5	5.5
Chemicals	17.0	17.0	8.5	8.0

Sources: A: O'Mahoney and Wagner (1994), Tables 1a, 1b; B: GATT (1991) *World Trade 1990–1991*, Tables IV.43, 34, 39, 29.

To date there has been no convincing analysis of German economic performance which has been able to reconcile the various performance indicators and allow a clear judgement to be made about the 1980s. Table 2.2 presents a summary of data on productivity and export market performance which highlights the conflicting indicators.

Germany has weaker productivity performance than the UK in the 1980s, but seems to have better defended its (already much stronger) export market performance in key sectors. Office equipment stands out as a sector in which relatively weak German productivity performance is consistent with a weaker export performance than the UK.

In spite of the deep disagreements between interpreters of German performance, there are also some threads in common. An important point of agreement is the notion that direct government intervention in industry has been largely unsuccessful in this period. Neither in 'sunset' industries (such as ship-building, steel and coal) nor in 'sunrise' ones (such as electronics and biotechnology) have attempts by the government to foster competitiveness met with success. This is also consistent with the French experience in the 1960s and 1970s. By contrast, the government stayed largely clear of the three core manufacturing sectors (chemicals, vehicles and engineering) and banking (Katzenstein 1989, p. 19).

It is possible that in the core sectors which account for the bulk of German exports, export market shares have been maintained through innovation and increases in quality but that average productivity for manufacturing as a whole has been pulled down by slow rationalization of ailing sectors – as compared, for example, with the UK. In the UK, productivity increased faster than in Germany in the 1980s, but the size of the manufacturing sector shrank much more dramatically. Klodt (1990) and Giersch et al. (1992) provide evidence of the role of increased government subsidies and higher effective protection in slowing the decline in employment in mining, agriculture and ship-building. An extreme example comes from the coal industry: between 1980 and 1992 employment in the UK fell from 294 000 to 44 000, whereas in Germany it fell from 187 000 to 115 000.

GERMAN REUNIFICATION

The immediate impact of German reunification was to impart a powerful demand shock to the West German economy. Political and economic euphoria coincided to produce a strong expansion in economic activity. Growth in the number of jobs was remarkable: employment in West Germany increased by 1.5 million between 1989 and 1992 (by contrast it had remained virtually constant at 26 million over the period from 1960 to 1988). Reunification occurred when West Germany was experiencing a strong cyclical upswing. The economy had been expanding since 1983, and both exports and investment were growing strongly and unemployment falling before the protests against the East German regime began in the autumn of 1989. The simplest way to think about the macroeconomic consequences of reunification is to view it as a large increase in aggregate demand. The boom in private and public spending that accompanied reunification brought about a deterioration in the current account by 5.5 per cent of German GDP: between 1989 and 1991, West Germany's current account swung from a substantial surplus into deficit. In the face of such a boom in demand, bargaining power in the labour market shifted in favour of the unions and claims for higher wage increases were successful. Wage claims were also boosted as the unions sought to shift the burden of the tax increases associated with financing reunification.

There are two routes through which the inflationary consequences of the demand expansion could have been offset. The first would have involved the willingness of Chancellor Kohl to negotiate an incomes policy with the unions so that the tighter labour market and higher taxes did not result in higher wage claims. In the absence of the negotiation of such bargaining restraint, a real appreciation of the Deutschmark would be necessary. A real appreciation would allow for constant inflation at lower unemployment as the real cost of imports was reduced, thus accommodating the higher real wages. The only non-inflationary method of securing a real appreciation would have been through the realignment of exchange rates in the European Exchange Rate Mechanism. The Deutschmark would have had to have been revalued relative to the other currencies. The Bundesbank supported such a realignment but it proved impossible to negotiate. As a consequence, the real appreciation had to occur through higher inflation in Germany; but the Bundesbank would not tolerate increased inflation and reacted by raising interest rates. The key interest rate set by the Bundesbank (the Lombard rate) more than doubled between 1988 and the end of 1991 (to peak at 9.75 per cent). The reunification boom was sharply curtailed: in 1993, the West German economy shrank by more than 2 per cent in real terms. The associated collapse of the ERM is discussed later.

Reunification brought short-term disruption to the West German and European economy, but also considerable costs to West Germany that will persist well beyond the end of the century. The source of the costs lies in the conseqences of the economic union between two economies at vastly different levels of productivity. Pre-reunification manufacturing productivity in East Germany was between 25 and 30 per cent of the West German level. German Economic and Monetary Union in July 1990 entailed the creation of a unified economic area with a single currency in which there was a free flow of labour, capital, goods and services. West German law, administration and institutions, including wage bargaining, were extended to the East. In the face of open competition with the West, East German industry collapsed. Output halved by early 1991 and employment had also fallen by half (that is, by over 2 million) when the trough was reached in 1993. In 1993, East Germany had one-fifth of the population of the united Germany and less than 10 per cent of the GDP.

East German industry was crushed by a collapse in demand and rising costs. East German consumers switched to Western products; western purchasers stopped buying East German goods when the previous subsidies required to produce low prices for exports were removed and purchasers in the former markets of Eastern Europe lacked the Deutschmarks to buy East German output. The previous trading arrangements in Eastern Europe had collapsed and the economies there were suffering from severe recessions. Moreover, wage costs rose after reunification, reinforcing the damage to competitiveness done by the conversion of the East German currency at a rate of one Ostmark for one Deutschmark – a political decision with which the Bundesbank had been unhappy. The increase in wages was the result of the success of the West German unions in having the principle of rapid adjustment to wage parity between the two parts of the country accepted by the employers' associations and the government.

The organizational form of large enterprises in East Germany had been designed to fit an allocation system and an international division of labour which were unrelated to market incentives. Large-scale restructuring of enterprises was required as well as finding new owners and markets. In the process of restructuring after reunification, enterprises went from being much larger than their counterparts in the west to being smaller (Carlin and Mayer 1995).

The dependence of East on West Germany is illustrated by the fact that whilst GDP per capita in East Germany is less than half that of the country as a whole, consumption per head is nearly two-thirds that of the national level and investment is 10 per cent higher than for the country as a whole. East German imports are running at the level of two-thirds of regional GDP. A country cannot run such a trade deficit – a region can, provided it is financed by the rest of the country. About 5 per cent of West German GDP is being transferred to the East each year. Estimates of the rate of regional convergence of East to West Germany based on historical experience of regions in the US, Europe and Japan produced the gloomy prediction that 35 years after reunification, only half of the initial difference between the two regions would have disappeared (Barro and Sala-i-Martin 1991). The experience of Italy since unification in 1862 would provide an even gloomier perspective: the per capita GDP gap between the Centre-North and the South (the Italian Mezzogiorno) appears to be greater now than it was at unification (Boltho et al. 1995), despite massive injections of capital and income transfers for most of the post-war period (see Chapter 4). A striking difference between the East German case and other situations of regional backwardness is that before the Second World War, East Germany had attained a level of GDP per capita slightly higher than that of West Germany at the time. The cultural traditions of successful manufacturing and entrepreneurship, along with the fact that the two regions were on a par 50 years ago, may prove significant in accelerating convergence.

Moreover, the huge regional problem in East Germany is being met by a massive policy-led investment effort. Initial indications are that high levels of

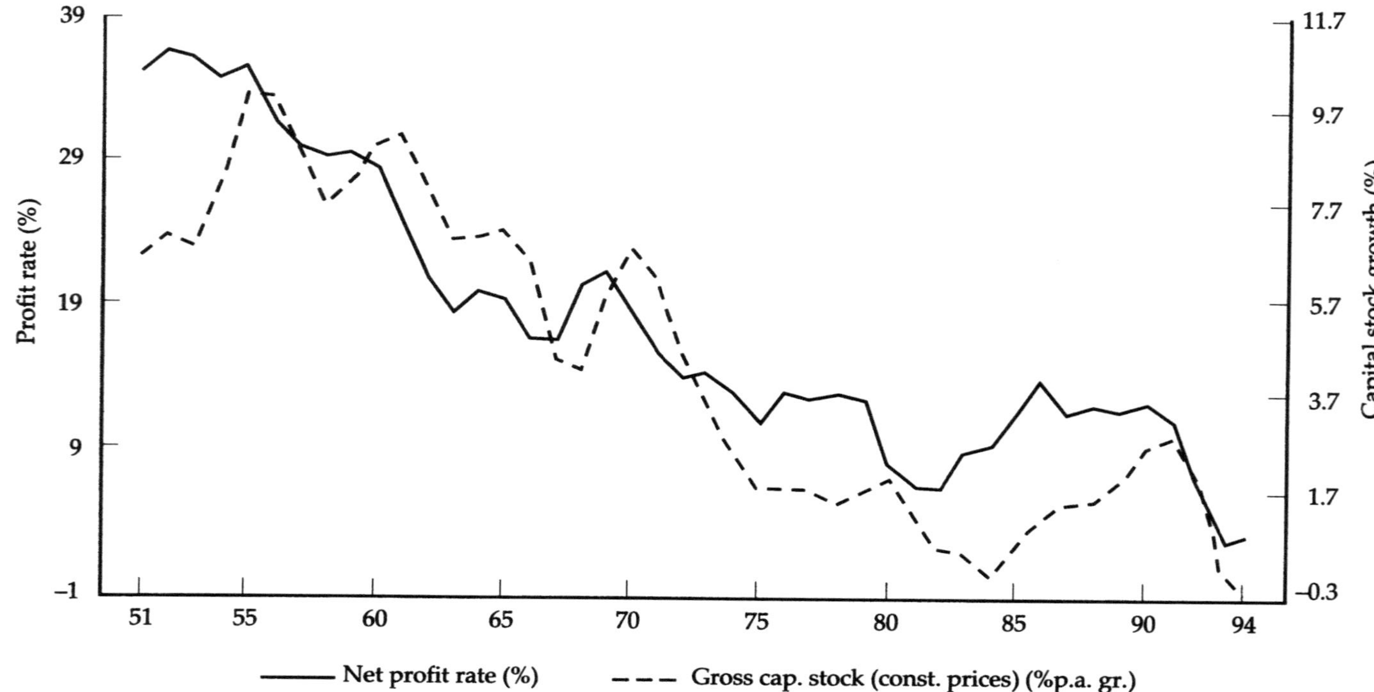

Figure 2.1 *West German manufacturing: profit rate and growth of capital stock 1951–94*

investment are promoting convergence in manufacturing: those industries in which there has been most investment have experienced the most rapid convergence toward West German productivity levels (Boltho et al. 1995). Although most investment is by private (including privatized) firms, the state is playing a large role in its financing. By the end of 1994, the privatization process was virtually complete: East German firms had either been sold – typically to a West German company or family – or closed down (Carlin and Mayer 1995). An eventual reduction in the burden this is placing on the German economy depends on the success of the investment projects which are being financed.

A major cause of the deterioration in West Germany's economic performance through the 1990s lies with the unexpectedly heavy costs of reunification. Unemployment has risen to the highest rate recorded in the post-war period and the recovery from recession in the early 1990s has been weak in comparison with earlier upswings. Figure 2.1 demonstrates the seriousness of the situation for West German manufacturing industry in 1993–4. Profitability has fallen to an extremely low level relative to West Germany's historical experience and relative to that of its competitors (Carlin and Soskice 1997). The gross capital stock in West German manufacturing fell in 1994.

The West German bargaining system worked fairly well over the post-war period to provide a high degree of economy-wide coordination, permitting low inflation to coexist with modest rates of unemployment. However, it seems that the need to finance reunification through tax increases placed a burden on workers that they were not prepared to accept. The result was a change in bargaining behaviour as unions sought compensation for the increased tax burden. As we have seen, the consequence of this was a tough response from the Bundesbank followed by a recession in West Germany and its ERM partners. West Germany may no longer be able to rely on its traditional recovery route of an export-led upswing. The economy is very large and half of its trade is with the rest of Europe, where growth is hindered by tight fiscal policy due to the simultaneous attempt of its European partners to meet the Maastricht criteria for budget deficits and public debt.

STRUCTURAL CHANGE, INSTITUTIONS AND POLICY IN POST-WAR WEST GERMANY

Policy

Contrasts are frequently drawn between the weakness of growth in the period of the Weimar Republic (1918–33) and the rapid growth after 1945 – at least until 1973. The post-1948 investment share was historically high (25 per cent in 1949) and rising through the 1950s while the investment share in the Weimar years was historically low and remained around the 18 per cent level from 1924 to 1929 (Mendershausen 1954, Table IX, p. 49).

One hypothesis links the investment failure to the operation of cartels in Germany. At the end of the nineteenth century, anti-trust legislation in the US was paralleled in Germany by a law making cartels legally binding. The possibility of price fixing had the effect of delaying and distorting the process of industrial restructuring associated with the new manufacturing technologies (James 1986). The propensity of German firms to form cartels and profit-pooling arrangements prevented the industry-wide rationalization that was required to exploit fully the economies of scale and scope available (Chandler 1990). This goes some way to explaining the failure of German industry to modernize before the Second World War: the old industries of coal, iron and steel with highly authoritarian management practices were not yet eclipsed by the industries of the so-called second industrial revolution – chemicals, vehicles and electrical goods.

After the war, Erhard and other so-called 'ordo-liberal' economists were opposed to the reformation of cartels. This was reinforced by the policies of the US occupation:

> [T]he aim and the effect of American industrial policy in occupied Western Germany had been to get the business community to abandon the cartel tradition and to adopt a market organization which resembled the American one and which, though oligopolistic, remained wedded to the principle of competition. (Berghahn 1986, p. 282)

A policy of openness of the economy to international trade was supported by domestic policy makers and was reinforced by West Germany's participation in the post-war international trade and payments arrangements. This proved to be an effective competition policy and a powerful weapon for modernization.

Structural Change: Deindustrialization

Changes in the balance of employment between agriculture, industry and services have long been linked to the process of economic development. In a closed economy, one would expect the process of development to be accompanied by a phase of decline in the share of employment in agriculture as underemployed labour in agriculture is pulled into higher productivity and higher wage employment in industry. Furthermore, the process is compounded by the inelastic demand for agricultural products as incomes rise as this limits the growth of markets for agricultural outputs. Later, with the demand for manufactured goods and for services growing in line in real terms, the higher productivity growth in manufacturing than in services produces a falling share of employment in industry and a rising share in services. This simple prediction of deindustrialization as development proceeds is modified in an open economy by the pattern of comparative advantage and specialization

(Rowthorn and Wells 1987). Germany is a good example of how open economy effects modify the simple prediction: between 1960 and 1990, during which the level of real income per head increased threefold, there was scarcely any change in the share of employment in manufacturing: in 1990, Germany's share (31.5 per cent) was markedly above that of all other OECD economies and 10 percentage points above the OECD average.

In the UK, unlike elsewhere in Europe, the share of employment in agriculture was already very low by 1950, with the result that a growing share of employment in services reflected the decline in manufacturing. In Germany, by contrast, industry's share declined relatively little, so the rising share of services reflected the shift of employment out of agriculture. There is clearly no simple relationship between these structural shifts and economic performance. Germany's relatively slow deindustrialization, by contrast with the UK and the US, for example, reflects its poor endowment of raw materials including energy and its ability to export manufactured goods successfully.

Institutions

Manufacturing has continued to play a more important role in the German economy than elsewhere in Europe and it has been argued that Germany's institutional structure is particularly well adapted to successful manufacturing. The institutional basis of the German economy has deep historical roots, but there were important innovations after the war. In industrial relations, there was a rationalization of union organization through the creation of industrial unions with comprehensive coverage – somewhat ironically following the advice of leading figures in the British trade union movement. This replaced the fragmentation along confessional and craft lines that had characterized the Weimar period. Secondly, state involvement in collective bargaining was abolished and, thirdly, the institutionalized participation of employees in management was established (through codetermination).

There are a number of routes through which these changes can be seen to have been growth promoting. For example, workers may be more willing to exercise bargaining restraint if they have confidence that, by postponing consumption, their wages and hence consumption in the future will be greater because investment by firms will be higher than it would otherwise have been (for a formal model, see Lancaster 1973). One way in which workers may be persuaded to act in this way is if they have institutionalized access to information about the firm's strategy through works councils and board representation (in large companies).

In economic models of bargaining, a situation of wage setting at industry level by industry unions can be more inflationary than one in which wage setting is decentralized to the level of the firm or when there is a single bargaining unit for the economy as a whole (centralized bargaining) (see, for example, Calmfors and Driffill 1988). This theoretical result emerges from the fact that when unions bargain at industry level, they are not worried about the impact of their wage increase on the employment of their members because the costs and prices of all products in the industry will rise in line and consumers will not have the choice of cheaper goods. Moreover, they are not worried about the impact of their wage settlement on the setting of macroeconomic policy because they are just one industry among many. The prediction that industry unionism would be inflationary does not square with the low inflation outcome achieved by Germany in the post-war period. It seems that the German collective bargaining system achieved a coordinated outcome – that is, one in which the consequences of inflation for the economy as a whole was taken into account in the wage bargain – without centralization. One factor of importance in producing this outcome is likely to have been the independence of the Bundesbank. The commitment of the Bundesbank to low inflation had the effect of deterring cheating by the wage negotiators by making them more sensitive to the consequences of any increase in inflation.

The new theoretical work on growth theory highlights the contribution which investment in human capital can make to growth. The distinctive feature of human capital formation in the German economy compared to others in Europe as well as the US and Japan is the extensive vocational training system. Twelve years after leaving school, 80 per cent of Germans had received a training certificate or post-secondary education degree, and almost all of the remainder had received some formal post-secondary education or training (Buechtemann et al. 1993, p. 101). Both in studies of matched plants in Germany and the UK, and in econometric work, skill differences, especially at the intermediate level, are a major explanatory factor for the productivity gap between British and German manufacturing (Daly et al. 1985; Steedman and Wagner 1987, 1989; Prais et al. 1989; O'Mahony 1992; Mason et al. 1993). The provision of marketable skills to an unusually broad section of the workforce in Germany can be explained by the presence of a set of specific institutional arrangements (Soskice 1993). For the German system to work it must provide incentives for school leavers to work hard at school in order to compete for apprenticeships; for apprentices to contribute to the cost of training through low training wages; for firms to offer and partially fund training places and to be willing to have their standards of training to be supervised. The state, unions, employers' associations and chambers of commerce are all involved.

The state contributes to vocational training by providing schools where trainees spend one or two days per week, and by establishing national standards for vocational qualifications. Unions and employers' associations cooperate closely in defining the detailed content of apprenticeships and in setting low training wages. The monitoring of training standards within companies is the responsibility of the local chambers of commerce. The coordinated wage-setting system and monitoring by works councils prevents employers from poaching trained workers, and by eliminating the free-rider problem, creates incentives for firms to contribute to investment in training. The legal protection of the artisanal (*Handwerk*) sector plays a vital role in the supply of training places at the bottom end of the ability scale (Steedman 1993). There is competition for apprenticeship places because of the difference in quality of the internal labour market to which the training place provides access and the value of the training in the external labour market (the best places are in large companies and in specific sectors such as banking).

This is a complex training system which has retained its effectiveness over a long period. Since the bulk of training occurs within firms, its success hinges on a stable population of firms. It would appear to be less well suited to meet the needs of a rapidly changing industrial structure.

The existence of differences in national institutional arrangements and their effect on performance is perhaps most hotly disputed in the case of the German banks and their links with industry (Shonfield 1965; Cable 1985; Edwards and Fischer 1994). Many empirical questions about the role of banks remain unresolved. What is clear, however, is that the business sector has a structure in Germany which is quite distinct from that found in the UK and the US. A far smaller part of the business sector is characterized by firms in which there is a split between those who own the firm and the managers who control it. In Germany, only about one-fifth of the turnover in the economy is accounted for by joint stock public companies, compared with over 50 per cent in the UK. Even in public companies, share holdings are much more concentrated in Germany than in the US or the UK – in the 200 largest listed German companies almost 90 per cent had a shareholder (usually another company) with a stake of at least 25 per cent. By contrast, in the UK, in more than four-fifths of the largest 200, the largest shareholding was less than 25 per cent.

This difference in structure means that German business as a whole is far less influenced by the behaviour of external investors on the stock exchange, and the phenomenon of the hostile take-over is virtually unknown. Banks appear to play a role of some significance in those (relatively few) large German companies which are widely held (Franks and Mayer 1994). All large companies have a supervisory board which monitors the managers. On the supervisory board are represented the owners (for example, other companies) and other stakeholders in the business (for example, suppliers, banks, and, by law, employees).

The other striking feature of German business is the size and strength of its small and medium-sized firms, especially in manufacturing. One hypothesis is that the German banking system provides important support for the SME sector. There are highly developed savings and cooperative bank sectors which compete with the commercial banks for the business of SMEs. These banks help to overcome the problems of credit rationing which typically face SMEs. Although much empirical work remains to be done, it appears that it is features of the structure of ownership of German firms and the broader structure of the banking system (rather than the specific relationship between the large commercial banks and large firms) which distinguishes Germany and which may be important to understanding the stability of German business and its continuing strength in manufacturing.

The institutional structure of the German economy is dense as compared with Anglo-American economies in that there is a complex set of non-market relationships which appear to be important to economic decision making. For example, firms and unions have relationships not just concerning wages, but also regarding vocational training. From this perspective, German 'long-termism' should be interpreted in terms of such non-market relationships between companies and other companies, employees, banks and institutions such as vocational colleges, industry associations and chambers of commerce. This interpretation provides a way of understanding the less than wholehearted embrace by German business of financial and labour market deregulation in the 1980s.

Germany's rigidities of employment protection, highly structured wage setting and compulsory consultation of management with the workforce ruled out the adaptation to increased international competition in the 1980s through cost-cutting strategies. Companies were forced to move into high value added products and processes. By the same token, the West German institutional structure permits forms of innovation which are not available to economies which are unable to sustain long-term relationships between companies, their employees and financial institutions. But it also militates against success in fields in which radical innovation is required, such as new technology fields of electronics, biotechnology and pharmaceuticals (Carlin and Soskice 1997). An open question is whether adaptation of the German economy in its core industries is rapid enough for competitiveness to be maintained and whether those core sectors will remain sufficiently central to economic activity. It is striking that Japanese manufacturing success is more highly concentrated than Germany's – in vehicles and electronics.

The regions of East Germany are obliged to operate under the labour market and other forms of regulation transferred from West Germany and will not have the option of being a low-wage economy. If they are to develop an indigenous economic base, the institutional structure must be created in which the long-term relationships which seem essential to West Germany's high wage economy can be built up.

GERMANY'S ROLE IN THE EUROPEAN ECONOMY

At the end of the 1960s German confidence in the ability of the US authorities to maintain and transmit stable inflation through the dollar's role as the anchor currency in the Bretton Woods system began to wane. The obvious solution to this would be to move to a floating exchange rate system in which each country could choose its own inflation rate. However, Germany was committed to the process of economic integration in Europe in which stable exchange rates between EEC members were viewed as important both in promoting trade and in facilitating the operation of the Common Agricultural Policy. Germany's interest in low inflation and in stable exchange rates in Europe could be met by a monetary union in the EC with a single currency that would float against the dollar – this would permit the revaluation of the EC currency against the dollar which would dampen imported inflation from the US without the destruction of the EC. These ideas were discussed at The Hague Summit in 1969, one result of which was the so-called Werner Plan (named after the Luxembourg Minister of Finance) for monetary union.

The Bretton Woods system finally fell apart in the early 1970s, but it was not until 1979 that an effective exchange rate system for Europe was established. There is considerable empirical evidence that although the ERM was set up with the intention of operating as a symmetric system, in practice it represented a continuity with the history of exchange rate arrangements: just as the US had played the key role in the Bretton Woods system, West Germany was the key currency country in the ERM. In an asymmetric system with Germany at the centre, the Bundesbank would set monetary policy and, in order to maintain the parity of their exchange rates, the other members would have to bring their monetary policy into line. In principle, this provided a useful external support for countries which sought to lower inflation, but in which the domestic monetary authorities lacked a reputation for imposing monetary discipline – France and Italy being prime examples. Countries with higher inflation than Germany would find their competitiveness and their current account deteriorating. In the ERM, periodic adjustments of the nominal parities were allowed for but they were typically not large enough to offset the deterioration in competitiveness that had occurred – hence the real exchange rate tended to be maintained at a higher than comfortable level. The system therefore operated to provide some discipline for domestic wage and price setters. Depending on the extent of wage restraint achieved, domestic fiscal policy had to be set tightly enough to contain inflationary pressure.

During the operation of the ERM from 1979 to 1992, Germany played an important role in facilitating the reduction of inflation in Europe. However, its importance should not be exaggerated. In general the ERM held together because there was a general policy objective in Europe to bring down inflation even at the cost of higher unemployment. The Bundesbank's reputation assisted with the realization of low inflation objectives elsewhere. However, there is neither strong evidence that ERM membership helped to reduce the cost of disinflation in terms of higher unemployment, nor that it operated as a mechanism for excessive deflation in Europe. All the members benefited from a reduction in exchange rate volatility. For Germany, there was also a reduction in the swings in the Deutschmark vis-a-vis the dollar and the yen as compared with the period before (or after) the existence of the ERM.

The shock of German reunification contributed to the demise of the ERM in the autumn of 1992, but there were two other important contributory factors:

the failure of inflation rates to converge fully to German levels, and the effects of the abolition of capital controls. The German authorities were actively seeking a realignment of rates through a revaluation of the Deutschmark. The unwillingness of the British and French to accept the associated devaluation of their currencies meant that the contractionary measures taken by the Bundesbank to raise interest rates through 1991 and 1992 transmitted a recessionary impact around Europe. The combination of the impending recession and the underlying misalignment of several currencies in the ERM (in particular the pound and the lira) fuelled the speculation on foreign exchange markets in the autumn of 1992 and the withdrawal of both currencies. Later, following further speculation against the Franc in the August of 1993, the intervention bands were widened to +/–15 per cent so that it could only barely be described as a continuation of the ERM.

The events of 1992 and the much higher than anticipated costs for West Germany of economic and monetary union with the former GDR have undoubtedly affected the prospects for monetary union in Europe. Because of the simultaneous currency union and transfer of institutions such as wage bargaining and income support to East Germany, the adjustment problems for the weak region and the financing burden on the strong region have been extraordinarily high. This has served as a warning to those seeking a rapid move to a single currency in Europe. Moreover a by-product of the ERM episode has been the demonstration that nominal exchange rate changes can have a considerable effect on real economic activity: UK and Italian exports have performed strongly following the devaluations. It has also become clear over the course of this episode that even in exceptional circumstances a number of countries, and in particular, France, are deeply reluctant to use exchange rate changes as a tool of economic policy. For these countries, there is little to lose from a currency union in which monetary policy is set by Germany.

It has been argued above that Germany could have operated a less restrictive macroeconomic stance in the early to mid-1980s and that this would have boosted growth. In view of the higher pressure of demand in the economy which accompanied German reunification, a tolerance by the Bundesbank for a slightly higher inflation rate may be necessary for steady growth to be achieved.

The openness of German markets to competition has provided a crucial incentive for adaptation in the post-war period and it is through the pressure of product market competition, especially from abroad, that changes in the production system appear to be negotiated. The Single Market has increased competitive pressure on German firms, especially in sectors which were previously highly protected by regulation. A recognition of the role of external competitive threats is likely to reinforce German support for the extension of economic integration in Europe (including the widening of the EU to include the Eastern European economies) and to oppose the formation of a 'Fortress Europe'.

CONCLUSION

Although benefiting from special growth factors in the immediate post-war years, West Germany's experience in the Golden Age up to 1973 was broadly similar to the general pattern in Europe. Growth was unprecedentedly high and stable and compatible with moderate inflation and full employment. Inequalities in income distribution declined and access to education, health care and social protection became universal. In the post-1973 period, and especially after 1979, divergences have become more pronounced between the economic policies and performance outcomes of the advanced economies.

Change occurred more slowly in West Germany in the 1980s than in many other countries. The labour market provides a good illustration of this. In unemployment, West Germany suffered moderate increases – fitting neither the Scandinavian pattern of holding unemployment below 3 per cent nor suffering from double-digit unemployment common to the other large European countries. In Scandinavia, low unemployment was maintained until the 1990s in spite of a substantial increase in the participation of women in full-time work. There was little increase in wage inequality. By contrast, in the UK, women's participation in part-time work increased and, in common with the US, there was a sharp rise in earnings inequality across the workforce. West Germany fits neither pattern: there was little increase in women's participation, which remained at a much lower level than typical of northern Europe. Wage inequality, if anything, decreased (Freeman and Katz 1994). The relatively modest changes in labour market outcomes is consistent with the continuity of the German institutional structure and the slow changes in industrial structure. There was no parallel in Germany to the sweeping deregulation of the labour market and weakening of the unions that took place in Britain.

The German economy faces formidable challenges from increased competition in world markets. It is unclear how well suited the virtues of incremental innovation and adaptation of existing products and processes based on a highly skilled workforce are to these conditions. The problems of integrating the new eastern states of Germany is not only creating strains on German public finances and on the willingness of taxpayers in West Germany to contribute to footing the bill, but it is also testing the resilience and adaptability of the core institutions of the German social market economy.

* This chapter draws on more detailed papers: W. Carlin (1996) 'West German growth and institutions, 1945–90', in N. Crafts and G. Toniolo (eds), *Economic Growth in Europe since 1945*; and W. Carlin and D. Soskice (1997) 'Shocks to the System: The German Political Economy under Stress', *National Institute Economic Review*, No. 159, pp. 57–76.

REFERENCES

Armstrong, P., Glyn, A. and Harrison, J. (1991) *Capitalism since 1945*, Oxford: Blackwell.

Barro, R. J. and Sala-i-Martin, X. (1991) 'Convergence across states and regions', *Brookings Papers on Economic Activity*, No. 1, pp. 107–82.

Berghahn, V. R. (1986) *The Americanisation of West German Industry*, Leamington Spa and New York: Berg.

Boltho, A., Carlin, W. and Scaramozzino, P. (1995) 'Will East Germany become a new Mezzogiorno?', *Journal of Comparative Economics*, Vol. 24, pp. 241–64.

Buechtemann, C. F., Schupp, J. and Soloff, D. (1993) 'Roads to work: school-to-work transition patterns in Germany and the United States' *Industrial Relations Journal*, Vol. 24, No. 2, pp. 97–111.

Cable, J. R. (1985) 'Capital market information and industrial performance: the role of West German banks', *Economic Journal*, Vol. 95, pp. 118–32.

Calmfors, L. and Driffill, J. (1988) 'Bargaining structure, corporatism and macroeconomic performance', *Economic Policy*, No. 6.

Carlin, W. and Mayer, C. (1995) 'Structure and ownership of East German enterprises', *Journal of the Japanese and International Economies*, Vol. 9, pp. 426–53.

Carlin, W. and Soskice, D. (1997) 'Shocks to the System: The German Political Economy under Stress', *National Institute Economic Review*, No. 159, pp. 57–76.

Chandler, A. D. (1990) *Scale and Scope: The Dynamics of Industrial Capitalism*, Cambridge MA: Belknap / Harvard.

Crafts, N. F. R. and Toniolo, G. (1996) *Economic Growth in Europe since 1945*, Cambridge: Cambridge University Press.

Daly, A., Hitchens, D. and Wagner, K. (1985) 'Productivity, machinery and skills in a sample of British and German manufacturing plants: results of a pilot enquiry', *National Institute Economic Review*, No. 111, pp. 48–61.

Dowrick, S. and Nguyen, D.-T. (1989) 'OECD comparative economic growth 1950–85: catch-up and convergence', *American Economic Review*, Vol. 79, pp. 1010–30.

Edwards, J. and Fischer, K. (1994) *Banks, Finance and Investment in Germany*, Cambridge: Cambridge University Press.

Flanagan, R., Soskice, D. and Ulman, L. (1982) *Unionism, Economic Stabilization and Incomes Policies: European Experience*, Washington: Brookings.

Franks, J. and Mayer, C. (1994) 'Ownership and control'. Paper presented at an International Workshop in Kiel, June 1994. Unpublished Ms. London Business School.

Freeman, R. and Katz, L. (1994) 'Rising wage inequality: the United States vs. other countries', in R. Freeman (ed.), *Working Under Different Rules*, New York: Russell Sage Foundation.

GATT (1991) *World Trade 1990–1991*, Geneva: GATT

Giersch, H., Paqué, K.-H. and Schmieding, H. (1992) *The Fading Miracle: Four Decades of Market Economy in Germany*, Cambridge: Cambridge University Press.

Hellwig, M. and Neumann, M. (1985) 'Economic policy in Germany: was there a turnaround?', *Economic Policy*, No. 5, pp. 103–45.

James, H. (1986) *The German Slump: Politics and Economics 1924–1936*, Oxford: Oxford University Press.

Katzenstein, P. (1989) 'Stability and change in the emerging third republic', in P. Katzenstein (ed.), *Industry and Politics in West Germany*, Cornell: Cornell University Press.

Klodt, H. (1990) 'Industrial policy and repressed structural change in Germany', *Jahrbücher für Nationalökonomie und Statistik*, Vol. 207, No. 1, pp. 25–35.

Krengel, R. (1958) *Anlagevermögen, Produktion und Beschäftigung der Industrie im Gebiet der Bundesrepublik Deutschland von 1924 zu 1958*, Berlin: DIW.

Lancaster, K. (1973) 'The dynamic inefficiency of capitalism', *Journal of Political Economy*, pp. 1092–109.

Maddison, A. (1991) *Dynamic Forces in Capitalist Development*, Oxford: Oxford University Press.

Marglin, S. A. and Schor, J. B. (eds) (1990) *The Golden Age of Capitalism: Lessons for the 1990s*, Oxford: Clarendon Press.

Mason, G., van Ark, B. and Wagner, K. (1993) 'Productivity, product quality and workforce skills: food processing in four European countries', *Discussion Paper FSI*, Berlin: Wissenschaftszentrum, pp. 99–309.

Mendershausen, H. (1954) *Two Post-war Recoveries of the German Economy*, Amsterdam: North-Holland.

O'Mahony, M. (1992) 'Productivity levels in British and German manufacturing industry', *National Institute Economic Review*, No. 139, pp. 46–63.

O'Mahoney, M. and Wagner, K. (1994) 'Changing fortunes: an industry study of British and German productivity growth over three decades', *Discussion Paper FSI*, Berlin: Wissenschaftszentrum, pp. 94–304.

Prais, S. J., Jarvis, V. and Wagner, K. (1989) 'Productivity and vocational skills in services in Britain and Germany: hotels', *National Institute Economic Review*, No. 130, pp. 52–74.

Rowthorn, R. and Wells, J. (1987) *Deindustrialization and Foreign Trade*, Cambridge: Cambridge University Press.

Shonfield, A. (1965) *Modern Capitalism: The Changing Balance of Public and Private Power*, Oxford: Oxford University Press.

Soskice, D. (1990) 'Wage determination: the changing role of institutions in advanced industrialized countries', *Oxford Review of Economic Policy*, Vol. 6, pp. 36–61.

Soskice, D. (1993) 'Reconciling markets and institutions: the German apprenticeship system', in L. M. Lynch (ed.), *Training and the Private Sector: International Comparisons*, Chicago: University of Chicago Press.

Steedman, H. (1993) 'The economics of youth training in Germany', *Economic Journal*, Vol. 103, No. 420, pp. 1279–91.

Steedman, H. and Wagner, K. (1987) 'A second look at productivity, machinery and skills in Britain and Germany', *National Institute Economic Review*, No. 122, pp. 84–96.

Steedman, H. and Wagner, K. (1989) 'Productivity, machinery and skills: clothing manufacture in Britain and Germany', *National Institute Economic Review*, No. 128, pp. 40–57.

van de Klundert, T. and van Shaik, A. (1993) 'On the historical continuity of the process of economic growth', *CEPR Discussion Paper*, Series No. 850.

3 France: A Case of Eurosclerosis?

Bernard J. Foley

INTRODUCTION

In the aftermath of the Second World War until the late 1950s, France was perceived as politically unstable and economically fragile. This perception changed sharply in the early 1960s, however, when the effects of rapid economic growth on living standards became apparent and President de Gaulle consolidated the political structures introduced by the Fifth Republic. By the 1990s, France could justifiably claim to be the second most important economy in Western Europe: according to the OECD (*Economic Survey of France* 1995), only Germany had a bigger GDP and, in purchasing power parity terms, French citizens were the third most affluent in the European Union (see Maddison 1995, Table D-1a).[1]

In this chapter we look at the factors that transformed post-war France such that, for a time at least, the economy outperformed most of the OECD economies and was held up as an example for others to follow. We also examine what has happened since the deceleration of the 1970s.

In the immediate post-war period French policy was driven by two major objectives: first, to modernize and renovate the economy; and, second, to avoid future conflict in Europe. Initially it was felt that the latter could be achieved by keeping Germany weak, but by the late 1940s, policy became concerned to incorporate Germany into various types of organization so as to preclude the possibility of future hostilities. These economic and foreign policy objectives were in the event mutually reinforcing: first, modernizing France meant that its industries would compete more effectively with their foreign counterparts – hence in due course economic integration with France's neighbours could be portrayed as an opportunity as much as a threat; second, the incorporation of West Germany into organizations such as the European Coal and Steel Community and the EEC implied a reciprocal opening-out of the economy by the French authorities. This changed France from its traditionally protectionist stance and accelerated the growth trajectory upon which the country was already embarked.

1945–58: RECOVERY, PLANNING AND THE CLOSED ECONOMY

The transformation of the French economy from the devastation which war and occupation had inflicted was a considerable feat. Eck (1988) describes the economy at that time as 'wrecked': the basic infrastructure – ports, roads, railways and energy production and distribution – were in ruins. Caron (1979) estimates the loss of capital stock at nearly one half, while manufacturing production was only a third of its 1938 level. Despite this, pre-war levels of GDP were reached in 1948/9.[2] France was the second largest recipient of Marshall Aid – approximately $2.7 billion as compared to the UK's $3.17 billion between 1948 and 1952 (Price 1955). Recovery was not simply a question of the replacement of physical assets, however: the stagnation of the 1930s had severely undermined the confidence of French business so that a defensive protectionism seemed the likeliest outcome in the post-war period. This was partly a function of the fact that the economy had badly underperformed other advanced economies in the 1930s: in 1939, GDP had barely recovered the level reached in 1929 and real living standards had declined. In addition much of the political elite was demoralized and humiliated by the collapse of 1940, while important sections of the business community were tainted by active collaboration with the quasi-fascist Vichy regime during the war.

In 1945 the authorities were clear that a break with the past was imperative. A rapid return to normal levels of economic activity was urgent but a reversion to the neo-liberal agenda of the inter-war period was impossible given the existing constellation of political forces which included a large, confident and vociferous Communist Party enjoying the halo effect of its role in the war-time Resistance. Hence reconstruction meant more than restoration: *modernisation ou decadence* became the slogan around which 'progressive' forces rallied.

The problem was to make this slogan a reality. A key institutional innovation was the development of medium-term national planning focused on the supply side of the economy. Compared to the UK and the US, France has traditionally been more centralized and interventionist in economic affairs and this was reinforced in the immediate post-war period via an emerging technobureaucracy which was to become a bridge between government and the business sector.[3] Hence the adoption of 'indicative planning' fitted into a *dirigiste* political culture looking to modernize archaic social and economic structures. Petit (1988), for example, argues that,

> The essential factor seems to have been a *consensus of opinion concerning the main economic options* which was shared by a group of people for whom the Plan was a useful (and neutral) meeting ground but whose connections, influence and ideas extended far beyond the thousand or so people directly involved in its elaboration. (p. 47; emphasis added)

By the late 1950s the role of planning in the recovery was beginning to achieve almost quasi-mythical status in the public mind, but its contribution to the growth of the post-war economy was already in doubt by the mid-1960s (Sheahan 1963; Lutz 1965). Opinion has become even more sceptical since: Adams (1989), for example, suggests that the effect of Common Market entry in 1958 was crucial to maintaining the rate of growth precisely because it corrected earlier policy errors. More recently, Sicsic and Wyplosz (1996) deploy econometric evidence to show that the authorities misallocated resources in the early phase.

The First Plan was only partly about economics, however – it also served political purposes. Lynch (1984) argues that its preparation served foreign policy objectives: in line with the desire to weaken Germany, the Plan was designed to win support for international control of the energy resources of the Ruhr. It was also explicit about the need to build up French heavy industry which had been vastly inferior to Germany's before the war. Hence it concentrated on industries – coal, electricity, cement, steel, transport and agricultural machinery – which were 'basic' and whose outputs were relatively homogeneous, so that quantitative targets were easier to formulate. Two other features were important: first, these were sectors where the government enjoyed direct influence – coal, electricity and railways had been nationalized in 1946; and, second, control of finance gave the authorities further leverage – four of the major commercial banks were nationalized and specialist organizations such as *Le Fond de Modernisation et d'Équipement* were established to finance the Plan. This constitutes the thrust of the recent argument by Sicsic and Wyplosz (1996): given their control over finance, planners and the state favoured energy and transport to the detriment of manufacturing. The latter, they suggest, was largely constrained by a lack of liquidity which resulted in a lower rate of growth than would otherwise have occurred. By implication, the private sector would readily have taken up the resources that the state sector was absorbing.

There is clearly some truth to this: for example, in the first official survey of French business in 1951, 30 per cent of the sample mention credit constraints as 'limiting their activities' (INSEE 1952). But this was not the complete story, there were other important factors holding firms back – for example, business expectations at the time were not uniformly optimistic. In the same survey nearly half of the sample suggested that they were mainly concerned about outlets or markets (*debouchés*). This response could have simply been the result of an expected cyclical downturn as government was struggling with inflation. However, the Economic Commission for Europe (1955) reported that, as late as November 1954 when business appeared more optimistic about markets, only half of their respondents in engineering and one-third of those in food were planning to increase investment while in textiles two-thirds were planning to reduce capital expenditure. It is not until the 1955 survey that 'outlets / markets' slip down the list of constraints to be replaced by concern for manpower (INSEE 1956). Bouvier and colleagues (1982, p. 1168) also point out that up until the mid-1950s French business had not shaken off the fear of overinvestment (*surcapitalisation*) which had been prevalent in the 1930s. One might argue therefore that significant segments of manufacturing industry were reluctant to invest until convinced that the climate of expansion was well founded. Indeed, Sicsic and Wyplosz (1996) themselves observe that, 'It is only after investment had started to soar in 1955 that the prospect of a long lasting stagnation evaporated' (p. 218).

One could easily argue this the other way round – perhaps it was only after business expectations adjusted to the reality of expansion that investment began to soar? Given the apparent pessimism of French business, state directed and/or supported investment at this juncture may have been appropriate even if at the risk of some misallocation.

Throughout the period of recovery the emphasis was on physical production even at the expense of financial outcomes: inflation was persistent and substantial at an annual rate of over 45 per cent between 1945 and 1949 (Bank for International Settlements 1949). This was in one sense unavoidable as the build-up of liquid assets during the war had been very considerable. Patat and Lutfalla (1990) suggest that when France was liberated in 1944, on average each citizen was holding 15 500FF in banknotes compared to 3800FF before the war. In addition bank deposits and postal accounts had grown by 147 per cent and 237 per cent respectively. The inflation then was driven by excess demand and this was duly reflected in the international value of the Franc which became progressively weaker: despite the existence of a web of controls to protect the balance of payments, several devaluations took the official parity of the Franc from 49.6FF : $ in 1945 to 350FF : $ in 1949.[4] There were signs that the authorities were beginning to contain the situation by 1949 via strict fiscal and monetary policy when they were driven off course by the outbreak of the Korean War. After an effective stabilization package in 1952–3, inflation remained broadly under control for the first half of the 1950s and then, after a sharp rise to 7.5 and 8.5 per cent in 1957 and 1958, deflation was combined with a devaluation of almost 20 per cent which helped to usher in what has been called the '*Grande Époque*' of the Fifth Republic.

With hindsight it is clear that the impact of planning was not all benign, but this was decidedly not the perception at the time, so that successive plans became more ambitious. The expansion of the economy throughout the 1950s, therefore, was commonly attributed to the policy regime: it seemed to provide continuity in a period characterized by serious difficulties for France. The Fourth Republic (1946–58) was synonymous with political instability: for example, there were 26 changes of government between 1946 and 1958 and, in addition, from 1946 until 1962 France was embroiled in successive colonial wars, first in Indo-China (Vietnam) and then in Algeria – a problem which at one time threatened to degenerate into civil war. In the late 1950s and early 1960s received wisdom among economists suggested that political and economic instability ('stop–go') increased business uncertainty with adverse effects on investment and the long-run growth rate. Hence France's unprecedented annual growth (in excess of 4 per cent) in the face of so much domestic volatility was ascribed to the planning regime. Indeed, by the time the Fourth Plan (1962–5) was in preparation, the prestige of French planning was such that other European governments, for example, the UK and Italy, attempted to introduce their own versions.

Even as it reached its zenith, however, critics were becoming more vocal. The preparatory documents for the Fifth Plan laid out a detailed rationale for the practice, which itself suggests that the planners were becoming sensitive to these criticisms. Lutz (1965, 1969) argued that the first four Plans had not only failed to meet many of their objectives, but they also suffered from serious technical deficiencies. Supporters were blithely unconcerned about technical flaws, however, as it was argued that accuracy was unimportant compared with influencing business decisions in ways which favoured expansion (Shonfield 1965). Whatever conclusion one arrives at with regard to the efficacy of planning, it is clear that in the 1960s, for a variety of reasons, its influence diminished while the growth of the economy gathered momentum (Estrin and Holmes 1983).

THE 'GRANDE ÉPOQUE' OF THE FIFTH REPUBLIC – 1958–73

Rapid growth in the 1950s was a surprise, but even in the latter part of the decade there was a view that it was simply the lingering effects of post-war recovery, so the acceleration in the 1960s was hailed as little short of miraculous. Only fifteen or so years before, opinion, in the US as well as Europe, was predicting macroeconomic instability and a return to the slump of the 1930s.

The magnitude of the acceleration can be seen in Table 3.1.

Table 3.1 *Growth of GDP and GDP per capita in France 1938–94*

	%GDP	*%GDP per Capita*
1938–50	1.3	1.4
1950–60	4.5	3.6
1960–73	5.2	4.2
1950–73	5.0	3.9
1950–58	4.3	3.6
1958–73	5.2	4.1
1973–94	2.1	1.6
1973–79	2.8	2.3
1979–94	1.8	1.3

Source: Calculated from Maddison (1995), Tables C16a/D-1a.

In accounting for this growth, successive studies refined the original inputs of capital and labour to allow for qualitative changes as well as the contribution of phenomena such as the age–sex profile of the labour force, economies of scale and foreign trade effects, but the residual component, 'Total Factor Productivity', turned out to be the largest contributor. Denison's (1967) early study found that, for France in the period 1950–62, almost three-quarters of the rate of growth was unexplained. Similarly Carré, Dubois and Malinvaud (1972) quantified *seven* contributory elements and, in their case, the proportion of the growth of GDP unaccounted for remained close to 50 per cent. More recently, Maddison (1991), with a set of eight variables, reduced the size of the residual yet further. But even in the period when its contribution is smallest, that is, 1973–87, it still accounted for over a quarter (28 per cent) of the annual growth rate.

This residual element gave rise to a number of explanatory hypotheses, most of which attributed it to some notion of 'technological progress'. This should come as no surprise given that technological progress is a major force explaining the growth of capitalist economies over the past two centuries. However, the big acceleration in the post-war rates of growth requires a little more by way of explanation. The idea that technological innovations may be clustered or bunched (rather than occurring in a steady flow) so as to produce acceleration and deceleration in the pace of growth, has a long pedigree (see Maddison 1991, Chapter 4), but it is unnecessary to appeal to this line of argument here. Even if innovation occurs randomly in a steady stream, it is possible to explain the acceleration of growth in Western Europe between 1950 and 1973, by the fact that the *application* or *diffusion* of new technologies had been retarded by the Great Depression and the Second World War. Hence by 1945 there was a shelf of existing technologies which could be utilized. In this case a substantial part of the acceleration would be the result of catching up on opportunities previously foregone. Thus the experience of the Golden Age (1950–73) is explicable in terms of the implementation of new technologies, new managerial techniques and new methods of production assimilated from the leading economy in the post-war period – the US. The US had established a clear lead across a whole range of industries in terms of modern production techniques from the 1920s onward, and that lead had been consolidated during the Second World War.

Levine and Renelt (1992) lend support to this view. Reviewing and analysing a very large number studies, they found that three features give a robust explanation of growth performance: the proportion of resources devoted to investment, the openness of the economy, and the capacity to catch up leader economies.

Catch-up is now recognized as a significant factor explaining convergence in the level of labour productivity and hence GDP per head, over a wide range of OECD economies (Maddison 1995; Verspagen 1996). France was no exception. Even to the casual observer, catch-up opportunities appeared to be considerable in the 1950s – this impression of backwardness showed up in several ways:

- First, at that time, nearly 30 per cent of the labour force was in agriculture and much of this in small undercapitalized farms in the South and West.

- Second, only some 65 per cent of France's exports were manufactured goods, compared with approximately 80 per cent for Germany, the UK and Italy (calculated from ECE 1955, Table 8).
- Third, excluding trade with the affiliated territories of the Franc zone, France was a *net importer* of machinery by comparison with the UK, West Germany and Italy (ECE 1955).
- Finally, the capital stock in France was on average older than that of her comparators (Maddison 1991, p. 143), and within this sector the vitally important machine tools industry was very dated – at the outset of the 1950s over half of France's equipment was over 20 years old compared with less than one-third in Germany and about one-fifth in the US.[5]

Table 3.2 *Age of machine tools (1952) percentages*

Years	*France*	*Germany*	*US*
<10	30	30	57
10–20	17	39	22
>20	53	31	21
	100	100	100

Source: *Les industries de transformation dans le second plan de modernisation* – Report of an ad hoc Commission (1953) Paris.

The effect of catch up-can be see in Table 3.3 which indicates the degree to which some follower countries in the OECD group were converging on the leader – the US – after the Second World War.

Table 3.3 *Comparative levels of productivity (GDP per man hour 1913–92)*

	1913	*1950*	*1973*	*1992*
France	56	45	76	102
Germany	68	35	71	95
UK	86	62	68	82
Italy	41	34	66	85
US	100	100	100	100

Source: Maddison (1995), Table 2.7a.

On this criterion, France had actually surpassed the US by the 1990s. Economies such as Germany, Italy and Japan experienced even faster rates of catch-up than France in the period 1950–73, but they started from a much lower base in the initial year.

However, the mere presence of catch-up opportunities does not guarantee that they will be exploited: there also has to be the capacity and incentive to absorb the techniques the leader has developed. The institutional context of Western Europe by comparison, say, with the former Soviet bloc (that is, relatively free markets, profit-driven attitudes to innovation, open information systems, a willingness to accept inflows of direct investment, and high levels of education) meant that these economies were well placed to absorb these advances and catch up with the leader. Furthermore, one must also recognize that political authorities in the US were very keen to encourage the process – partly for economic reasons, but also for strategic, geo-political reasons, given post-war competition with the communist bloc.

In the 1950s, GDP expanded at 4.35 per cent per annum with very little by way of additional factor supplies. The labour force was virtually static: employment rose, but only by 46 000, while the number of working hours per year actually fell. In addition, as Table 3.4 illustrates, France's gross capital stock was increasing more slowly than the growth of output so the capital stock was being used more effectively.

Table 3.4 *Annual average rate of growth of gross capital stock (Non-residential structures and machinery and equipment)*

	France (%)	*Germany* (%)	*Netherlands* (%)	*UK* (%)	*US* (%)
1950–60	3.3	5.5	4.0	4.8	2.9
1960–73	5.8	6.6	4.8	5.2	3.5
1973–92	4.3	3.3	3.0	3.2	3.3

Source: Maddison (1995) – calculated from Appendix Tables A5–D10.

Hence growth in the 1950s was described at the time as mainly a result of rising productivity, and France's economy was held up as 'a study of the efficient use of scarce productive resources' (ECE 1965 Chapter VI, p. 7). In the 1960s the rate of growth picked up momentum to 5.2 per cent per annum – partly attributable to the conventional route of increased factor supplies. The labour force increased at an annual rate of just over 1 per cent – and there was more rapid accumulation of capital at 5.8 per cent. The major part, however, again came from improvements in total factor productivity – driven by a historic reorientation of policy – what is termed, in France, *l'Ouverture*, the opening of the economy to international competition.

Recent evidence overwhelmingly suggests that the more open economies are, the faster their rate of growth (IMF 1993; Sachs and Warner 1995). The boom in international trade in the post-war period was a common experience for the whole of the capitalist world and reflects the process of trade liberalization embarked upon under the tutelage of the US. For France this had implications which were much more significant than for economies such as the Netherlands, the UK, Germany and Sweden. The latter have historically been open to international competition whereas, by contrast, France had leaned toward autarky and vested interests sheltered behind an array of quotas and other restrictions (OEEC 1953). Tariff barriers too were much higher than elsewhere: prior to reductions under the Treaty of Rome the average tariff (on consumer durables, other consumer goods, and fixed assets – excluding food, beverages and tobacco) imposed by individual members of the EEC was as shown in Table 3.5.

Table 3.5 *Average tariff rates, EC(6)*

	%
France	17.2
Italy	14.5
Benelux	9.9
Germany	8.3

Source: Warta (1966).

Within the EEC, tariff barriers disappeared by 1968, and after the Kennedy Round of GATT was completed in 1972, the average common external tariff on manufactures for the EEC as a whole was 7.6 per cent, compared with 11.2 per cent for the US, 10.2 per cent for the UK and 9.8 per cent for Japan. Hence, in terms of tariffs at least, France had gone from one of the most highly protected to one of the least protected of the OECD economies. This of course overstates the degree of openness as non-tariff barriers such as preferential state purchasing, customs classification and differential standards (for example, on safety requirements, and so on) remained available as protectionist devices but the impact on efficiency of lower tariff barriers was evident.

Opening-out, then, was significant for the following reasons. First, France obtained reciprocal access to other fast-growing economies within the EC, so there was a sustained increase in demand in the domestic economy and a change in the geographical pattern of trade. Second, opening-out influenced the competitiveness of the French economy (Mistral 1975). These effects were enhanced by the aggressive devaluation undertaken by the authorities in 1958 in preparation for the Common Market.

The behaviour of French exports before and after the Treaty of Rome came into effect in 1958 can be seen in Table 3.6. From 1950 to 1958, exports were expanding at a rate less than the growth of GDP, but from 1959 exports grew twice as quickly as GDP and they also exhibited greater stability than in the previous sub-period. This relationship was maintained though at lower levels between 1973 and 1990.

Table 3.6 *Annual average rate of growth of output and exports*

	A. Output%	*B. Exports%*	*B/A*
1950–58	4.3	4.4	1.02
1959–73	5.2	9.5	1.83
1973–89	2.3	4.3	1.87

Source: Maddison (1991), calculated from Tables A.8 and F.4.

After 1959 the internationalization of the French economy was driven on by the EEC. In 1958 the ratio of exports to GDP was only 9 per cent, by 1968 it reached 13.7 per cent and rose further to average 21 per cent between 1974 and 1979; imports behaved in a like manner (OECD *Economic Survey of France* 1986). In the space of six years, between 1958 and 1964, exports to and imports from the other EC economies rose threefold, that is, French trade with its European partners was expanding at an annual rate of 18 per cent. Whereas, in the late 1950s, exports to these economies were some 27 per cent of total French exports, by the late 1960s they accounted for over 47 per cent. The new markets in Europe were based on more sophisticated outputs – those with a higher income elasticity of demand – and increasingly sophisticated consumers.

Table 3.7 *Shares of French trade with EC countries 1949–68 EC(6) 1992 EU(12)*

	1949 (%)	*1959 (%)*	*1968 (%)*	*1992 (%)*
Imports	15.2	26.8	47.3	65.9
Exports	17.5	27.2	42.9	67.7

Sources:
1949–68: Carré Dubois et al. (1972), p. 405;
1992: OECD (*Economic Survey of France* 1994).

In the 1990s approximately two-thirds of French exports and nearly 70 per cent of French imports are accounted for by the (much enlarged) EU. By comparison, trade with the economies of the Franc zone became less and less significant: in 1958 they had taken nearly a third of French exports; by 1973, it was only 3.5 per cent of imports and 5 per cent of exports, and in 1994 it was down to 0.2 per cent of imports and 2.0 per cent of exports.

A third way in which opening-out influenced France relates to the increase in foreign direct investment (FDI) in French industry. Until 1958 legal obstacles were problematical for FDI, but in 1959 the regime was liberalized and the Ministry of Finance actually opened a '*Bureau d'Acceuil*' for foreign investment. Comprehensive data therefore were not available until the early 1970s, but a study by Cohen and Fontanaiche (1974) demonstrates that the 'degree of foreign penetration' in industry had been rising sharply in the 1960s. In certain sectors of manufacturing, firms under foreign control or influence accounted for a high proportion (that is, over 20 per cent) of economic activity – whether measured by sales or investment. They accounted for a lower proportion of employment, but this is a reflection of their focus on high-tech, high value added outputs, such as electrical and electronic goods, precision machinery, chemicals and pharmaceuticals, plastics, non-ferrous metallurgy, oil and oil refining. By 1975 the presence of overseas influence in the industrial sector was very marked: firms in which foreign ownership was substantial (that is, participation over 20 per cent) accounted for 17.4 per cent of total employment, 25.9 per cent of sales and nearly 22 per cent of investment (Bremond and Bremond 1990, p. 60). This influenced the performance of the economy directly as firms involved in foreign ventures are among the more dynamic in their country of origin and they bring that dynamism with them in the quality of management and technology. Indirectly these firms also have a competitive effect on domestic firms whose own performance is thereby improved (Michalet and Chevallier 1985).

In effect, opening-out altered the supply side of the economy in ways more favourable to the growth process. Sharper competition has an allocative effect – greater specialization in the domestic economy produces 'one-off gains' as firms exploit their comparative advantage. In addition, two related dynamic effects are of continuing influence: the spread of new methods of production/technology and, with greater access to the international market, the possibility of exploiting economies of scale. Both phenomena resulted in faster growth in income per head (Carré et al. 1972, pp. 414–15).

The long period of growth in France and the OECD countries came to an end with the oil price hikes of the 1970s. There is some evidence to suggest that it would have ended in any case as a result of falling profit rates (Armstrong et al. 1984) and the rising tide of union militancy which was felt throughout Europe in the late 1960s. The fourfold increase in oil prices was a crushing blow and France faced major difficulties as 75 per cent of energy requirements were imported, compared with a European average of 50 per cent. The slowdown in the international economy and the sharp lift in the global rate of inflation – a condition referred to as 'stagflation' – became a feature of the late 1970s. While inflation fell in the 1980s it was accompanied by fragile growth and rising unemployment in most of Europe.

THE DECELERATION: 1974–95

In their investigation of the sources of economic growth in France, Carré, Dubois and Malinvaud (1972) concluded by suggesting that 'the extraordinary growth experienced by France and many other countries since the war *is unlikely to slow down significantly for a good many years*' (p. 506; emphasis added). Unfortunately, this prediction was brutally proven incorrect within two years as France, along with the rest of the developed world, was mired in recession. Furthermore, it soon became clear that this was not a one-off shift to a lower level of output from which point growth would resume its previous impetus. On the contrary, the underlying rate of growth decelerated to less than half of its previous rate (see Table 3.1) and it never regained the momentum experienced between 1950 and 1973.

Slower growth was common to all OECD economies, but experience of unemployment and inflation has differed: on these issues Europe has performed badly compared to the US and Japan. Within Europe, France's performance was close to the average in the 1980s, but deteriorated in the 1990s in terms of growth and unemployment. Indeed, if we take the period which encompasses the effects of the two oil shocks – that is, 1973–9 – despite international turmoil and the adjustment problems they posed, the real performance of the French economy was better than in the 1980s. Excluding the first three years of the 1970s because they fall within the Golden Age, from 1973 to 1979 the annual average rate of growth of GDP in France was 2.8 per cent while unemployment rose steadily from 2.8 per cent to 6.2 per cent. By contrast, annual GDP growth from 1979 to 1990 averaged 2.3 per cent (it collapsed further with the recession of the early 1990s), but in the meantime unemployment escalated into double figures (see Table 3.8).

Table 3.8 *GDP growth and rate of unemployment in France and the EU(12)*

	% Growth of GDP		*% Unemployment*	
	France	*EU(12)*	*France*	*EU(12)*
1961–70 (av.)	5.6	4.8	2.0	2.3
1971–80 (av.)	3.5	3.0	4.1	4.2
1981–90 (av.)	2.3	2.4	9.2	9.6
1991	0.8	1.6	9.4	8.5
1992	1.2	1.0	10.3	9.4
1993	–1.3	–0.5	11.7	10.9
1994	2.8	2.8	12.3	11.4
1995	2.2	2.5	11.6	11.0

Sources:
Decennial averages: *European Economy* (1995).
Data for 1991–95: OECD (1996), *Economic Outlook* No. 59, Tables 1 and 22.

Control of inflation was of course much better than the 1970s, as one might expect given the policy stance of the authorities: for the most part France kept inflation at or below the average for the EU – a considerably better performance than the UK or Italy.

Table 3.9 *Average rates of inflation (selected economies)*

	1951–60 (%)	*1961–70 (%)*	*1971–80 (%)*	*1981–90 (%)*	*1991–94 (%)*
France	4.4	4.3	9.8	6.2	2.3
Germany	1.2	2.8	5.2	2.6	3.4
UK	3.5	3.9	13.3	6.0	4.8
Italy	2.4	3.8	1.6	9.9	5.3
EU(12)	na	3.9	10.7	6.5	4.2

Sources:
1961–94: *European Economy* (1995).
1951–60: based on Maddison (1991), Table E.4.

But why was the performance of the real economy better in the 1970s compared to the 1980s? First, catch-up potential was clearly still available in the 1970s (see Table 3.3), but was gradually being exhausted by the 1980s – GDP per hour worked in France was only 70 per cent of the US level in 1970 and had reached over 90 per cent by the mid-1980s. Second, and perhaps more significantly, there were major policy errors in the early 1980s – largely connected with overoptimism in relation to the state's capacity to influence the national economy in the context of an open international system. Arguably these errors were then compounded by the policy of *le Franc fort* – the strong Franc – and the commitment to European Monetary Union later in the decade.

Table 3.10 *Discretionary impact of fiscal policy (% of GDP)*

	Annual average 1969–73	*Annual average 1974–78*
France	0.90	1.36
UK	0.86	–0.19
Germany	0.91	0.81
Italy	0.96	0.21

Sources:
OECD (1978) *Budget Indicators*, p. 12.
OECD (1978) *Economic Outlook*, No. 23, p. 18.

Initially most European governments reacted to the deflationary shock of the first oil price rise by pursuing expansionary macroeconomic policies in 1974 and 1975, but thereafter they moved into a contractionary mode. Table 3.10 shows that France attempted to offset recessionary forces by increasing demand via fiscal expansion more than was the case elsewhere. At the same time monetary policy was relaxed such that negative real interest rates emerged.

This halted the rise in unemployment temporarily, but at the expense of a faster rate of inflation – particularly when compared to Germany, the US and Japan. In relation to the EU, France was below the average, but this was no great comfort as the EU average was pulled up by several countries which had severe double-digit inflation – Spain (15.6 per cent), Italy (14.6 per cent), Ireland (14.6 per cent), and the UK (13.3 per cent) being the worst offenders. This acceleration in the rate of inflation was accompanied by a sharp deterioration in the balance of payments and a fall of 10 per cent in the value of the Franc when it was withdrawn (for a second time) from the European currency snake in March 1976. However, floating the exchange rate removed a major constraint and allowed the French government to tolerate more easily the balance of payments consequences of its inflationary stance. Given that wages were indexed to the cost of living, inflationary expectations became so deeply entrenched that squeezing inflation out of the system was to prove a prolonged and difficult process.

THE MITTERRAND PRESIDENCY

In 1981 the French people elected a Socialist President for the first time in the life of the Fifth Republic and also gave the left coalition a majority of deputies in the National Assembly. International opinion took the view that the new regime would address the problem of unemployment more actively and therefore was likely to be soft on inflation. The rhetoric of the left helped foster this perception: there was much talk of a 'rupture with capitalism', and declarations such as the following were typical:

> we must escape from capitalism in crisis ... Profit seeking must no longer sovereignly determine decisions about investment and goods. It must give way to the rationality of citizens democratically stating their needs through planning and the market. (*Parti Socialiste* 1980, – cited in Hayward 1986)

This of course was extraordinarily naive: it ignored the fact that decisions to open the economy and reduce controls on the movement of capital seriously limited policy independence. Mitterrand's ensuing experiment was largely a Keynesian reflation mixed with a series of structural changes in terms of working hours and nationalization – the details are discussed in Lombard (1995). But all the measures were taking place against the background of a developing recession in the world economy, hence they generated severe balance of payments problems. Meanwhile a hoped-for increase in the rate of investment from the private sector failed to materialize. The currency was vulnerable to the judgement of financial markets which had changed out of all recognition since the left had last been in power. Whereas governments and public institutions dominated the international financial system in the 1960s, by the 1980s foreign exchange in the hands of private banks and companies far outweighed the aggregate of publicly held reserves. Furthermore, the ability to trade these, and other short-dated assets, quickly, had also changed. Defending currencies in these circumstances required more than periodic intervention by the central bank and the verbal assurances of politicians. Thus, having suggested that his programme could be accomplished without devaluation, Mitterrand was humiliated on three separate occasions between 1981 and 1982 as the Franc fell in the foreign exchange markets.

By 1983, some in the government (for example, Pierre Chevenement, the Industry Minister) were prepared to contemplate leaving the EMS and reversing the process of European integration by reintroducing protectionist devices. Others (such as Jacques Delors) opposed leaving the EMS and instead advocated a policy of *rigueur* – retrenchment and austerity – which Mitterrand eventually accepted. Periodic devaluation of the currency was deemed incompatible with the political imperative of Franco-German parity in the construction of European unity and therefore the strategy of *le Franc fort* became a cornerstone of policy. The Maastricht Treaty (1991) underpinned this policy further with its objective of monetary union later in the decade.

The pursuit of monetary integration had a heavy cost in the short run, whatever its long-term promise. French governments did not have the inflation-fighting reputation of the German authorities, hence international holders of Franc assets demanded a substantial risk premium in the form of higher interest rates: in every year from 1974 onward nominal interest rates in France exceeded those in Germany, and in the early 1980s the disparity was as much as 5 to 6 per cent. The squeeze on demand yielded benefits in terms of falling inflation, but the downside was a depressed economy – with the exception of two years in the late 1980s. The interest differential has since contracted but France has been faced with slower growth, a continued serious rise in the rate of unemployment and problems with the public finances. Before turning to these matters, however, we look briefly at some of the structural changes which have accompanied the processes of growth and slowdown.

STRUCTURE OF THE ECONOMY

Despite the fact that France was the second country to experience industrialization, as we have suggested earlier, the structure of its economy in 1950 was antiquated and stagnant and in some sectors closer to the nineteenth than to the mid-twentieth century.

Agriculture

The significance of agriculture has already been mentioned, but the depth of change in this extremely conservative sector needs to be emphasized. Table 3.11 gives some indication of changes in the distribution of the labour force between 1950 and 1990.

Table 3.11 *Sectoral distribution of employment and value added 1950–90 (%)*

	Agriculture		*Industry*		*Services*	
	1950	*1990*	*1950*	*1990*	*1950*	*1990*
France						
Employment	28.3	6.1	34.9	29.9	36.8	64.0
Value added	9.0	4.4	29.3	31.8	61.7	63.8
UK						
Employment	5.1	2.1	46.5	29.0	48.4	68.9
Value added	1.6	1.7	41.9	38.3	56.5	60.0
Germany						
Employment	22.2	3.4	43.0	39.8	34.8	56.8
Value added	4.3	1.7	41.7	39.4	64.0	58.9
Italy						
Employment	45.4	9.6	28.6	29.7	26.0	60.7
Value added	11.3	4.2	25.8	34.6	62.9	61.2

Note: Agriculture includes fisheries and forestry; industry includes mining, energy supply and construction as well as manufacturing; services includes public and private sector.

Sources:
Employment: OECD *Labour Force Statistics*, various years.
Value added calculated from van Ark (1996), Appendix Tables, pp. 131–41.

Contraction of agriculture in Britain occurred largely in the nineteenth century before universal suffrage when farmers' political leverage was weak: as early as 1911, employment in agriculture was only 8 per cent of the total labour force (Tracy 1989). In France, however, the agricultural population was politically much stronger so the process was delayed.

After 1950 the decline in agricultural employment and population was largely a result of mechanization and rising productivity. But there were also a series of agricultural reforms and various legal changes, particularly in the 1960s, which made the consolidation of smaller units more easily attainable and facilitated the retirement of older farmers. In terms of mechanization, numbers of tractors expanded from 137 000 in 1950 to almost 1 million by the mid-1960s, and combine harvesters rose from 4900 to over 100 000. Barral, in Bouvier et al. (1982), details the efforts to modernize agriculture by the use of state subsidies for capital goods, cheap finance via *Credit Agricole*, the provision of fuel at lower prices for farmers, improvements in the mechanisms of distribution and changes in the laws on inheritance.

As a result of these efforts agricultural productivity increased sharply – the annual rate of growth was 4.1 per cent in the 1950s and 6.4 per cent from 1960 to 1973. Even after the 1974 slowdown, output per person in agriculture rose at 5.1 per cent per annum.

Unfortunately, these changes did not benefit farmers greatly – the low income elasticity of demand for foodstuffs limited the growth in their markets, while increases in the price of inputs squeezed profitability. Hence falling employment and a diminishing share of agricultural incomes in the GDP was the outcome (Tracy 1989, p. 301). The contraction of farming and the depopulation of the countryside would have been even more rapid but for government intervention and the Common Agricultural Policy which maintained the size of French agriculture when market criteria would have imposed faster decline.

Industry and Services

From 1950 to 1973 the contraction of agriculture was facilitated by the expansion of services and industry. The former saw employment expand by some 35 per cent and this was combined with an annual growth of productivity of 3 per cent. Employment growth in industry was not as rapid – some 20 per cent more were employed compared to 1950, and its share of total employment rose from 34.9 to 38.5 per cent. But the growth of output per person at 4.9 per cent per annum (5.5 per cent in manufacturing alone) was unexpected.

Despite these annual productivity gains the competitive performance of industry and particularly manufacturing remained of major concern to policy makers: it was suggested that further gains were possible by pursuing amalgamation and concentration. The size distribution of French manufacturing establishments, for example, was different from comparators such as Germany, the UK and the US. A higher proportion of small establishments and a lower proportion of very large establishments was a long-standing feature and by the 1950s and 1960s there was a growing awareness of this issue (see, for example, INSEE 1953; Bouvier et al. 1982, p. 1133).

Table 3.12 illustrates that shortly after the signing of the Treaty of Rome, within the EC, only Italy was characterized by a similar sized distribution of establishments in the manufacturing sector.

The inference was drawn that competitiveness could be increased by shifting toward a size distribution more nearly resembling that of France's competitors. This inference, however true in the 1950s and 1960s, is less true of the 1980s and 1990s when, as West Germany and the 'Third Italy' indicate, a thriving small/medium-sized firms sector is a vital feature of flexible manufacturing processes and job creation.

Table 3.12 *Manufacturing labour force by size of establishment 1962*

Nos employed	*France*	*Germany*	*Belgium*	*Netherlands*	*Italy*	*US*
10–49	21	16	17	17	26	13
50–99	12	10	11	24	14	10
100–499	34	29	31	15	30	32
500–1000+	33	45	41	44	30	45

Source: Nioche (1969).

Nevertheless, concern about competitiveness became particularly acute during the 1960s when there was growing fear of US dominance of high-tech industries. This produced two sorts of policy response: first, the pursuit of *grands projets* such as the nuclear programme, the TGV, Concorde, the modernization of telecommunications, and so on; and, second, the encouragement of a small number of French firms to maintain control of sectors considered vital to the national interest, that is, the selection of 'national champions' which were nurtured by state aids such as direct subsidies, cheap finance and preferential treatment in state procurement to enable them to compete internationally. A handful of firms such as CGE, Dassault, Thomson-Brandt and Aerospatiale, located in the high-tech sector, were the major recipients of this largesse. Size and public support, however, do not guarantee success and the record has been distinctly patchy and in some cases appalling. Thus attempts in the late 1960s to maintain an independent domestic computer industry centred on *Machines Bull* misfired ignominiously, and likewise the Concorde project was an abject failure commercially.

After the election of the Socialists in 1981, a programme of nationalization was undertaken, with large industrial firms in diverse sectors such as electronics (Thomson-Brandt, CGE, Honeywell-Bull), glass (St Gobain), aluminium (Pechiney), chemicals (Rhone-Poulenc) and steel being fully nationalized while the state took a majority stake in Matra and Dassault. Industrial policy shifted to the idea of supporting *filieres industrielles* – that is, connected or linked industrial activities – and not merely the leading firms in the sector. This ran into difficulty almost immediately as the government found itself embroiled in dealing with unemployment resulting from the declining sectors of the economy. For example, textiles, ship-building and heavy engineering contracted sharply as a result of intensifying competition, while the iron and steel industry was a disaster area of accelerating losses and massive overcapacity constructed in areas far from its traditional location (Hayward 1986). The state was no more successful with its liberal support of Air France and the banking system. Indeed, some of these firms – Air France and Credit Lyonnais in particular – have continued to require large injections of public capital to keep them going in the 1990s. This has strengthened calls for privatization – a policy embarked upon hesitantly in the 1980s, interrupted by the Stock Market Crash of 1987, and only recently and tentatively revived.

The public authorities can claim some limited success in a number of sectors: for example, in 1970 just over 10 per cent of French households had telephones and the system was antiquated and unreliable, but within a decade it was one of the most advanced in the world. Similarly, the French motor vehicle industry came through major financial difficulties in the mid to late 1980s, and maintained a presence across the board in terms of the range and volume of production, so that it is now the fourth largest producer in the world. However, the industry remains sensitive to competition from East Asian producers, which from time to time leads to incipient protectionism. As late as the summer of 1995 Peugeot-Citroen PSA put pressure on the government to subsidize the purchase of new cars, and this was conceded.

Finally, aerospace and defence goods have been major export earners, but once again this has required considerable support from the public purse, and in the case of aircraft the development of joint European projects. French authorities remain susceptible to calls for 'temporary' help, but periodic injections of capital or debt write-offs have become increasingly problematical because the EU's competition rules, when enforced, require the elimination of selective support. This will be no bad thing as the ability to resort to the public purse means the absence of a hard budget constraint and, as evidenced in Eastern Europe, a major incentive to improve performance disappears.

More recently, therefore, policy in France has been moving towards a watered down version of 'Thatcherism' with greater emphasis on the market and intervention confined to supply side measures such as improved training, reduced taxation and deregulation, but there is a long way to go in terms of reducing further the role of the state.

Since the 1960s, the service sector in France, as in most developed economies, has grown rapidly to become the major source of employment and output (van Ark 1996, Tables A.1–A.4). By 1990 nearly two-thirds of employment derived from services, and the contribution of private and public sector services to total output (GDP) had risen to 69 per cent. Most services are non-tradable internationally and therefore do not face the problem of external competition – some, such as education and health, are largely driven by demographic change and are income elastic so that their share in total spending has risen particularly sharply. Internationally traded services such as insurance and banking enjoyed protection for much longer than manufacturing as they were explicitly outside the remit of the old GATT arrangements. Even within the EU, it was not until the 1980s that governments began seriously to dismantle the barriers to competition in financial services, and the result has been a considerable increase in cross-border investment. The French have followed the general trend to deregulation of the banking system and capital markets and in 1984 carried through a comprehensive series of reforms which modernized and liberalized the financial sector. This reflects a number of factors: pressures at the level of the EU, a determined attempt to raise the profile of Paris as a competitor to London as a centre of international finance, and not least the wish to deepen the domestic capital market so that privatizations could be successfully carried through. The latter has received more attention of late as a result of the need to maximize government revenues to close the fiscal deficit as required by the Maastricht criteria for monetary union.

PUBLIC FINANCES

Government spending and public borrowing in France has tended to exceed the European average for much of the post-war period. Also, as elsewhere, there has been a secular upward drift in the ratio of government spending to GDP. As can be seen from Table 3.13, general government spending as a proportion of GDP is higher than is the case in any of the larger European economies.

Table 3.13 *General government expenditure (% of GDP)*

	1961–73	*1974–85*	*1986–90*	*1995*
France	35.5	39.4	52.2	54.5
Germany	33.8	44.4	46.5	49.7
Italy	29.4	34.4	50.7	53.8
UK	31.4	43.1	42.9	42.3
US	28.3	32.3	37.1	36.5

Source: *European Economy* (1995).

Until 1991 budget deficits in France were less than 3 per cent of GDP (in the 1960s surpluses were not uncommon) and the ratio of public debt to GDP was well below 40 per cent. Since 1991, however, matters have deteriorated with a deficit of over 5 per cent of GDP in 1995 and the debt ratio increasing to over 50 per cent. Hence the need to deal with the public finances became urgent. This is the case in the short term because of the wish to meet the timetable for EMU, but in the medium- to long-term there are more fundamental difficulties: the age structure of the French population implies rapidly rising pension commitments and health spending which together will bring further demands on the public purse. In the absence of an acceleration in economic growth, which would increase tax revenue, the authorities face the problem of a rising budget deficit or an unenviable mix of higher taxes and deeper spending cuts. The latter appears to be the chosen route but it will prove difficult to implement. The problem is considerably exacerbated by the nature of unemployment and the labour market in France.

THE LABOUR MARKET

The most serious result of the stagnation of the 1980s has been the steady rise in the level of unemployment. After having averaged less than 2.0 per cent between 1950 and 1973, over the period 1973–9 it deteriorated to an average of some 4.3 per cent. Between 1980 and 1995 the average exceeded 10 per cent despite a small drop in the late 1980s, and the rate was rising once more by the 1990s reaching some 12.5 per cent of the labour force by 1996. The OECD (*Economic Survey of France* 1995) estimates that some three-quarters are 'structurally unemployed'. In 1995, unemployment was marginally higher than the EU average (see Table 3.8) and with approximately 3 million people out of work, and some 1.5 million people on various job support schemes, it remains of crucial political significance. Unemployment of this magnitude has grave consequences: it diminishes the capacities of those affected, increases public expenditure, feeds protectionist sentiment and fuels the politics of the extreme right.

On the supply side, demographic developments have not helped – France experienced a rise of nearly 3 million in the population of working age (16–64) in the 1970s just at a time when the post-war boom was coming to an end. In addition, the 1980s were marked by faster population growth in France while other economies were undergoing deceleration. Hence one might argue that the record on unemployment is not so bad when compared with the rest of the EU. Unfortunately, the extent of the problem is disguised by participation rates which are lower in France – 66/67 per cent of the labour force – than, for example, in Germany (69 per cent), the UK (75/76 per cent), the US (77 per cent) and Japan (77 per cent) (OECD *Economic Survey of France* 1996).

On the demand side the overall cost of labour in France is pushed up by non-wage costs which effectively act as a tax on employment. By 1995, on average they accounted for nearly 30 per cent of total labour cost (Grimond 1995). The authorities have recognized the problem but have addressed it piecemeal by mitigating social charges for certain types of labour. None the less, the extra expenses have undermined the competitiveness of employers and stimulated the growth of part-time and temporary work: only 5 per cent of workers were in this category in 1980, but by 1985 the numbers had risen to 13.2 per cent and by 1994 the proportion was approaching 18 per cent.

It has been suggested that at the root of this unemployment lies the 'rigidity' of the labour market. What truth is there to this? If rigidity is defined as a condition where real wages and/or the volume of employment do not respond to shifts in supply and demand, the evidence is mixed. For example, the OECD

(*Economic Survey of France* 1985) in a sample of nine member countries found that only Holland and the UK (which had not long embarked on its labour market reforms) displayed greater rigidity than France. By contrast, Layard et al. (1991) suggest that, compared with other EU economies, real wage rigidity is not markedly greater in France. Indeed, France comes out as close to the average.

It is frequently suggested in the UK that the minimum wage (*Salaire Minimum Interprofessionelle Garantie* – SMIG) is the explanation as it prevents real wages from adjusting downward. In 1970 a reformed version – the SMIC (*Salaire Minimum Interprofessionelle de Croissance*) – was introduced to prevent disadvantaged workers from falling behind: the value of the SMIC was now to increase by at least half the annual rate of increase of average hourly wage rates.

Evidence on the effect of the minimum wage is again mixed – for example, the OECD (*Economic Survey of France* 1985) pointed out that two-thirds of those qualifying for the minimum – the *Smicards* – were found in small firms (that is, those with less than 50 workers), yet this was the very sector where employment growth was strongest over the period 1974–84. Furthermore, Martin (1983) suggested that the SMIC had little discernible impact in the case of younger workers, a group whose lower productivity would make them vulnerable to wages set above market clearing level.

By the 1990s, however, the OECD (*Economic Survey of France* 1995) was arguing that 'the SMIC *does* appear to have an appreciable impact on unemployment among the least skilled workers and especially the young' (p. 59; emphasis added). The contradiction is perhaps explicable if the minimum wage had been pushed up over time such that the market disequilibrium had worsened. This may have happened from the late 1970s to 1985 when the gap between the SMIC and the average wage fell from 57 per cent to 43 per cent (OECD *Economic Survey of France* 1991), but the ratio has since remained broadly the same. At this stage, therefore, the best we can say is that the SMIC looks guilty, but the case is not proven. What of other explanations of rigidity?

Trade unions are frequently cited as a factor in labour market rigidity and this seems particularly plausible for countries where unions organize a high proportion of the labour force and have a central focus. Neither of these things applies to France, however: compared with the UK, Germany, and Scandinavia, French trade unions have been numerically and organizationally weak. Estimates of union density in France in the early 1980s put it at 19 per cent of the workforce (Barker et al. 1984). Since then membership has continued to decline and Grimond (1995) suggests that it is below 10 per cent. Unions therefore seem an unlikely explanation for rigidity in the French labour market.[6]

Bean (1994a) reports that unionization per se is not an important factor: neither the extent of unionization nor the degree of solidarity (coordination) are significant in affecting the speed with which unemployment adjusts to external shocks. Instead, 'hiring and firing costs' and the 'progressive disconnection of the unemployed from the labour market' appear to offer better explanations for rigidity (Bean 1994b). These findings are consistent with an insider–outsider model of the labour market. Insiders – those already in employment – enjoy relative job security and are able to secure higher wages by using devices which limit competition from outsiders. Thus insiders may construct rules on dismissal which raise the cost of labour turnover for the firm. Normally such rules and procedures are a result of trade union action, but if the political authorities devise protective legislation this would have the same effect.

In 1975 Premier Barre introduced tight regulations on firms wishing to make redundancies. All redundancies had to be notified to the authorities to obtain permission, and periods of consultation with employee representatives were required. The difficulty of not being able to make redundancies easily is frequently cited by business as one of the factors constraining new employment growth. Only in 1994/5 were the French authorities considering relaxing these regulations.

With regard to 'progressive disconnection of the unemployed from the labour market', this too operates. As the duration of unemployment lengthens, the probability of getting another job diminishes and, by the 1990s, over two-fifths of the officially unemployed had been out of work for more than a year. Hence there is a 'discouraged worker effect' – people do not bother to compete effectively for jobs.

A final piece of evidence relates to the behaviour of the Non-Accelerating Inflation Rate of Unemployment (NAIRU) across the economies of the European Union. With the exception of Denmark, a rise in NAIRU has been a common phenomenon so that in the 1990s accelerating inflation occurs at higher rates of unemployment than in the 1970s.

Table 3.14 *Non-Accelerating Inflation Rate of Unemployment (NAIRU)(%)*

	1973	*1994*
Spain	8.5	13.8
Ireland	8.6	12.1
Belgium	6.3	9.0
France	4.4	7.9
Italy	6.5	7.9
Netherlands	4.1	7.5
Portugal	4.4	6.9
UK	6.0	6.8
Greece	2.4	6.4
W. Germany	2.1	3.8
Denmark	3.5	3.2
EC/EU(12)	3.7	6.1

Source: *European Economy Annual Economic Report* (1995).

This is prima facie evidence of labour markets becoming less flexible and, within the Union, France finds itself among the upper ranks.

Flexibility in labour markets will become more not less pressing because the locking-in of exchange rates in the move to EMU will mean that wages and the domestic price level and / or real output (rather than nominal exchange rates) will have to adjust to supply side shocks. If, in parts of the Union, wages and the price level are sticky downward, the growth of output there will be undermined and unemployment will rise further – an uneasy prospect for the French authorities.

CONCLUSION

In the 1950s France commenced a period of sustained economic expansion which surprised contemporary commentators, some of whom actually feared the social consequences of rapid growth. French success required the potential for catch-up to be appropriately mobilized and this was facilitated by a growth coalition comprising politicians, the technobureaucracy, academics and businessmen committed to the concept of modernization. The coalition was fortunate, however, as the international conjuncture was advantageous: after a faltering start, the US used its hegemonic position to nurture post-war recovery. Hence supporters of planning claimed some degree of success (whether or not such claims were valid). French policy had the virtue of focusing on long-term, supply side issues without the obsessive concern with the short-run management of aggregate demand prevalent in Britain in the 1950s and 1960s.

The growth coalition may have been necessary but it was not sufficient: opposition from the labour movement or a sceptical business sector could have frustrated its objectives, or external constraints may have been binding. In France, the trade unions were compliant and big business was chastened, while small business, initially resistant to change, dropped its resistance as the benefits of expansion became apparent. As to external constraints, even in the deeply conservative financial sector there was not the same commitment to defending the external value of the currency compared to the British financial community. Hence periodic and aggressive devaluations were deployed to maintain competitiveness and mitigate the deflationary effects of tight monetary policy.

The forces that helped to promote modernization were initially identified with planning but, by the 1960s, they were superseded by the opening-up of the economy and exposure to international competition. The Treaties of Paris (1950) and Rome (1958) were signal events as they demonstrated a willingness on the part of France to pool its jealously guarded sovereignty. With hindsight, such decisions appear well justified as the economy prospered mightily, but since the mid-1970s growth has fallen closer to its long-run average and a new set of rigidities appears to have taken hold, focused on the labour market.

Compared with eliminating the product market rigidities of the 1950s, however, this problem appears more intractable: the international context is less expansionary and the drive for Monetary Union in Europe limits exchange rate and monetary policy options. The authorities are engaged on a profoundly difficult course in which mounting unemployment and harsh fiscal decisions may serve to undermine social cohesion. However, it must be remembered that mundane economic interests are not necessarily uppermost here; instead policy may be better understood in terms of the issue which has dominated France and French politics since the late nineteenth century – relations with Germany.

NOTES

1. Excluding Luxembourg. The states with higher GDP per capita were Germany and Denmark.
2. Sicsic and Wyplosz (1996) suggest, on the basis of Dubois (1985), that France's recovery was disappointing. Using the growth rate of the economy from 1896 to 1929, Dubois projects a hypothetical level of GDP for the post-war period and shows that it was not until between 1955 and 1960 that the economy achieved that hypothetical level of GDP. This is not such a poor performance as it seems at first sight, however: using data from Maddison (1991) and applying the same technique to assess post-war recovery in most of the war-damaged nations, I estimate that very few had recovered their 'growth adjusted' level of GDP by the early 1950s. Belgium, Denmark, the Netherlands, Italy and even Japan all took between 1954/5 (Netherlands) and 1961/2 (Denmark).
3. The *Grandes Écoles* had traditionally provided the administrative elites of the state. With the founding of the *École Nationale d'Administration* (ENA) in 1945 a yet more concentrated layer was installed and the interpenetration of business and politics by *Énarques* became a feature of the post-war era.
4. With only one or two short periods of price stability, inflation and devaluation continued to be features of the economy for the next 30 years. The effects reverberated in the 1980s and 1990s when French governments found it difficult to convince the markets that their tolerance of inflation was truly a thing of the past. As a step towards establishing anti-inflation credentials, the Bank of France was given its independence from the political authorities in 1993.
5. This had been rectified by the 1980s, however, when the age profile of the stock of machine tools in France was broadly similar to that in Germany and the US (Prais 1986).
6. Numbers and union density may understate the influence of unions to some degree: first, because in France the negotiated wage is legally generalized to other workers; and, second, unions are more prominent in the public sector where their leverage is stronger than mere numbers suggest. Contrary to public perception, however, I would argue that the widespread unrest which affects France periodically is not evidence of strong unions. A close look at May 1968 and more recent events in 1995–6 shows that the official unions were rarely in the lead – they were frequently slow to catch up on a general mood of unease. The lack of collective discipline in the conduct of some disputes by, for example, lorry drivers and others may also be evidence of a lack of control by union leaders.

REFERENCES

Adams, W. J. (1989) *Restructuring the French Economy*, Washington: Brookings Institution.
Armstrong, P., Glyn, A. and Harrison, J. (1984) *Capitalism since 1945*, Oxford: Blackwell.
Bank for International Settlements (1949) *The Post-war Economic and Financial Position of France from the Liberation to the Beginning of 1949*, Zurich: BIS.
Barker, K., Britton, A. and Major, R. (1984) 'Macroeconomic Policy in Britain and France', *National Institute Economic Review*, No. 110, pp. 68–84.
Bean, C. R. (1994a) 'European Unemployment: A Survey', *Journal of Economic Literature*, Vol. XXXII, June, pp. 573–619.
Bean, C. R. (1994b) 'European Unemployment: A retrospective', *European Economic Review*, Vol. 38, No. 3, pp. 523–34.
Bouvier, J. et al. (1982) *Histoire Economique et Sociale de La France*, Tome IV, Vol. 3, Paris: Presses Universitaires de France.
Bremond, J. and Bremond, G. (1990) *L'economie francaise*, Paris: Hatier.
Caron, F. (1979) *An Economic History of Modern France*, London: Methuen.
Carré, J. J., Dubois, P. and Malinvaud, E. (1972) *French Economic Growth*, Oxford: Oxford University Press.
Cohen, J.-C. and Fontanaiche, P. (1974) 'Les participations étrangères dans l'industrie francaise en 1971', *Études et Statistiques*, No. 52, Paris: INSEE.
Denison, E. F. (1967) *Why Growth Rates Differ*, Washington D.C.: Brookings Institution.
Dubois, P. (1985) 'Rupture de croissance et progrès technique', *Economie et Statistique*, No. 181, pp. 3–31.
Eck, J. F. (1988) *Histoire d'Economie Francaise depuis 1945*, Paris: Armand Colin.
Economic Commission for Europe (1955) *Economic Bulletin for Europe*, Geneva: United Nations, pp. 26–7.
Economic Commission for Europe (1965) *Some Factors in Economic Growth in Europe During the 1950s*, Geneva: United Nations.
Economic Directorate of the European Commission (1995) *European Economy*, Brussels: EC.
Economic Directorate of the European Commission (1995) 'The Composition of Unemployment from an Economic Perspective', *Annual Economic Report*, Study No. 3, pp. 127–54.
Estrin, S. and Holmes, P. (1983) *French Planning in Theory and Practice*, London: George Allen and Unwin.
Grimond, J. (1995) 'A Survey of France', *The Economist*, 25 November.
Hayward, J. (1986) *The State and the Market Economy*, Brighton: Harvester.
INSEE (1952; 1956) 'Les Perspectives en France pour la deuxieme semestre d'après les chefs d'entreprises', *Études et Conjoncture*, Paris.
INSEE (1953) 'L'industrie francaise', *Études et Conjoncture*, Special Edition: Paris.
International Monetary Fund (1993) *World Economic Outlook*, May / June, IMF: Washington.
Layard, R., Nickell, S. and Jackman, R. (1991) *Unemployment: Macroeconomic Performance and the Labour Market*, Oxford: Oxford University Press.
Levine, R. and Renelt, D. (1992) 'A Sensitivity Analysis of Cross Country Regressions', *American Economic Review*, Vol. 82, pp. 942–63.
Lombard, M. (1995) 'A re-examination of the reasons for the failure of Keynesian expansionary policies in France 1981–1983', *Cambridge Journal of Economics*, Vol. 19, pp. 359–72.
Lutz, V. (1965) *French Planning*, New York: American Enterprise Institute.
Lutz, V. (1969) *Central Planning for the Market Economy*, London: Longman.

Lynch, F. M. B. (1984) 'Resolving the Paradox of the Monnet Plan: National and International Planning in French Reconstruction', *The Economic History Review*, XXXVII (2), May, pp. 229–43.

Maddison, A. (1991) *Dynamic Forces in Capitalist Development*, Oxford: Oxford University Press.

Maddison, A. (1995) *Monitoring the World Economy 1820–1992*, Paris: OECD.

Martin, J. (1983) 'Effects of the Minimum Wage on the youth Labour Market in North America and France', *OECD Occasional Studies*, June, Paris: OECD.

Michalet, C.-A. and Chevallier, T. (1985) 'France' in J. H. Dunning (ed.), *Multinational Enterprises, Economic Structure and International Competitiveness*, New York: John Wiley and Sons.

Mistral, J. (1975) 'Vingt ans de redeploiement du commerce exterieur', *Économie et Statistique*, No. 71, Paris: INSEE.

Nioche, J. P. (1969) 'Taille des établissements industriels dans sept pays developpés', *Collections de l'INSEE*, Entreprises E1, Paris: INSEE.

OECD *Economic Survey of France*, various years: Paris: OECD.

OECD *Economic Outlook*, various years: Paris: OECD.

OEEC (1953) *France*, Paris: OEEC.

Patat, J.-P. and Lutfalla, M. (1990) *A Monetary History of France in the Twentieth Century*, London: Macmillan.

Petit, P. (1988) 'The Economy and Modernisation: An Overview', in J. Gaffney (ed.), *France and Modernisation*, Aldershot: Avebury.

Prais, S. J. (1986) 'Some International Comparisons of the Age of the Machine Stock', *Journal of Industrial Economics*, March, pp. 261–77.

Price, H. B. (1955) *The Marshall Plan and its Meaning*, Ithaca, NY: Cornell University Press.

Sachs, J. and Warner, A. (1995) 'Economic Reform and the Process of Global Integration', *Brookings Papers on Economic Activity*.

Sheahan, J. (1963) *Promotion and Control of Industry in Post-war France*, Cambridge, MA: Harvard University Press.

Shonfield, A. (1965) *Modern Capitalism*, Oxford: Oxford University Press.

Sicsic, P. and Wyplosz, C. (1996) 'France 1945–92', in N. F. R. Crafts and G. Toniolo (eds), *Economic Growth in Europe since 1945*, Cambridge: Cambridge University Press, pp. 210–39.

Tracy, M. (1989) *Government and Agriculture in Western Europe 1880–1988*, Brighton: Harvester Wheatsheaf.

van Ark, B. (1996) 'Sectoral growth accounting and structural change in post-war Europe', in B. van Ark and N. F. R. Crafts (eds), *Quantitative Aspects of Post-War European Economic Growth*, Cambridge: Cambridge University Press, pp. 84–164.

Verspagen, B. (1996) 'Technology indicators and economic growth', in B. van Ark and N. F. R. Crafts (eds), *Quantitative Aspects of Post-War European Economic Growth*, Cambridge: Cambridge University Press, pp. 215–43.

Warta, J. A. (1966) 'Import Duties inside and outside the European Economic Community', *Statistical Information*, No. 2, Brussels: Statistical Office of the European Communities.

4 Italy: After the Rewards of Growth, the Penalty of Debt

Ruggero Ranieri

INTRODUCTION: RECONSTRUCTION 1945–51

At the end of the war, in common with much of Europe, Italy's economic infrastructure was seriously crippled. Very little of her merchant marine had survived, roads and railways were severely damaged, and the stock of houses, already badly in need of repair before the war, was severely depleted. Output was at a very low level, because of a lack of raw materials, a shortage of dollars and the general disorganization of the country, after a long period of bloody fighting, German and Allied occupation and civil war.

The stock of industrial capital, however, was less severely damaged. Granted some assets had been destroyed: the steel industry, for example, had suffered from Allied bombardment as well as German sabotage but the bulk of manufacturing was located in the North-West, which escaped the worst of the fighting and where the Germans, thanks to the Resistance, were prevented from carrying out their demolition plans. There had also been a considerable amount of war-time investment, particularly in engineering which was obviously an important component of post-war recovery (Daneo 1975).

After 1945, investment picked up in energy facilities, as well as in petrochemicals and steel, while textile and engineering exports rapidly gained ground. The picture of postwar recovery in Italy was, therefore, far from bleak and high rates of growth of output and investment were helped, in the initial stages, by substantial injections of dollars. Between 1946 and 1948, Italy received about $850 million from the UNRRA programme and between 1948 and 1952, $1.3 billion of Marshall Aid. These sums were mostly conferred in the form of grants for the import of fuel, raw materials and machinery and were the equivalent of some 2.2 per cent of GNP in 1947–51 (Zamagni 1993, p. 332).

Politically, there was a short period of 'governments of national unity', composed of all the main anti-fascist parties. In May 1947, however, the Socialists and Communists were ejected by De Gasperi, the leader of the Christian Democratic Party (DC). Within a year, in April 1948, the Popular Front of the left was defeated in the first general election held under the new Republican Constitution. Thereafter Italy was run by unstable coalitions built around the Christian Democrats and including smaller parties of the centre and the right.

Differences of approach to economic policy partly reflected this picture: a liberal faction, led by orthodox economists such as Einaudi and Corbino, gained the upper hand in the months immediately following the war. They were committed to abolishing war-time controls, which they considered a legacy of the inter-war period and linked to fascist autocracy and mismanagement. Not surprisingly, however, measures of sweeping deregulation stoked up an inflationary boom, encouraging commodity, stock exchange and currency speculation (De Cecco 1972). By 1947 therefore a sharp deflationary squeeze was imposed, failing which the lira would have collapsed. Thereafter more cautious policies prevailed: orthodox monetary and fiscal approaches were combined with public sector investment and some protectionist measures were retained while the economy was opened up gradually. This policy was essentially a supply side strategy, strongly export and growth oriented, but unwilling to tackle unemployment and low incomes by simply reflating the economy. As a member of the Organization for European Economic Co-operation (OEEC) Italy took part in the liberalization of trade and payments. It was also a founder member of the European Coal and Steel Community, albeit needing special transitional protection for steel (Holbik 1959; Ranieri 1988).

The fate of the state-owned sector reflected the new mood. Italy came out of the war with one of the largest state-dominated economies in Western Europe. The IRI (*Istituto per la Ricostruzione Industriale*) had been created during the 1930s to take over from a crisis-torn banking system, the management of a constellation of industrial, financial and utility holdings. After brief tinkering with plans for privatization, IRI assumed a pivotal role in the economy: sub-holdings, in steel, engineering, electricity, shipping and telecommunications, were encouraged to proceed with long-term plans for modernization.

Among the managers of the state-owned sector were former private industrialists. Men such as Sinigaglia, the architect of the post-war steel industry, Vignuzzi in engineering, Reiss Romoli in telecommunications, Mattioli in banking, and Mattei in the energy sector, enjoyed a significant period of ascendancy. Key appointees, such as Menichella, Governor of the Bank of Italy from 1948 to 1960, were drawn from IRI's inner circle. The *Cassa del Mezzogiorno* (CASMEZ), established in 1950 to tackle the problem of the underdevelopment of the South, was the brainchild of IRI's Pasquale Saraceno and Francesco Giordani. This group of people constituted a powerful and effective technocracy (Mortara 1984; Amatori 1987).

To sum up, therefore, Italy emerged from the war with a weakened economy but a fairly robust industrial sector. Reconstruction proceeded rapidly: by 1949 the pre-war level of manufacturing output had been restored while pre-war per capita income was attained in 1950. Exports were buoyant and large-scale investment projects were initiated. Political parties were inexperienced, having been largely suppressed since the 1920s, and this played into the hands of a group of pragmatic, expansion-minded technocrats who effectively took charge of economic management with the aim of modernizing industry. Many Italian firms were technologically backward and productivity was low while unemployment and underemployment were severe. Hence governments were happy to encourage large-scale emigration (Romero 1991).

THE YEARS OF RAPID GROWTH 1950–73

Structure and Performance

Following reconstruction, Italy, like much of Europe, experienced a long period of rapid growth facilitated by rising inputs from capital (some 5.3 per cent per annum) and the labour force (0.8 per cent per annum). Once again, as elsewhere, the greater proportion of this growth – nearly three-fifths in Italy's case – was not directly attributable to measurable factor inputs but to rising Total Factor Productivity. Clearly the economy was taking advantage of gaps in technology and managerial techniques which had emerged since the period of fascist dictatorship and inter-war autarky. Maddison (1996, Table 2.15a), for example, shows that labour productivity in Italy relative to that in the US rose from some 34 per cent in 1950 to 66 per cent by 1973 (the European average was 40 per cent in 1950 and 64 per cent in 1973). The rate at which the gap was closing was clearly among the fastest in Western Europe: of the 12 most advanced economies in Europe, only Germany and Austria were converging on the US level of productivity at a faster rate than Italy (Maddison 1995, Table 2.8).

Selected indicators in Table 4.1 illustrate the performance of the economy across successive stages of the long boom.

Table 4.1 *Selected macro-indicators: Italy 1951–73 (average annual growth rates at constant prices) (%)*

	1951–8	*1959–63*	*1964–9*	*1970–3*	*1951–73*
GDP (market prices)	5.3	6.5	5.3	4.2	5.4
Agricult. output	3.2	2.3	3.1	–0.3	2.3
Industrial output	8.1	9.1	5.7	4.9	7.1
Private consumption	4.8	7.4	5.8	5.0	5.7
Public consumption	3.9	4.4	3.5	4.0	3.9
Exports	13.1	14.3	13.3	6.3	11.6
Gross fix. invst.	10.8	10.1	5.0	2.8	7.5

Source: Rossi et al. (1993).

Growth peaked between 1959 and 1963, a period that has gained the reputation of an 'economic miracle'. Overall the annual rate of growth of industrial production averaged 7 per cent while for manufacturing alone it was even higher. It is important, however, to note that the 5.4 per cent GDP growth rate must be adjusted downwards in per capita terms, given that the resident population increased by an average 0.6 per cent per annum.[1]

Exports and gross fixed investment were clearly star performers. Export growth was strong enough to offset the rising imports of raw materials, fuel and capital goods, characteristic of a rapidly industrializing economy. Gross fixed investment, which stood at 17 per cent of GDP in 1951, climbed to 24.1 per cent in 1958 and to 29.2 per cent in 1963, and although it fell slightly thereafter, was still at 27 per cent in 1973. By contrast, private consumption fell by three points as a percentage of GDP during the 1950s to a share of about 56.5 per cent in 1963. Thereafter it grew slightly more rapidly than the whole economy, signalling the advent of a consumer society.

These changes were accompanied by massive shifts in the structure of the economy with rapid contraction of employment in agriculture and substantial gains in services and industry – again rather typical of an economy involved in modernization.

Table 4.2 *Share of the workforce employed by sector in selected years (%)*

	1951	*1958*	*1964*	*1973*
Agriculture	43.9	34.1	25.0	16.6
Industry	29.5	34.6	40.2	38.3
Services	20.8	24.9	26.7	30.1
Public Admin.	5.8	6.4	8.1	15.0

Source: ISTAT (1986).

The outflow from agriculture was highest in the South: net migration was 1.8 million between 1951 and 1961 and a further 2.3 million between 1961 and 1971, compared with a population of around 18 million. About two-thirds of those leaving went to the North and Centre, attracted largely to bigger cities such as Rome, Turin and Milan (Saraceno 1988, p. 53). Urbanization affected the whole country, however, also touching towns with populations numbering between 100 000 and 250 000. In 1951, only about 20 per cent of Italians lived in urban communities of more than 100 000 residents. Ten years later this had grown to 25 per cent, while in 1971 it was close to 30 per cent. Each year during the boom, approximately 400 000 people were added to the numbers of those living in the larger towns (ISTAT 1986). Others migrated to foreign parts; Switzerland, West Germany and France being the most important. Nationally, net emigration amounted to 750 000 from 1946 to 1950, 1.6 million from 1951 to 1961 and 800 000 in the following decade, among the highest rates ever experienced in Italy (ISTAT 1986). The outflow decelerated in the second part of the 1960s, and petered out in the early 1970s.

These changes had important economic consequences. First, the shift between sectors raised productivity in the whole economy, given that agriculture was by far the least efficient sector. After leaving the land, however, many did not take up new jobs, thus contributing to a declining rate of activity: women's participation in the labour force ranked among the lowest in Western Europe, and activity rates among the young and in the South were also particularly low. However, the departure of marginal workers and impoverished peasants raised the productivity of those who remained. Agricultural productivity, in fact, grew in step with industrial productivity, if not faster, at a yearly rate estimated as somewhere between 5 and 7 per cent.[2]

From 1951 to 1958 there was a sustained build-up of fixed capital: public investment schemes were launched related to agricultural reform, housing, and infrastructural development in the South. State-owned industry completed the first wave of post-war modernization. Rising productivity in manufacturing (about 6 per cent a year) outstripped money wage growth. Hence, despite high employers' social charges, unit labour costs maintained a marginally downward drift. As a result Italy enjoyed the benefits of a virtuous circle: firms enjoyed good profits, lowered export prices and became more competitive (Ciocca et al. 1975, p. 299). There was a danger that a low wage economy with high unemployment could generate stagnation, but domestic private consumption managed to grow at 4.8 per cent per annum, thanks to urbanization bringing into the market families previously living at the margins.

After a fragile performance in the early 1950s the balance of payments was in surplus by the end of the decade, and the period after the signing of the Treaty of Rome saw the rapid opening-up of the economy: the ratio of foreign trade to GDP rose from 20 per cent in 1958 to 25 per cent in 1964 with the EEC becoming progressively more important. Some 800 000 new jobs in manufacturing and construction, coupled with greater emigration to West Germany, reduced unemployment to a record low of 3.9 per cent: in the Centre/North it was 1.5 per cent, a condition of virtually full employment (Ciocca et al. 1975, pp. 302–5; Rey 1982, p. 511).

Unfortunately the economy was overheating: capacity was overstretched and unable to accommodate further increases in demand. Furthermore, 1961–2 had seen substantial wage settlements so that labour costs in manufacturing increased by 5.3 per cent in 1962 and 14.5 per cent in the following year with a corresponding fall in profits (Podbielski 1974, p. 104). Rising imports during 1963 generated a current account deficit, topped up by substantial capital flight, largely to Switzerland, in response to the inclusion of Socialists in the government.

The payments crisis, however, was easily overcome: the Bank of Italy had considerable reserves and an international rescue package was assembled to counter fears of devaluation. A credit squeeze slowed the economy, and inflation, which had climbed to 7.5 per cent in 1963, decelerated as GDP growth fell back in 1964 and 1965. The most serious repercussions of this deflation were on investment which only recovered after 1967. Such investment that did take place was directed at rationalizing production so that there were few new jobs and working hours were increased by overtime. Manufacturing productivity increased by more than 7 per cent per annum from 1964 to 1969, surpassing the rate achieved between 1959 and 1963, but this time without the net injection of fixed capital. These efficiency gains clearly reflected the forces of catch-up which were particularly significant in the manufacturing sector. Exports too continued to grow rapidly as, within the Common Market, tariff barriers fell and Italian firms took advantage of the booming French market.

Visible trade surpluses combined with earnings from remittances and tourism to the tune of $2 billion a year, produced a healthy foreign position: the current account being positive in the late 1960s by an average 2.8 per cent of GDP.[3] As a result Italy turned into a net exporter of capital, although capital flight continued seeking a safe haven away from Italy's social and political tensions. Year on year these outflows made the payments position erratic, but the fundamentals were strong and the Bank of Italy was again accumulating reserves (Allen and Stevenson 1974).

In late 1969 there was an upsurge in union militancy during the so-called *Autunno Caldo* – the 'hot autumn' – a phenomenon experienced elsewhere in Europe. Wages increased by over 20 per cent in 1970 and 13.5 per cent in 1971. Labour unrest at plant level became a feature of the 1970s and as a result the cost of labour moved into line with the rest of the EEC. Investment and output decelerated as wage increases dented profits and the resulting rise in consumption stoked up inflation and imports.

The Growth of Exports

Italy's share of world exports more than doubled between 1950 and 1972, rising from 2.1 to 4.9 per cent (Britton et al. 1986, pp. 48–9). This was achieved through several successive export booms: the first, based mainly on textiles, occurred in 1946 when the existence of a vast overhang of capacity in the mechanical and textile sectors enabled Italian firms to take advantage of post-war shortages and the temporary absence of German exporters. In the early 1950s, sales of textiles and foodstuffs to Western Europe were further helped by the OEEC trade liberalization programme (Holbik 1959, p. 79). Further booms followed based on the remarkable growth of intra-Western European trade, especially within the Common Market. The composition of Italian exports changed: manufactures as a whole, and mechanical goods and chemicals became more significant, while textiles and primary goods, such as fruit and vegetables, declined (see Table 4.3). This also shows the growth of EEC markets and the dominance of West Germany, which not only attracted an increasing share of exports but was also by far industry's largest supplier of equipment and machinery (Milward 1992).

Table 4.3 *Selected shares of the value of exports of goods by composition and destination (%)*

Share of Italian exports	*1951–2*	*1962–3*	*1971–2*
By composition:			
all manufactured goods	85.1	89.6	95.0
of which			
textiles and clothing	31.0	20.5	18.8
mechanical	20.3	34.8	40.0
chemical	11.7	15.7	14.0
By destination:			
W. Germany	8.8	18.5	22.8
France	7.9	9.8	13.9
Total EEC	20.9	33.9	45.0
EFTA	25.0	19.7	13.6
US	8.3	9.4	9.8

Source: ISTAT, *Statistica del Commercio con l'Estero*, various years.

Exports to the heavily protected French market, by contrast, were stuck at below 8 per cent of the total. The prospect of easier access to that market convinced industrialists to support Italy's membership of the EEC. Their calculations proved correct and during the 1960s France became Italy's second most important partner (Ranieri 1996).

By the mid-1960s the EC was a trading bloc with high reciprocal import and export propensities for manufactured goods (Maizels 1959; ECE 1988). This rapidly growing market required firms to keep abreast of technological innovation and to score high productivity gains, offering in return new opportunities for economies of scale. The more dynamic the export trade of a particular category of goods, the more it could benefit from this 'virtuous circle'. Exports of mechanical goods, for example, shown in Table 4.4, grew most rapidly and within that category cars, electrical machinery and precision instruments were most successful.

Italian exporters were competitive partly thanks to labour and production costs, as suggested earlier, but continuing success when they no longer enjoyed this advantage implies that non-price factors were important. For machinery this involved rapid delivery and good after-sales service, while for consumer goods, it was mostly the ability to offer innovative style and design. Nor should export-maximizing strategies of a neo-mercantilist nature be overlooked: despite the more liberal climate of the 1960s, governments could still deploy a variety of protective devices. When quotas were lifted, there were tariffs, and when these were gradually reduced a formidable array of non-tariff barriers was disclosed. Thus, in several cases the Italian authorities raised the competitive advantage of exports by sheltering producers in the home market and offering tax rebates, hidden subsidies or generous export credits. All these were made easier by the fact that Italy's exports concentrated on a narrow range of goods, produced by a limited number of firms.

Table 4.4 *Percentage share of visible exports of selected mechanical goods going to the EEC (by value)*

Export shares to the EEC	*1953–5*	*1959–61*	*1969–71*
all mechanical goods	18.6	24.6	34.7
all vehicles	17.4	28.8	40.2
cars	18.4	39.1	50.1
electrical machinery	26.3	23.4	40.1
non-elec. machinery	21.2	22.2	28.0
precision instruments	16.6	36.4	60.0

Source: Cao-Pinna (1975).

Economic Policies

Economic management remained for a long time in the hands of the generation of technocrats clustered around the Bank of Italy and IRI. They kept politicians at arm's length and implemented their supply side, investment-based strategy, with a mixture of paternalism and ruthlessness (De Cecco 1989a). Within their ranks were also a number of managers committed to modernization, technological innovation and reform in industrial relations and business organization.

In the 1960s, however, once this elite had moved on, the governing parties, particularly the Christian Democrats, subjected economic management to their political imperatives. State-owned industry lost its former freedom of action and increasingly became a vehicle for patronage and political influence: what once had been the spearhead of expansion was turned into a sickbed for inefficient, loss-making firms (Osti 1993).

Up to 1973, however, the achievements of state-owned industry were still remarkable. Doubling its workforce and increasing by tenfold the volume of investment between 1955 and 1970 to a share of 30 per cent of gross fixed investment in industry, it occupied the commanding heights of the economy via IRI and ENI. IRI was the largest group in Italy, employing 450 000 people.

Its core lay in heavy industry, with steel, ship-building and heavy engineering covering over half of its sales, but it was also engaged in infrastructure, utilities and transport – such as the construction of the autostrade – and the telephone network (Posner and Woolf 1967; Allen and Stevenson 1974). ENI, created in 1953 for the development of energy resources, was given a monopoly of exploitation in the Po valley, where gas discoveries had taken place. Helped by favourable pricing arrangements it moved upstream into refineries, pipelines, petrochemicals and fertilizers. By 1972 it employed nearly 80 000 workers and controlled 180 companies (Allen and Stevenson 1974, pp. 231–4).

State-owned companies were able to enjoy the best of both worlds. The state, via IRI/ENI, was the major shareholder, giving them privileged access to finance and public support. They were not, however, formally part of the state in as much as they were run as private corporations: thus they were supposed to fend for themselves in the market and could raise capital by selling shares – but only up to a point, since they were never allowed to break free of state ownership.

Nevertheless, this ambiguous status paid dividends, allowing for a kind of informal but effective industrial policy. State-owned companies fostered projects which were particularly capital intensive, sometimes in conjunction with private firms – for example, the development of strip-mill steel production was accomplished together by IRI-Finsider and Fiat. At other times they were deeply involved in international negotiations – thus Italy's membership of the ECSC largely reflected Finsider's priorities (Ranieri 1988). In some instances, as, for example, with electricity, cement and fertilizers, they were called upon to break private monopolies. Finally they could act in a countercyclical fashion, stepping up investment during economic slowdowns, and they launched into the industrialization of the South. The ability to act swiftly allowed them to accomplish what the state itself, with its cumbersome administrative practices and inefficient bureaucracy, could never hope to achieve.

Meanwhile the Bank of Italy operated fiscal, monetary and exchange rate policies which were conducive to stability and prudence, at least up to 1958: a balanced budget and restrained money supply growth did not hurt investment, as large investment projects were backed up by subsidies and private firms relied on a high rate of self-financing. The exchange rate had been set in 1949 at the slightly undervalued level of 625 lira to the dollar, and this rate was maintained for the duration of the fixed exchange rate regime. The Bank of Italy felt strong enough by 1959 to make the lira freely convertible and Italy became a full adherent to the Bretton Woods system (Kaplan and Schleiminger 1992). During the miracle years the authorities allowed the money supply to grow faster than GDP, but the 1963 crisis elicited harsh deflation and in the following years credit remained tight. At this stage fiscal policies became more adventurous so that deficit financing reflated the economy in 1964 and 1965 and again in 1971 and 1972, but spending decisions were carried out with long delays, while on the revenue side the tax system was lax.

Politically, in the early 1960s, Italy turned left, with the inclusion (in 1963) of the Socialist Party (PSI) in the majority coalition. Unfortunately the new coalition proved ineffective and disappointed its supporters and it became clear that the political edge remained with the conservative core of the Christian Democrats, such that necessary reforms were delayed and diluted, while patronage and corruption increased insidiously.

Attempts at economic planning were particularly inconsequential. Planning bodies were created but were powerless: governments were too precarious and divided to be seriously motivated, public administration was inefficient and uncooperative while attitudes of trade unions and business ranged from lukewarm to adversarial. There is of course an argument that planning can never work in a market economy, and certainly the kind of detailed objectives of the first planning document covering the 1965–70 period were all but unattainable. Among the reasons for this failure was the fact that business elites in Italy were not as cohesive as elsewhere and there was little cross-fertilization between politicians and technocrats. Moreover, it would have been necessary to accommodate planning with the informal technocracy that already existed – something which was not even clearly acknowledged, let alone accomplished (Shonfield, 1965; Podbielski 1974).

State intervention remained important but only partially coordinated. During the 1960s, the electricity industry was nationalized, capital was poured into the industrialization of the South, and tax breaks were introduced to encourage amalgamations designed to stave off foreign competition and foster 'national champions'. Unfortunately, governments failed to rise to the challenge of massive urbanization. For example, social expenditures fell as a proportion of national income from 18.3 per cent of GDP from 1951–8, to 17.3 per cent by 1965–71 (Podbielski 1974, pp. 154–5). As a result there was congestion and crisis in metropolitan areas: cheap accommodation was lacking, hospital facilities were overstretched, urban transport and education were inadequate. For many who had coveted the consumer society, urbanization turned out to be a bitter disappointment. The workforce reacted by escalating wage demands. Meanwhile political extremism found a fertile breeding ground. In the trade-off between equity and economic success, Italian society, more consciously perhaps than it was prepared to admit, had chosen the latter.

PURSUIT OF GROWTH AND FINANCIAL DISTRESS: 1973–95

General Features

The broad pattern after 1973 was one of adaptation to slower growth. There were, however, question marks about Italy, stemming from its being a 'latecomer'. How would the structural transformations undergone during the years of rapid growth be absorbed? Would the catch-up process continue?

Would the country be able to discharge the responsibilities of a leading EU/OECD nation?

The economy continued to exhibit structural change similar to other developed countries: the service sector by 1993 accounted for 60 per cent of the workforce and 65 per cent of value added (see Table 4.5).

Table 4.5 *Selected structural indicators 1973–93*

	1973	*1980*	*1989*	*1993*
Agriculture				
% of workforce	17.5	14.0	9.3	7.5
% of value added	6.9	6.0	3.5	3.0
Industry				
% of workforce	39.3	36.0	32.4	33.0
% of value added	41.1	40.0	33.9	32.0
Services				
% of workforce	43.2	48.0	58.2	60.0
% of value added	52.1	54.0	62.6	65.0
Unemployment %	5.3	7.5	11.8	10.8
% male	3.5	4.8	7.9	8.3
% female	9.4	13.1	18.6	15.1

Source: OECD various years, Venturini (1993).

The growth of GDP throughout the whole period from 1973 to 1993 averaged 2.3 per cent a year, better than other major European economies, largely as a result of a good performance between 1973 and 1979. Italy's 3.7 per cent average annual growth exceeded the UK's 1.5 per cent, France's 2.8 per cent and the Federal Republic's 2.4 per cent.

How did Italy perform so successfully during the 1970s, when it was beset by double-digit inflation, disruptive strikes and political instability? Part of the answer lies with currency devaluation which boosted exports, and, in addition, despite steeply rising labour costs, the government succeeded in engineering a shift back from wages to profits. Although total investment fell, there was a strong investment performance in machinery and equipment and manufacturing output remained fairly robust (Table 4.6; D'Adda and Salituro 1989). On the other hand, during the 1970s inflationary expectations became deeply ingrained in the system.

While monetary policies were tight, fiscal policies were not, so that budget deficits remained high and public debt rocketed to over 100 per cent of GDP. Readjusting to a tighter fiscal stance has proved very demanding, since it has been attempted during a recession. The depreciation of the lira following Italy's exit from the ERM in September 1992 provided scope for export growth, but with state expenditure reined in and no more room for domestic spending sprees, the path to further growth has looked particularly narrow.

Table 4.6 *Selected macro-indicators: Italy 1973–95 (average annual growth rates at constant prices) (%)*

	1973–9	*1979–89*	*1989–94*	*1973–95*
GDP market prices	3.7	2.4	1.0	2.4
Agricult. output	1.4	0.9	1.0	1.1
Industrial output	3.1	2.1	0.7	2.0
Manuf'g output	5.5	2.8	0.9	3.0
Dom. private consumpt.	3.7	3.2	0.9	2.7
Public consumption	2.7	2.6	0.9	2.2
Exports (volume)	7.9	2.7	6.9	5.3
Gross fixed invst.	0.4	2.2	–2.3	0.5
Machinery*	3.8	4.5	–2.7	2.4

* Investment in machinery and equipment.
Source: OECD various years.

A broad comparative perspective of the last 20 years, however, reveals that some of the peculiar advantages of the Italian economy have persisted. As Table 4.7 indicates, Italy outperformed her main European partners both in manufacturing and in machinery and equipment investment.

Table 4.7 *Comparative performance indicators 1973–93 (average growth rates (or average shares)) (%)*

	Italy	*UK*	*France*	*W. Germany*
GDP per capita	2.3	1.5	1.5	2.0
Manuf'g output	3.0	n.a.	0.8	0.9
Exports of goods by value	5.6	3.4	n.a	3.6
Gross fixed invst.	0.8	1.3	0.9	1.3
of which				
machinery/eqpt	2.7	2.1	1.7	2.0
(as % of GDP)	10.0	8.2	8.8	8.8
Labour productivity* in manufacturing	2.3	1.6	1.9	1.9
Inflation rate (annual av.)	11.7	9.4	7.4	3.6

* Real GDP per person employed.
Source: OECD various years.

Exports performed strongly, allowing Italy to retain a share of 4.6 per cent of world markets in 1993, at a time when all the major European countries were losing ground.[4] Italy's advantage in labour productivity growth can probably be explained by one-off gains accruing from the ongoing shift out of agriculture, but higher productivity growth in manufacturing was the result of comprehensive rationalization and flexible adjustment allied to greater residual catch up possibilities than in Germany, France, the Netherlands and Belgium.

A weak spot was the slow overall growth rate of investment, despite the dynamism of investment in machinery. There was, in fact, net disinvestment in residential and non-residential construction, resulting in deteriorating infrastructure and housing conditions. A further weakness was the poor productivity performance in services: poor standards in rail transport, a poor postal service, inadequate telecommunications and high costs in the tertiary sector impaired overall efficiency and raised prices.[5] Inflation remained high and persistent and ensuing exchange rate instability meant that the country failed to live up to its ERM commitments.

Italy shared with most of Europe the rise in unemployment: in 1980 the rate was 7.5 per cent, by 1990 10.3 per cent, and by 1995, adopting the same definition, approximately 15 per cent.[6] A key factor here was an increase in the population of working age, because of the relatively high birth rates prevailing in the 1950s and 1960s. Emigration no longer provided an outlet: indeed, there were more repatriations than there were new departures. Furthermore, the participation rate of women rose via the expanding service sector and the evolution in social attitudes consequent on better access to education. Youth unemployment was partly the result of the inability of the labour market to accommodate larger numbers of well qualified applicants seeking white-collar jobs; partly also it reflected protected job tenure of existing employees – the insider–outsider syndrome observed elsewhere in Europe. The weakness of the labour market was particularly evident in the South: in 1980 the difference between the rate of unemployment in the Centre-North and the South was less than 4 percentage points; since the end of the 1980s it has measured 10 points or more (Venturini 1993; OECD 1996a, pp. 10–13).

Managing Inflation in the 1970s

Inflation proved to be a serious problem for most of Europe in the 1970s, but for Italy it proved to be a decade when it became particularly deep-rooted. This reflects a number of errors in policy making as well as certain aggravating political pressures.

The first oil shock hit the Italian economy severely. The response to rampant inflation should have been deflation but this was all but ruled out given the prevailing climate of rising trade union influence and shopfloor unrest. Furthermore, the Communist Party, having polled over one-third of the vote in 1976, was asked and agreed to support 'Governments of National Solidarity', thus re-entering government for the first time since 1947. This had contradictory effects: on the one hand the Communists showed themselves willing to win the trade unions over to a policy of restraint; on the other hand they tried to deflect deflationary measures and push through a number of ambitious spending reforms in health care, pensions, housing and other fields (Sassoon 1990).

The authorities, therefore, and in particular the officials of the Bank of Italy, had little choice but to meet the crisis with 'stop–go' policies, seeking to contain the worst excesses of inflation. Their immediate concern was to restore business profitability and to boost exports through a fairly lax exchange rate management.

To minimize labour unrest employers conceded substantial wage settlements and shorter hours. Moreover, new legislation known as the '*Statuto dei Lavoratori*' (Workers' Statute) introduced a degree of labour market rigidity as it curbed employers' power to hire and fire, to check absenteeism and bring about labour mobility. As a result labour costs in manufacturing rose substantially and profitability fell. There is no reason, however, to believe that industrialists could not have met the challenge: exports continued to perform well and private companies continued to enjoy productivity gains and the benefits of a wider domestic market.

The international environment, however, was not conducive to stability. The demise of the Bretton Woods system removed the dollar's role as an anti-inflationary anchor. In 1972, EC countries tried to limit fluctuations inside the so-called 'snake'. The lira's participation, dubious from the start, was short-lived. Following heavy speculation it was withdrawn early in 1973 and allowed to float downwards (Templeman 1981, p. 313). Inflationary pressures built up as investment in the public sector increased while the government undertook a host of spending commitments in the form of transfer payments. The budget deficit rose from 3 per cent in 1969 to 7 per cent of GDP in 1973.[7] These increases in domestic demand added to higher prices for primary products and culminated in a double-digit inflation rate.

The oil shock of autumn 1973, therefore, came at the worst possible time. Imported oil accounted for about 80 per cent of primary sources of energy so that the hike in prices ran up the import bill by 3 per cent of GDP. The balance of payments came under strain, the lira fell and inflation received a further fillip. Commercial international borrowing in the Euro-dollar market, through which the capital account had been sustained, dried up, and the Bank of Italy was forced to turn to the IMF. An agreement was struck in March 1974, amounting to a loan of $1.2 billion, all which was drawn down within a year. Additional lines of credit in the form of oil facilities and other borrowing from international institutions were arranged, while in return the authorities were to restrict the money supply and redress the non-oil current account deficit (Spaventa 1983). Direct credit ceilings and portfolio requirements were imposed on the commercial banks, the discount rate was raised and so were indirect taxes and utility prices. These measures aggravated the effects of the international slump so that domestic demand and GDP fell back sharply. Strong concerns were voiced from all quarters and during 1975 the measures were reversed.

This overlooked the inflationary threat: the brief recession had reduced inflation's international component, but domestic pressures, especially generous wage settlements, were still pushing prices up. Inflation peaked at an annual rate of 25.3 per cent in December 1974. Within a year it had more than halved to 11.1 per cent, but by the end of 1976 it was again over 20 per cent. The window of opportunity had been lost, inflationary expectations had been stoked up such that inflation stayed above the 10 per cent mark for the rest of the decade and beyond (Templeman 1981, p. 148).

Equally seriously, this decision to reflate overlooked the fact that foreign exchange reserves were thin and confidence in the lira brittle – speculation proved so damaging that the foreign exchange markets had to be closed for 40 days in 1976. As soon as they were reopened, there was sharp depreciation followed after a few months by yet another crisis. Loans from the EEC, the Bundesbank and the Federal Reserve helped, but monetary and fiscal policy had to be set into reverse gear: interest rates rose, ceilings on credit were reintroduced and expenditure decreased. A new tougher standby arrangement was reached with the IMF in April 1977 which committed the government to bringing down public sector deficits and inflation over a period of 20 months. This was partly retribution for the way Italy was seen to have squandered the previous loan (Spaventa 1983, p. 459). Meanwhile, support in managing the crisis was sought from the Communist Party and the trade unions and there was a measure of agreement on ending shopfloor confrontation.

The response of the economy was encouraging: the current account returned considerable surpluses and there was also a resurgence of investment in manufacturing. The resulting recovery of output gained strength all the way up to 1979, when the growth of GDP accelerated from 3.7 to 6 per cent in the final year of the decade. Despite nominal wages rising by over 20 per cent a year, business profitability improved. Various factors were at work: first, there were continuing large productivity gains; second, real interest rates on business loans remained negative for most of the period; third, the state took on the burden of employers' social charges. This so-called 'fiscalization' was funded by revenue generated by fiscal drag: as taxes were imposed on money incomes, high inflation resulted in rising revenues as people moved into higher tax brackets (Giavazzi and Spaventa 1989; Micossi and Trau 1994).[8]

As the recovery progressed, however, the quest for fiscal probity was abandoned. With commercial creditworthiness fully restored, there was no need to draw upon the new IMF loan, and targets for the public sector deficit were overshot. Another chance was missed to tackle a major structural flaw and by 1979 inflation was picking up again strongly.

Behind the twists and turns of policy one detects a relentless pursuit of growth through inflation. After each crisis, the money supply was expanded again so that firms could rebuild the profits they had just lost as a result of higher costs of labour and raw materials. Because of the floating exchange rate, inflation was accommodated by a steady depreciation of the lira, which allowed producers to remain internationally competitive.

Table 4.8 *Movement in Italy's nominal and real effective exchange rates 1973–9*

	Nominal rate	*Real*
1973	–9.0	n.a
1974	–9.5	n.a.
1975	–3.0	n.a.
1976	–17.5	–10.0
1977	–10.0	–4.0
1978	–6.0	–5.5
1979	–2.5	+3.5

Source: IMF *International Financial Statistics Yearbook*, various years.

The exchange rate was also managed in order to improve the terms of trade, particularly between 1977 and 1979, when it steered an intermediate course between the weakening dollar and the strengthening Deutschmark. Exports to the DM zone became more competitive, whereas imports, 50 per cent of which were invoiced in dollars, became cheaper (Giavazzi and Spaventa 1989, pp. 49–50).

The argument is not whether such a strategy worked in the short term, but whether by failing to address the problem of inflation and mounting public expenditure it was not in fact simply laying in trouble for the future. Taking an optimistic view, Giavazzi and Spaventa (1989) have claimed that by encouraging the investment boom of the late 1970s, the authorities ensured that firms were in a solid financial position at the time of the second oil shock. Massive UK-style cuts in capacity were avoided, and rationalization was carried out in the early 1980s when the resistance of the trade unions had weakened.

Disinflation in the 1980s: Going Through the Motions

The start of disinflation can be traced back to membership of the ERM, in March 1979. Monetary policy became tighter, with very high nominal interest rates and positive real ones. Although the lira was repeatedly devalued inside the ERM, the rate of nominal depreciation resulting from such realignments was less than that required by the cumulative inflation differential with the DM hence the real exchange rate rose.

The switch to a tougher monetary stance was reflected in domestic politics. Early in 1979 the Communists resumed their role of main opposition party. The following years were marked by centre-left coalition governments, in which the Christian Democrats and Socialists were the main players. There was some move toward liberalization and a more market-based approach, but it was accompanied by an increasingly pervasive regime of corruption and public sector inefficiency. The Craxi government, which lasted from August 1983 to April 1987, seemed to provide a measure of stability and leadership, but did not produce lasting change, and the worst habits of Italian politics were more rampant than ever during the late 1980s.

The Bank of Italy, whose autonomy was boosted in 1981 as a result of the so-called 'divorce' which lifted the obligation to purchase any government paper the Treasury failed to auction, took the main role in managing disinflation. Inflation had reached an annual rate of 25 per cent in the autumn of 1980: the differential with Germany increasing from 12 per cent in 1979 to 16 per cent. Hence Italy required a wider band of fluctuation within the ERM (+/– 6 per cent) and carried out four downward revisions of the lira's parity between 1979 and 1983. Even so, there was a *real appreciation* of the lira of about 3 to 4 per cent a year. Up to 1985, this was partially offset by a rising dollar but, as indicated earlier, Europe not the US was Italy's major partner.

There has been some debate as to how far joining the Exchange Rate Mechanism succeeded in bringing about a shift in inflationary expectations (Nardozzi 1993). The answer must be that it was only a beginning: clearly it provided an element of external discipline, but other signals were needed. When high real interest rates emerged in the US and Germany in the early 1980s, they were not matched in Italy by any significant adjustment in fiscal policy: in fact, between 1980 and 1981 the budget deficit widened. A shift of expectations did seem to occur, however, at the beginning of 1984 when Craxi stood up to a large section of the trade union movement and implemented a modest cut to wage indexation. The issue was fought out in a national referendum in June 1985, which resulted in victory for the government. Thus in the latter part of the decade the fall in inflation became more substantial and there was a downward adjustment of real wages.

Navigation inside the ERM, however, was never entirely safe. A credible anti-inflation stance required a substantial interest rate premium over the German level while liberalization of capital movements, initiated haltingly in Italy after 1985, deprived the authorities of one of their main anti-speculative weapons. A major realignment took place in 1987 followed by five years of a virtually fixed exchange rate regime, and in January 1990, the lira joined the narrower band. Interest rate differentials contracted but the inflation differential persisted at some three points higher than Germany and France. The resulting real appreciation of the lira undermined competitiveness and produced a growing deficit on the current account. After 1990 the situation was aggravated as interest rates rose in Germany following reunification (Farina 1992).

By the late 1980s the increasingly restrictive approach of the German monetary authorities sparked a debate over the merits of the system, with some claiming that the link with the Deutschmark was counterproductive. Germany, it was said, wanted the best of both worlds – a fixed exchange rate regime with the DM at its centre, combined with a structural trade surplus with its neighbours – but it was not prepared to pay the price of a creditor country (De Cecco 1989b). Critics suggested that there might have been some merit in following the Germans in the early 1980s because of their anti-inflationary virtue, but their embrace was proving deadly. Such arguments, though containing some truth, neglected the deep, structural interdependence that had been built up since the 1950s with the German economy: Germany might not be a generous banker, but it had proved a key trade partner, whatever the monetary picture. The real question lies elsewhere: why did Italy engage in the battle against inflation using an overvalued fixed exchange rate as the only weapon?

In the early 1980s economic performance was discouraging. The second oil shock in 1979 seriously affected the terms of trade, hampering exports. While inflation peaked, GDP contracted – the first year-on-year fall since 1975 and only the second since the war. In the next three years, growth averaged less than 1 per cent per annum. After 1984 there was substantial recovery but growth during the rest of the decade remained less than between 1973 and 1979. The inflation rate declined to 5.9 per cent in 1987, but refused to sink any further. More positive notes came from investment and productivity, particularly in manufacturing as the investment performance of the late 1970s carried over into the early 1980s. These productivity gains allied to moderate rises in wages reduced unit labour costs and there was a surge in profitability. Despite the rising cost of capital and in the face of deflation, re-equipment and restructuring occurred, particularly in large firms: the industrial workforce declined by 14 per cent between 1980 and 1988 (Ranci 1993). Given that the unions maintained considerable bargaining power and were unwilling to allow more flexibility, the government helped rationalization via the *Cassa Integrazione Guadagni* (Wage Supplementation Fund) – a subsidy for workers made temporarily redundant which amounted to as much as 80 per cent of the actual wage (Venturini 1993). Hence these changes meant that even within the constraints of the ERM, exports rose rapidly in the mid-1980s as manufacturers displayed a high degree of adaptability (see Table 4.9).

Table 4.9 *Shares of Italian visible exports by destination 1971–93 (%)*

	1971–2	*1978–9*	*1984–5*	*1992–3*
W. Germany	22.8	19.0	16.2	20.0
France	13.8	14.5	14.0	13.9
Total EEC	45.0	48.7	45.7	55.5
US	9.8	6.8	11.6	7.4
Middle East	3.1	7.6	8.2	4.8
Eastern Europe	4.6	4.1	3.4	3.8
Far East	2.8	3.3	4.7	8.0

Source: ISTAT various years.

Exports consisted mainly of traditional consumer goods such as textiles, clothing, leather goods and furniture as well as engineering goods, usually of a low to intermediate technological content (ECE 1990). However, in machine tools, Italy ranked just behind the world leaders, Germany and Japan, by keeping abreast of latest developments in computerization and process innovation. Indeed, the capital goods sector as a whole was particularly dynamic: export performance was matched by a rising share of total industrial value added – by 1990 it was nearly 30 per cent (Ginsborg, 1994 p. 388). On the other hand, performance in other high-tech goods was less impressive, reflecting a remaining significant R&D gap with more advanced industrial countries (Antonelli 1995).

The 1980s, however, were marked, above all else, by lax fiscal policy: budget deficits were increasingly bloated by the burden of interest payments on accumulated debt. In fact, whereas the *primary* deficits (that is, excluding interest payments), which were the norm since the mid-1970s, began to decline, interest payments rose ominously: during the period 1980–5 they averaged 7 per cent of GDP and in 1987 reached 8.1 per cent – thus a primary deficit of 2.4 per cent became an overall budget deficit of 10.5 per cent of GDP (OECD *Economic Survey of Italy* 1989, p. 12).

Although there was some borrowing in the international markets, much of this mountainous debt was financed by domestic private savings. Encouraged by tax exemptions, the share of government paper in the financial wealth of households increased from about 5 per cent in the mid-1970s to approximately 30 per cent in the late 1980s and households held about 60 per cent of all negotiable government debt. When capital movements were fully liberalized in 1988 (OECD *Economic Survey of Italy* 1989, pp. 21–2) the risk that households might seek to diversify into new financial instruments required the authorities to keep yields on government bonds as attractive as possible, thereby adding to the servicing costs of the debt.

After the Binge: Paying the Penalty in the 1990s

The combination of fiscal profligacy and monetary stringency made the lira's position within the ERM problematical. When speculation built up following the rejection of Maastricht in the Danish referendum, eventually, in September 1992, the lira was forced (along with the pound) to leave the system. Politically also the country entered a long tunnel, from which it has yet to emerge. As endemic corruption was unveiled by magistrates, the leading political parties, particularly the Christian Democrats and Socialists, saw their support crumble. Protest movements emerged, with vague, even contradictory, agendas. In 1993 a new majority-based voting system was ushered in by a national referendum, but stability was elusive. A right-wing coalition was voted into power in 1994, but soon fell apart. In 1996 fortunes were reversed and a broadly based left-wing coalition obtained a narrow mandate.

More importantly economic management was formally entrusted to technocrats at the Bank of Italy. In 1993 the Governor, Ciampi, was asked to become Prime Minister in a 'technical' capacity and during 1994 and 1995 Lamberto Dini, a former top Bank official, moved from being Treasury Minister in the Berlusconi government to Prime Minister. Finally in 1996, Ciampi was again put in charge of economic policy in the new centre-left coalition. This was hardly surprising: the admonitions of the Bank had long been ignored by a political class which seemed intent on committing political suicide. Who else could be entrusted with the painful job of pulling the country back from the brink of bankruptcy?

The leitmotif of policy has since been the need to correct fiscal imbalances to meet the Maastricht criteria and join the Single Currency. The task remains daunting as conditions in the 1990s have proved difficult: the recession of 1992–3 was shorter than that of 1980–3, but it was deeper and was followed only by a mild rebound led by exports in the wake of currency depreciation (OECD 1995). Between 1992 and 1995 there was a decline in the nominal effective exchange rate of about 30 per cent, while relative unit labour costs fell by 34 per cent. Half of this was passed on by manufacturers into lower export prices (OECD 1996b, p. 21) and manufactures made strong gains world-wide, despite competition from newly industrialized countries: in two years they recovered the ground lost between 1987 and 1992. Given that internal demand remained depressed, imports stagnated and did not pick up until 1995. The current account swung into surplus, but the direction of capital flows was uneven, affected by bouts of fear over the free-floating lira.

In 1993 employers and trade unions negotiated a comprehensive wage accord, removing indexation, fixing nominal increases within the projected rate of inflation and matching any eventual above-inflation pay rise to gains in productivity (OECD *Economic Survey of Italy* 1993, pp. 19–20). Rising unemployment caused the trade unions to embrace moderation: the result was a sharp fall in real wages such that internal demand flagged far more than in any other European country. While this concentrated the minds of exporters, it held down industrial production and investment. Investment in machinery revived in 1994, but construction investment remained depressed. Cuts in public investment were substantial and they jeopardized the recovery of the South. Unemployment rose to historic records while productivity gains were substantial: there was no doubt as to who was shouldering the heaviest burden of the crisis.

Striving for fiscal rectitude increased the strains. The options facing the authorities were limited: given the stock of accumulated public debt, estimated in 1993 at 114 per cent of GDP, and the burden of yearly interest payments which surpassed 10 per cent of GDP in 1991, any improvement necessitated substantial primary surpluses (Wolf 1996). How could they be achieved? Italian governments have long dodged the issue of tackling key areas of expenditure such as pensions, the health service and local government. These areas comprised the core of the post-war consensus and although progress was made after 1992, cuts remained inadequate: there was a stubborn holding on to illusions. Generous pensions and social benefits were not tackled decisively and preference was given to increasing taxation: in 1980 fiscal receipts accounted for 33.3 per cent of GDP; by 1993 they were up to 48.3 per cent. This bore heavily on the most productive sectors, engendering frustration, particularly in the North, and bringing hints of fiscal revolt and secession. The picture has improved, thanks to primary surpluses from 1993 to 1996, but the crisis is not resolved. Privatization designed to contribute to this process as well as to bring about fuller economic liberalization has been slow and patchy: between 1992 and 1995 it yielded receipts equivalent to little more than 1 per cent of GDP and only marginally dented the size of the huge state-holding sector (OECD *Economic Survey of Italy* 1993; OECD 1996b).

DUALISM AND THE REGIONAL PROBLEM

The Mezzogiorno

Most of the economies of Europe face regional problems, but Italy's are often portrayed as particularly intractable. How serious is the position of the Mezzogiorno and what has been the result of over 40 years of state intervention? Clearly some progress has been made, but considerable problems remain: in 1951, GDP per head in the South was 51.9 per cent of the rest of the country's and it climbed to 57.3 per cent by 1973. In 1987 it was down again to 55.6 per cent and has fallen further since (OECD *Economic Survey of Italy* 1990). In 1950 three segments of the country enjoyed different levels of development: the industrialized North-West, the semi-industrialized North-East and Centre, and the rural Mezzogiorno. Today the North-East and Centre have caught up with the North-West, whereas the South, even its most prosperous regions, remains considerably behind. Lombardy, which is one of the richest areas of the EU, enjoys an income per head which is two and a half times that of Calabria.

The Mezzogiorno accounts for 41 per cent of Italy's territory, and over one-third of her population, but only about one-quarter of her output. The regional balance of payments shows a large deficit: in 1990 net imports of goods and services accounted for 20 per cent of the area's GDP, financed by net income transfers, from the rest of Italy. Put another way, the revenues accruing to the state from the South amount to about 18 per cent of national revenue, whereas public expenditure channelled *into* the South amounts to 36 per cent of the total. Herein lies the root of the growing unease of northern taxpayers (Trigilia 1992, pp. 60–1).

The annual growth of southern GDP throughout the post-war period has been far from negligible, averaging 4 per cent between 1950 and 1986. Special development investment from CASMEZ was sizeable and sustained, peaking at some 3.6 per cent of southern GDP between 1962 and 1974 (OECD *Economic Survey of Italy* 1990). Initially it was directed at land reform and the provision of basic infrastructure (irrigation, aqueducts, roads and railways). Later in the 1950s there was a switch to subsidies to encourage industrialization. State-owned companies played a major role in this context, particularly in metallurgy (the Finsider Taranto steelworks) and petrochemicals (in Sicily and elsewhere), as well as engineering (with the Alfa Sud plant near Naples). Large private companies such as Fiat and Montedison followed suit. Fixed industrial investment in the South by the early 1970s had doubled its share of the national total to over 30 per cent (OECD *Economic Survey of Italy* 1981, pp. 37–44).

After 1975 CASMEZ's funds were cut, industrial investment in the South fell and public expenditure became increasingly geared towards income maintenance. In 1986 the Cassa was replaced by the *Agenzia per il Mezzogiorno* with a more decentralized approach to project financing with local authority involvement. The outcome, however, was unsatisfactory, leading to a fragmentation of investment into many small uncoordinated projects. In 1993 special aid was brought to an end (Castronovo 1995, p. 540).

Intensive investment targeted on a number of key areas produced large capital-intensive firms derisively known as 'cathedrals in the desert', since it was claimed that they failed to generate local spin-off in terms of services or supplier industries. This, however, was an exaggeration and a host of connected manufacturing activities did often emerge, while large-scale industry provided the rudiments of an industrial culture in formerly underdeveloped areas (Saraceno 1988). During the 1970s and 1980s, moreover, the section of the Mezzogiorno lying alongside the Adriatic exhibited features of the so-called 'Third Italy', based on clusters of small firms. Consequently industrial output there has grown sharply and the income gap with northern Italy has narrowed (De Vita 1992; Trigilia 1992).

Thus there have been some success stories, although in the South as a whole, creation of new jobs has been slow. The rate of unemployment at over 20 per cent is dangerously high, and for the young especially job prospects are dim: only about half of them get a chance to enter the workforce. The expansion of public administration has helped to alleviate the problem, but at the same time it offers very low-quality services. Moreover, high inflows of public expenditure, accounting for over half of total economic activity, have discouraged enterprise creation and encouraged a culture of dependency. The spread of organized crime and its bid to gain control of public subsidies, particularly in the large metropolitan areas, has also acted as a brake on the development of local entrepreneurship and as an obstacle to a more efficient targeting of state aid.

Manufacturing in the 'Third Italy'

Small firms have been a long-standing feature of Italy's manufacturing sector, but their organization and technology were primitive and their capabilities limited. This pattern started to change with the rise of new markets during the 'economic miracle'. During the 1970s the process gained momentum and led to the emergence of the so-called 'Third Italy' – new areas of light industrialization, spreading out mainly to the Centre and the North-East.

Two developments were at work. First, the breakdown in industrial relations originating in the *Autunno Caldo* affected the profitability of the large firms in the North-West. By contrast, small firms were more flexible: unionization was low, some of the provisions of the Workers' Statute did not apply and employers were able to dodge social security contributions. Large firms, therefore, sub-contracted an increasing number of their operations. Second, there was a change in demand away from mass-produced standardized goods toward more sophisticated, customized goods facilitated by the introduction of flexible technologies, suited to small-scale production, which lowered barriers to entry and increased competition (Paci 1992).

The relationship between the new small-scale firms and the larger ones was complex: sometimes sub-contracting played an important role in fostering activities which then acquired more autonomy and became self-sustaining (hosiery at Brescia); at other times small entrepreneurial activities arose out of attempts to replace large-scale firms which had failed (household equipment in Novara); yet other areas of light industrialization originated out of multiple small-scale manufacturing (tiles in Sassuolo in Emilia). These various patterns apply to their further evolution: in some cases there has been a move to vertical integration; in others, collaboration between small producers has intensified (Nuti 1992; Bruno 1995, pp. 396–402).

Social factors also contributed to the emergence of the 'Third Italy'. Some manufacturing grew in areas which formerly had been farmed either on a share-cropping basis (*mezzadria*) or in small peasant-owned plots and had concurrently developed handicraft traditions and entrepreneurial skills. The extended family played a key role in fostering the accumulation of capital and the regulation of the labour supply. The outcome was a diffuse socialization of small industries over large areas (Bull and Corner 1993).

Attempts to quantify the significance of these new forms of production have proved difficult. A useful approach has been to divide the national economy of 1981 into 955 functional areas of economic activity (Sforzi 1990). Within these, 161 areas of light industrialization were identified, more than half of which could be further categorized as 'industrial districts', in as much as they were more specialized and were dominated by one leading sector. Moreover, alongside these areas constituting the 'Third Italy' proper, there were other systems of non-urban manufacturing activity, situated in the Alpine regions, which shared many of the same features. It must be added, however, that these areas, despite having greatly increased their share of manufacturing activity during the 1970s, still accounted for little more than a quarter of manufacturing employment in 1981, compared to 60 per cent found in urban locations, dominated by large and medium-sized firms. Since then there seems to have been further expansion, but not enough to really change the balance (Rey 1989; OECD *Economic Survey of Italy* 1991, pp. 61–5).

The strength of the districts was particularly evident in a number of light industries such as textiles, clothing, footwear, tanning, wooden furniture, ceramics and toys. A few developed specialization in engineering and metal goods, but these were more successful in the northern Alpine systems.[9] Districts are also characterized by high birth and mortality rates of companies. Positive externalities take the form of common services, ranging from marketing to quality control and training arrangements, and useful channels for conflict resolution were set up by trade associations and trade unions, as well as by local authorities. Finally, further support derives from local banks possessing extensive knowledge of the firms' activities (Goodman and Bamford 1989; Zeitlin 1990).

The emergence and growth of the 'Third Italy' is evidence of the resilience and adaptability of Italian business, which seems capable of flourishing despite a climate of economic instability, corruption and incompetence engendered by a succession of political elites.

NOTES

1. In 1987 ISTAT re-estimated Italian GDP upwards by 18 per cent to take account of the existence of the black economy. This resulted in a revision of the historical statistics from 1970 onwards. Indexes by Maddison (1991) and Rossi et al. (1993) have reconstructed the series before 1970. We have used the latter to chart the performance of the economy up to 1973 while relying on OECD and ISTAT figures thereafter.
2. Value added per person in agriculture grew at 5.3 per cent annually between 1951 and 1963 (Rossi and Toniolo 1996, Table 14.3). Rey (1982) using ISTAT and OECD sources, estimates rates of growth of 6.2, 7.3, 7.5, and 4.8 for the periods 1951–8, 1958–63, 1963–9 and 1969–73 respectively.
3. The figure is based on the old series – see Allen and Stevenson (1974). It would be lower based on the Rossi et al. (1993) revisions.
4. Less than Germany (10.4 per cent), France (5.7 per cent) and the UK (4.8 per cent), but only Italy did not experience a substantial decrease (OECD 1996b, Table 46).
5. Services tend to be characterized by slow productivity growth. Rossi and Toniolo (1996) estimate the annual change of productivity in services at +0.6 per cent for 1974–89. For public administration it was negative at –0.1 per cent, squaring with qualitative evidence cited in OECD (*Economic Survey of Italy* 1991).
6. In 1963 official unemployment was revised downward by about 3 percentage points based on new definitions of the labour force and job seeking (OECD 1996a, Table 4).
7. Rey (1982, p. 521) on the older series – see note 1 above.
8. Some kind of dialogue was inescapable. The employers in March 1975 had chosen to avert confrontation by granting the unions the *scala mobile* agreement entailing wage indexation. However, reciprocal trust was limited as the fiscal drag effect showed: only in the 1980s did the unions fully equip themselves to neutralize its effects. Agreed plans for industrial restructuring were aborted and a kind of informal industrial policy implemented in the state-owned sector, acting as a lever for fiscal expansion as well as an emergency lifeboat for ailing private companies (Giavazzi and Spaventa 1989).

9. The importance of small firms was not decisive – for example, in metal goods and engineering, firms employing 20 to 100 workers produced about 25 per cent of sales in 1985. Across the whole of industry the share was about 30 per cent with 70 per cent being accounted for by firms with 100+ employees (Rey 1989, Table A4.6).

REFERENCES

Allen, K. and Stevenson, A. (1974) *An Introduction to the Italian Economy*, London: Martin Robertson.

Amatori, F. (1987) 'Iri: From Industrial Saviour to Industrial Group', *Annali di Storia dell'Impresa*, Vol. 3, pp. 203–19.

Antonelli, C. (1995) 'Il cambiamento tecnologico: innovazione e modernizzazione (1945–90)', *Storia dell'Italia Repubblicana -volume secondo – Le trasformazioni dell'Italia: sviluppo e squilibri, 1 – Politica, economia, societa'*, Torino: Einaudi.

Britton, A., Eastwood, F. and Major, R. (1986) 'Macroeconomic policy in Britain and Italy', *National Institute Economic Review*, No. 118, pp. 38–52.

Bruno, G. (1995) 'Le imprese industriali nel processo di sviluppo (1953-75)', *Storia dell'Italia Repubblicana – volume secondo -Le trasformazioni dell'Italia: sviluppo e squilibri, 1 – Politica, economia, societa'*, Torino: Einaudi.

Bull, A. C. and Corner, P. (1993) *From Peasants to Entrepreneurs: the Survival of the Family Economy in Italy*, Oxford: Berg.

Cao-Pinna, V. (1975) *Le esportazioni italiane – Prospettive al 1970*, Torino: Boringhieri.

Castronovo, V. (1995) *Storia Economica d'Italia – Dall'Ottocento ai giorni nostri*, Torino: Einaudi.

Ciocca, P., Filosa, R. and Rey, G. M. (1975) 'Integration and development of the Italian economy 1951–1971: a re-examination', *Banca Nazionale del Lavoro Quarterly Review*, Vol. 114, pp. 284–320.

Covino, R., Gallo, G. and Mantovani, E. (1976) 'L'industria dall'economia di guerra alla ricostruzione', in *L'economia italiana nel periodo fascista*, a cura di P. Ciocca e G. Toniolo, Bologna: Il Mulino.

D'Adda, C. and Salituro, B. (1989) 'L'economia italiana negli anni Settanta e Ottanta', *Rivista di Politica Economica*, Vol. LXXIX, IV, pp. 317–44.

Daneo, C. (1975) *La politica economica della Ricostruzione 1945–1949*, Torino: Einaudi.

De Cecco, M. (1972) 'Economic Policy in the Reconstruction Period, 1945-1951', in S. J. Woolf (ed.), *The Rebirth of Italy, 1943–1950*, London: Longman.

De Cecco, M. (1989a) 'Keynes and Italian Economics', in P. A. Hall (ed.), *The Political Power of Economic Ideas: Keynesianism across Nations*, Princeton: Princeton University Press.

De Cecco, M. (1989b) 'The European Monetary System and National Interests', in P. Guerrieri and P. C. Padoan (eds), *The Political Economy of European Integration: States, Markets, Institutions*, New York: Harvester Wheatsheaf.

De Vita, P. (1992) 'L'industria nel Mezzogiorno: Mutamenti strutturali nel decennio 1980–1990', *Rassegna Economica*, lvi, 1, pp. 173–99.

Economic Commission for Europe (1990) 'Europe's trade in engineering goods: specialization and technology', in *Economic Survey of Europe in 1989–90*, Geneva: United Nations.

Economic Commission for Europe (1988) 'Aspects of intra-west European trade in manufactures 1962–1985', in *Economic Survey of Europe in 1987–88*, Geneva: United Nations.

Farina, F. (1992) 'Monetary Policy' in F. Francioni (ed.), *Italy and EC Membership Evaluated*, London: Pinter.

Giavazzi, F. and Spaventa, L. (1989) 'Italy: the real effects of inflation and disinflation', *Economic Policy*, No. 8, pp. 135–71.
Ginsborg, P. (ed.), (1994) *Stato dell'Italia*, Milano: Mondadori.
Goodman, E. and Bamford, J. (eds) (1989) *Small Firms and Industrial Districts in Italy*, London: Routledge.
Holbik, K. (1959) *Italy in International Cooperation – The Achievement of her Liberal Economic Policies*, Padova: Cedam.
IMF *International Financial Statistics Yearbook*, various years.
ISTAT (1986) *Sommario di Statistiche Storiche Italiane 1926–1985*, Roma.
Kaplan, J. J. and Schleiminger, G. (1992) *The European Payments Union – Financial Diplomacy in the 1950s*, Oxford: Oxford University Press.
Maddison, A. (1991) 'A Revised Estimate of Italian Economic Growth 1861–1994', *Banca Nazionale del Lavoro Quarterly Review*, No. 177, pp. 225–41.
Maddison, A. (1995) *Monitoring the World Economy* 1820–1922, Paris: OECD.
Maddison, A. (1996) 'Macroeconomic accounts for European countries', in B. van Ark and N. F. R. Crafts (eds), *Quantitative Aspects of Post-War European Growth*, Cambridge: Cambridge University Press, pp. 27–84.
Maizels, A. (1959) 'Trade in World Trade in Durable Consumer Goods', *National Institute Economic Review*, No. 6, pp. 15–36.
Micossi, S. and Trau, F. (1994) 'The Role of Monetary and Financial Policies in the Restructuring of Industry', in M. Baldassarri (ed.), *The Italian Economy. Heaven or Hell?*, Basingstoke: Macmillan.
Milward, A. S. (1992) *The European Rescue of the Nation State*, London: Routledge.
Mortara, A. (1984) a cura di, *I protagonisti dell'intervento pubblico in Italia*, Milano: Angeli.
Nardozzi, G. (ed.) (1993) *Il ruolo della banca centrale nella recente evoluzione dell'economia italiana*, Milano: Angeli.
Nuti, F. (1992) *I distretti dell'industria manufatturiera in Italia*, Milano: Angeli.
OECD *Economic Survey of Italy*, various years, Paris: OECD.
OECD (1995) *Historical Statistics 1960–1993*, Paris: OECD.
OECD (1996a) *Historical Statistics 1960–1994*, Paris: OECD.
OECD (1996b) *OECD Economies at a Glance: Structural Indicators*, Paris: OECD.
Osti, G. L. (1993) *L'industria di Stato dall'ascesa al degrado – Trent'anni nel gruppo Finsider, conversazioni con R. Ranieri*, Bologna: Il Mulino.
Paci, P. (1992) 'Italy', in D. A. Dyker (ed.), *The National Economies of Europe*, London: Longman.
Podbielski, G. (1974) *Italy: Development and Crisis in the Postwar Economy*, Oxford: Clarendon Press.
Posner, M. V. and Woolf, S. J. (eds) (1967) *Italian Public Enterprise*, Cambridge: Cambridge University Press.
Ranci, P. (1993) 'La strategia della Banca d'Italia vista dal sistema delle imprese', in G. Nardozzi (ed.), *Il ruolo della banca centrale nella recente evoluzione dell'economia italiana*, Milano: Angeli.
Ranieri, R. (1988) 'The Italian Steel Industry and the Schuman Plan negotiations', in K. Schwabe (ed.), *Die Anfange des Schuman Planes 1950–1: The Beginnings of the Schuman Plan*, Baden: Nomos Verlag.
Ranieri, R. (1996) 'L'integrazione europea e gli ambienti economici italiani', in R. H. Rainero (ed.), *Storia dell'integrazione europea, volume 1, L'integrazione Europea dalle origini alla nascita della CEE*, Milano: Marzorati.
Rey, G. M. (1982) 'Italy', in A. Boltho (ed.), *The European Economy Growth and Crisis*, Oxford: Oxford University Press.
Rey, G. M. (1989) 'Small firms: profile and analysis 1981–5', in E. Goodman and J. Bamford (eds), *Small Firms and Industrial Districts in Italy*, London: Routledge.

Romero, F. (1991) *Emigrazione e integrazione europea*, Roma: Edizioni Lavoro.
Rossi, N., Sorgato, A. and Toniolo, G. (1993) 'I conti economici italiani: una ricostruzione statistica 1890–1990', *Rivista di Storia Economica*, Vol. 10, No. 1, pp. 1–47.
Rossi, N. and Toniolo, G. (1996), 'Italy', in N. Crafts and G. Toniolo (eds), *Economic Growth in Europe since 1945*, Cambridge: Cambridge University Press.
Saraceno, P. (1988) *L'Unificazione economica italiana e' ancora lontana*, Bologna: Il Mulino.
Sassoon, D. (1990) 'Italy', in A. Graham and A. Seldon (eds), *Government and Economies in the Postwar World*, London: Routledge.
Sforzi, F. (1990) 'The quantitative importance of Marshallian districts in the Italian economy', in F. Pyke, G. Becattini and W. Sengenberger (eds), *Industrial districts and inter-firm cooperation in the Italy*, Geneva: International Institute for Labour Studies.
Shonfield, A. (1965) *Modern Capitalism: The Changing Balance of Public and Private Power*, Oxford: Oxford University Press.
Spaventa, L. (1983) 'Two letters of intent: External Crises and Stabilization Policy, Italy 1973–77' in J. Williamson (ed.), *IMF Conditionality*, Washington: Institute for International Economics.
Templeman, D. C. (1981) *The Italian Economy*, New York: Praeger.
Trigilia, C. (1992) *Sviluppo senza autonomia. Effetti perversi delle politiche nel mezzogiorno*, Bologna: Il Mulino.
Venturini, A. (1993) 'Il Mercato del Lavoro negli anni Ottanta: sue trasformazioni e sviluppi', in G. Nardozzi (ed.), *Il ruolo della banca centrale nella recente evoluzione dell'economia italiana*, Milano: Angeli.
Wolf, M. (1996) 'To seize the moment', *Financial Times*, 24 September.
Zamagni, V. (1993) *The Economic History of Italy 1860–1990*, Oxford: Clarendon Press.
Zeitlin, J. (1990) 'Industrial districts and local economic regeneration: Models, institutions and policies'. Paper 10, *International Conference on Industrial districts and Local Economic Regeneration*, Geneva 18/19 October.

5 The Benelux Countries

Peter M. Solar and Herman J. de Jong

INTRODUCTION

The Benelux countries – Belgium, the Netherlands and Luxembourg – are surrounded by the great powers of northern Europe, and their population, taken together, has never amounted to more than half that of France, Britain or Germany. Over the centuries the central location and small size of the Benelux countries have created both dangers and opportunities. These countries have been traversed by the armies and buffeted by the economic policies of their large neighbours. But being at the crossroads of Europe, the Belgians, Dutch and Luxemburgers have often been able to profit by acting as commercial and financial intermediaries. These countries have been among the ranks of the most developed economies since the Middle Ages, and at the beginning of the twentieth century, along with Britain, were at the top of the European league table of income per capita.

For these small countries the post-war world has offered more opportunities than dangers. The reduction of trade barriers in Europe and in the world at large has opened markets for their products. Political stability in Europe has created a favourable environment for international capital movements, and the Benelux countries have benefited greatly, though in different ways, from the growth of direct and portfolio investment. This is especially true of Luxembourg which has one of the world's highest concentrations of foreign banks. All three countries have, not surprisingly, been strong proponents of European economic integration. The Benelux customs union, launched even before the Second World War had ended, served as a model for the European Union, of which Belgium, the Netherlands and Luxembourg were founder members.

Over the post-war period as a whole the Benelux economies have grown more or less in line with the economies of Germany and France, which has kept them among the richer European countries. But growth has not always been steady and it has involved major structural changes. Belgium was a notable laggard in the 1950s when it faced severe problems in adapting to the decline of its coal industry. From the mid-1970s to early 1980s both Belgium and the Netherlands had difficulties as growth slowed and unemployment rose. A legacy of this episode in Belgium has been its huge public debt, a hindrance to economic policy making ever since.

This chapter surveys economic growth and structural change in Belgium and the Netherlands since the war. (Luxembourg, much smaller than its two partners in Benelux, will receive only passing mention.) The emphasis will be on how the two countries performed relative to their large neighbours and on certain peculiarities of the Belgian and Dutch cases.

BENELUX GROWTH IN HISTORICAL AND COMPARATIVE PERSPECTIVE

The long-run contours of economic growth in Belgium and the Netherlands are shown in Table 5.1. The most striking difference between the two countries has been the Netherlands' rapid rate of population growth. The Dutch population has consistently grown faster than that elsewhere in northwestern Europe, while Belgium's population growth has been somewhat slower than the average. This has changed the relative size of the two countries: before the First World War Belgium was a quarter larger; today it has only two-thirds the population of the Netherlands.

Table 5.1 *Major growth indicators: Belgium, the Netherlands and Northwest Europe 1938–94 (annual compound growth rates %)*

	GDP			*Population*		
	Bel.	*Neth.*	*NW Eur.*	*Bel.*	*Neth.*	*NW Eur.*
1938–50	1.29	2.41	2.81	0.26	1.28	0.73
1950–94	3.05	3.46	3.29	0.34	0.96	0.59
1950–60	3.00	4.61	4.44	0.58	1.28	0.82
1960–73	4.93	4.83	4.52	0.48	1.22	0.79
1973–94	2.10	2.10	2.30	0.20	0.60	0.30
	GDP per capita			*GDP per hour*		
	Bel.	*Neth.*	*NW Eur.*	*Bel.*	*Neth.*	*NW Eur.*
1938–50	1.03	1.11	1.41	1.17	0.43	1.74
1950–94	2.70	2.47	2.61	3.65	3.37	3.43
1950–60	2.40	3.29	3.45	3.15	4.16	3.90
1960–73	4.43	3.57	3.63	5.48	4.39	4.89
1973–94	1.90	1.40	1.80	2.90	2.20	2.60

Note: 'NW Eur.' is an unweighted average of the growth rates in Austria, Belgium, Denmark, Finland, France, Germany, Netherlands, Norway, Sweden, Switzerland and the UK.

Sources: Maddison (1991, 1995).

Faster population growth in the Netherlands is echoed in faster rates of output growth, though the patterns of growth in the two countries have similar shapes. The similarities show up more clearly in the growth of output per capita. After relatively strong growth in the 1920s, both Belgium and the Netherlands were particularly hard hit by the world depression of the 1930s. In the 1950s per capita incomes grew more slowly than in the rest of northwestern Europe; in the 1960s more rapidly. The acceleration in Belgian growth from the 1950s to the 1960s was especially marked. Since the early 1970s, when growth has slowed down everywhere in Europe, output per capita in Belgium has grown somewhat faster than the northwest European average, while in the Netherlands per capita output growth has been relatively slow, especially during the early 1980s.

When allowance is made for changes in hours worked, most of the similarities between the two countries remain, but the 1950s and 1960s take on a different aspect. Until 1950 output per hour worked grew more slowly in Belgium and the Netherlands than in the rest of northwestern Europe. During the 1950s Belgium was a notable laggard while the Netherlands' performance was quite respectable. The increases in Dutch hourly productivity continued apace in the 1960s, but were far surpassed by the exceptionally high rates in Belgium. During the 1970s and early 1980s hourly productivity growth in the two countries, while a good deal lower than in the 1960s, was above the northwest European average. Since then it has been rather disappointing.

STRUCTURES AND STRUCTURAL CHANGE

Throughout the post-war period the Benelux economies have been characterized by certain structural features that formed the context for growth and for the economic policies that might influence it. These economies have long been very open to international trade. Over the post-war period the share of exports in available resources (GDP plus imports) remained at around a third in the Netherlands. In Belgium it rose from an already high one-quarter in the early 1950s to over two-fifths in the early 1990s. Openness to trade has meant that international competitiveness and external balance have been central concerns for business, unions and government. Trade is all the more important because both Belgian and Dutch production and exports have a high import content. These countries essentially import raw materials and export the value added that has gone into transforming them. For centuries the Netherlands was a major processor of colonial goods such as cocoa, sugar and tobacco. Today industries like paper, foodstuffs and oil refining rely heavily on imported materials. In Belgium textile and non-ferrous metal production were totally dependent on imported raw materials. But the best example is probably the automobile industry, in which Belgium has no native manufacturers, produces relatively few components, but has been one of Europe's major assemblers. Belgian and Dutch commercial policies have reinforced this sort of specialization by maintaining low or no duties on raw materials. High import content has been the other side of having few natural resources, the major exception being energy. In Belgium coal was a major resource during its early industrialization and continued to be mined into the 1980s, but its importance declined markedly from the early 1960s. In the Netherlands, by contrast, the development of the huge Groningen gas field from the 1960s stimulated the development of energy-intensive activities such as petrochemicals and metallurgy.

Both countries started the post-war period with small and relatively efficient agricultural sectors (see Table 5.2). In the late 1940s only 12 per cent of the labour force worked in Belgian agriculture. In the Netherlands the share was higher, at 16 per cent, but Dutch agriculture had long been quite specialized and geared to exports, and remains so today. By the 1970s these shares had each fallen, but post-war growth was not characterized, as it was in many other countries, by a massive shift from rural to urban employment.

Table 5.2 *Sectoral shares of employment: Belgium and the Netherlands 1937–87 (% of total employment)*

	1937		*1960*		*1987*	
	Bel.	*Neth.*	*Bel.*	*Neth.*	*Bel.*	*Neth.*
Agriculture	15.4	20.2	8.2	10.7	2.8	5.2
Extractive ind's	5.1	1.4	3.7	1.5	0.5	0.2
Manufacturing	33.0	24.2	32.8	30.0	20.5	17.7
Construction	4.4	5.9	6.7	9.7	6.0	7.0
Utilities	0.4	0.7	0.9	1.1	0.8	0.9
Trade and finance			13.9	16.2	23.3	29.7
Transport	41.7	47.5	6.1	6.9	6.4	6.5
Non-market services			27.8	23.9	39.7	32.8

Source: de Jong and Soete (1996).

Where the countries' economic structures did differ after the war was in the greater prominence of industry, especially heavy industry, in Belgium. Belgian production was concentrated in the traditional industries of the nineteenth century: coal mining, steelmaking, metalworking, and textiles. The decline of these industries during the post-war period would pose major problems of adaptation. The Dutch also had a substantial textile industry but the rest of their industry was quite diverse. During the 1950s and 1960s the industrial sectors of the two countries converged as the Dutch developed more heavy industry and as traditional industries in Belgium declined or were transformed. Since the mid to late 1970s the share of manufacturing employment in both countries, in common with many other OECD economies, has plummeted.

The Belgian and Dutch economies have been open not only to trade but to foreign investment as well. In the 1950s and 1960s they received a disproportionately large share of American direct investment in Europe. Foreign control of Belgian manufacturing has continued to increase, rising from 22 per cent of value added in 1968 to 59 per cent in 1990 (Daems and Van de

Weyer 1993). For many Belgians this degree of foreign control has been a matter of concern, perhaps because it has not been balanced by the growth of indigenous multinationals, as has been the case with the Dutch giants Shell, Unilever and Philips (Van Den Bulcke 1986; Gales and Sluyterman 1992). Financial capital has also been highly mobile, with both countries having long traditions of lending abroad. Luxembourg, which forms a monetary union with Belgium, has been a major haven for international and, more specifically, Belgian funds. Increased international capital mobility has become a major constraint on tax and exchange rate policies.

Certain peculiarities of social organization and politics have influenced growth and constrained policy in Belgium and the Netherlands (Lijphart 1981). Both countries have been characterized by long-standing and deep ideological divisions: in Belgium between Catholics and anticlericals and in the Netherlands between Protestants and Catholics, as well as between conservatives and socialists in both countries. In Belgium there has been the further complication of linguistic and territorial quarrels between Walloons (French speakers) and Flemish (Dutch speakers). The role of these different ideological groups goes beyond politics. From the late nineteenth century they each created distinct networks of institutions: trade unions, schools, youth movements; in Belgium even insurance companies. Belgian and Dutch societies have been described as being organized not so much horizontally, that is, by class, as vertically, by these 'pillars'.

The political results of this social organization have been fragmented yet very stable party systems and the prevalence of coalition governments able to act only on the basis of complex compromises (Frognier 1988). In Belgium there has also been a thorough politicization of public services – the police, judiciary, the administration – and persistent problems with the public finances. Pressures to satisfy all interest groups have inflated spending while making it difficult to raise more revenue, particularly in the frequent periods of political crisis (Vuchelen 1991). Another consequence of the excessively complicated Belgian political structure has been short-termism. During most of the post-war period it is difficult to discern any coherent Belgian growth policy. This has not been the case in the Netherlands, where there has been a remarkable consensus about economic policy (Abert 1969; Griffiths 1980). Parliamentary government in Belgium and the Netherlands coexists with other parallel decision making institutions. Representatives of trade unions, business and government come together frequently, not only in collective bargaining but in a dense network of institutions and advisory bodies developed in large measure since the Second World War. This corporatism has been a general feature of the small, open economies in Europe. In Belgium and Holland it has tended to be less centralized and less paternalistic than in Scandinavia (Katzenstein 1985). In Belgium, conflicts within the labour movement and weaknesses in the central employers' organization have hindered the functioning of the system. One result has been that the level of strike activity in Belgium has been distinctly higher than in the Netherlands.

These economic and political features provide the context for post-war growth and policy. Since the war the increasing internationalization of product and capital markets, along with the deterioration of public finances from the late 1970s, has steadily reduced the scope for classic macroeconomic policy. The great importance of foreign trade (and the system of wage indexation in Belgium) has inclined governments toward preserving stable exchange rates with their principal trading partners, notably Germany, with monetary policy generally dedicated to this goal. The use of fiscal policy has been limited by the public finances and in Belgium by the difficulties of securing agreement on tax and spending programmes. What has been left in the governments' arsenals are policies, either explicit or disguised, that have sought to influence the distribution of income between capital and labour.

THE LEGACY OF THE 1930s AND THE SECOND WORLD WAR

At the end of the Second World War Belgium and the Netherlands found themselves with productive capacities (machinery and equipment) largely unchanged since the late 1920s. During the 1930s output grew hardly at all, as both countries' adherence to gold delayed recovery from the depression (Keesing 1978; Cassiers 1989). Once they had left gold and devalued their currencies, in 1935 and 1936, there remained only a few years of limited prosperity before the threat of war put a damper on activity. In the 1930s net capital formation fell off markedly in Belgium, with investment probably at best only sufficient to maintain the overall capital stock (Van Meerten 1996). The Dutch invested more during the 1930s but it was concentrated in housing and infrastructure for their growing population. During five years of German occupation output in both countries was severely reduced by materials shortages. There was little new investment, though perhaps more in the Netherlands than in Belgium. The major difference between the two countries after the war was that Belgium's ageing capital stock and infrastructure had suffered relatively little war damage, while in the Netherlands losses were much greater (Groote et al. 1996).

Despite low levels of investment, labour productivity in the open sectors of the Belgian and Dutch economies appears to have grown rapidly during the 1930s. This was particularly evident from 1932, as firms started shedding labour previously kept on short time. Some inefficient firms closed, while others were merged into other concerns. But coherent programmes to rationalize capacity were rare and often failed due to the desire of family enterprises to remain independent (Hogg 1986). Most of the gains in productivity resulted from persistent pressures to reduce production costs in order to remain competitive on shrinking international markets.

These productivity gains were counterbalanced by relatively little change in the sheltered sectors. In both countries liberal economic policies gave way to protectionism and to many anti-competitive practices. Protection could do little for most manufacturing industries, dependent as they were on exports. But new legislation in Belgium and the Netherlands made it easier to cartelize the domestic market. In Belgium agriculture and the coal industry, both of which produced primarily for the home market but which had been open to international competition, managed to obtain quotas, import duties, and subsidies during the 1930s (Hogg 1986). Small shopkeepers, another powerful group, also secured protection against larger retailers. In the Netherlands farmers obtained price supports, and several manufacturing industries were protected by quantitative restrictions on imports (van Schaik 1986). Although these anti-competitive measures were intended to be temporary, many survived the Second World War.

Not all developments in the 1930s and during the war were so unpromising for post-war growth. In the Netherlands the search for new markets led to increased diversity in manufacturing; not only into 'new' industries such as electrical goods and synthetic fibres, but also into new branches of 'old' industries like textiles and mechanical engineering. Electrification also continued during the depression and the war. In Belgium there was continued improvement in the quality of the labour force. From a very low level, by northwestern European standards, the labour force's average educational attainment grew rapidly during the inter-war years and into the post-war period. Yet despite these changes, there were still persistent complaints during the 1930s about the Belgian labour force's lack of technical skills.

The depression and the war also saw movement toward corporatism as elsewhere in Europe. In both Belgium and the Netherlands, socialists were increasingly integrated into economic policy making from the late 1930s. Contacts between management and labour during the war furthered the entente, and employers reluctantly came to accept that organized labour would sit at the same table as business and government. The unions, for their part, came to acknowledge the legitimacy of management (Balthazar 1981; van Zanden and Griffiths 1989). A final legacy of the war for Belgium was a healthy foreign exchange position. The Belgian gold stock survived the war largely unchanged and sales of minerals from its African colony (the Congo, now Zaire) added to reserves. In the immediate aftermath of the war Belgium's foreign exchange position was further strengthened by dollars earned from billeting US forces and from traffic through Antwerp, the only major European port still largely intact. The Belgians thus had far more room for manoeuvre than did the Dutch and most other European countries, which had serious foreign exchange shortages.

RECONSTRUCTION IN THE LATE 1940s

Both Belgium and the Netherlands recovered relatively rapidly after the Second World War, but the ways in which they did so were markedly different. The

Belgian 'miracle' of 1945–8 was the result of much good luck and little planning. The Dutch faced much more difficult problems, but their highly centralized management of reconstruction, facilitated by a remarkable degree of social consensus and significant Marshall Aid, made for some of the fastest growth in Europe in the late 1940s.

In Belgium, output and consumption recovered with astonishing rapidity after the Second World War (Cassiers 1993). By 1948 Belgium's relative position seemed so enviable that it hardly appeared to need Marshall Aid at all, and indeed, neither asked for nor received very much. Yet this 'miracle' was short-lived. By 1950 most other countries in northwestern Europe had registered more growth in per capita output since before the war.

The 'miracle' owed much to strong external demand for Belgian goods in the first years after the war. As suggested above, the concentration of US troops on Belgian territory in 1945 gave rise to large dollar expenditures. Then, as reconstruction got under way elsewhere in Europe, Belgian specialities such as coal, metals, glass and cement were in great demand. Domestic demand was also strong, as the Belgian government quickly left the allocation of goods to the market, following what has been called alternatively the 'economics of abundance' or an 'exercise in supply side economics' (Baudhuin 1958; Kindleberger 1987). These policies favoured consumption. Belgians imported nylon stockings, Coca-Cola, and automobiles – even Cadillacs. The investment rate did increase after the war, to 15–16 per cent of national income, but it remained well below that in other European countries (Van Meerten 1996).

In the late 1940s there was surprisingly little public concern for modernizing industry (Camu 1961). The government's worries about its own finances kept public investment low. When, in 1950, the Belgians eventually requested direct Marshall Aid, they intended to use it for public investment and to assist agriculture, fishing and coal mining (Kurgan-van Hentenryk 1993). The aid they received went almost entirely down the mines, in a manner of speaking. The government's major concern after the war was maintaining social peace, a reason why it favoured consumption over investment (Kurgan-van Hentenryk 1993).

Labour and other input costs rose rapidly after the war. Up to 1948 unemployment was quite low and, with employers being particularly concerned to keep factories running, trade unions were well placed to push up money wages, despite government attempts to control increases (Dancet 1988). Extension of the social security system from 1945 also contributed to the rise in labour costs. Coal and electricity became more expensive than in neighbouring countries, which created problems for heavy industry (Dupriez 1951).

These increases in costs were not particularly damaging while the demand for Belgian goods was strong. But by the late 1940s industry elsewhere in Europe was recovering. In 1949 the difficulties faced by Belgian manufacturers were magnified when Britain and several other countries, including the Netherlands, devalued their currencies by 30.5 per cent against the dollar in 1949, while Belgium chose to devalue by only 12.3 per cent. Even this small devaluation – in effect, a relative revaluation – was opposed by the Socialist

Party, whose leader deemed it a 'measure against the common man' (Bismans 1992). Concern for maintaining a strong and stable franc would cast a shadow over much of the following decade.

In the Netherlands the impact of the war had been much more severe. Machinery and buildings were lost to war damage, lack of replacement investment, and plunder by the Germans (van Bochove and van Sorge 1989; Groote et al. 1996). During the winter of 1944/5 people starved in the western parts of the country. After the war, food and raw materials were critically short, as were the dollars needed to buy them on international markets. Income from abroad, traditionally a major component in the Dutch balance of payments, had been reduced by the running down of foreign investments during the war and by difficulties in the country's Indonesian colony.

Dutch economic policy during reconstruction was highly centralized and interventionist (Griffiths 1990). Prices and imports were controlled, and raw materials and finished products were rationed until 1949. The government also kept wages down, using special legislation passed in 1945 that gave it the legal right to intervene in wage negotiations. Wage restraint was intended both to keep down the costs of Dutch goods and to make more funds available to firms for investment. Rebuilding and modernization were also encouraged by low interest rates, though bank funding of investment projects had to be approved by the Ministry of Economic Affairs.

These policies, decided on and implemented with a remarkable degree of consensus, and the recovery of other European economies, especially that of Germany, were primarily responsible for the Netherlands' rapid recovery. Marshall Aid, of which the Dutch were major recipients, provided additional help. Some of these funds went to buy food and raw materials, but a large share was spent on industrial machinery (Tinbergen 1954; van der Eng 1986). More generally, the Marshall Plan involved sustained pressure to liberalize intra-European trade and provided funds to help relieve balance of payments problems, initiatives of the greatest importance to open economies such as the Netherlands and Belgium. When trade with Germany was made easier in 1949, there was a noticeable jump in Dutch exports.

The Benelux customs union was an early initiative to liberalize European trade. Although established in 1944, it could not become fully effective as long as the Dutch maintained strict import controls. Even then its practical significance should not be overstated. Agricultural products were excluded, much to the chagrin of the Dutch, and many quantitative restrictions hampered free trade. Like other early attempts at European integration, its major importance was symbolic (Gillingham 1995).

THE 1950s: BELGIUM LAGS BEHIND

Growth in Belgium and the Netherlands during the 1950s was faster than had ever been experienced before. The reduction of trade barriers and the rapid growth of world trade created great opportunities for small countries. The Dutch economy profited fully, but output and productivity growth in Belgium lagged behind neighbouring countries, even when allowance is made for its lack of war damage and its already high level of income (Crafts 1992). In the growing export markets Belgian manufacturers were losing market share, while Dutch manufacturers gained ground (Van Rijckeghem 1982). Unemployment in Belgium remained relatively high throughout the decade.

In Belgium, the 1950s can be seen as a prolonged and not entirely successful adaptation to large shocks caused by recovery elsewhere and by the relative revaluation of the franc in 1949. Much of the investment that took place has been described as 'defensive', that is, firms faced by a squeeze on profits – the result of high wage and energy costs and low export prices – reacted by limited investments designed to rationalize production (Lamfalussy 1961). Existing productive facilities were modified without being renewed or diversified. In some cases these defensive investments brought rapid productivity gains as old machines were replaced by up-to-date equipment. But by the early 1960s the potential for such vintage effects was being exhausted.

Belgian investment, though higher than before the war, was low by European standards. This was not for lack of savings: the household savings rate was high and rising, and a persistent trade surplus suggests that funds were flowing abroad (De Brabander 1981). Weaknesses in financial intermediation, caused in part by the requirement that commercial banks hold large amounts of government debt, may have left firms' investment constrained by the profits they could generate (Van Meerten 1996).

Growth was also held back by the lack of competitive pressure in the sheltered sectors of the economy. Most of the measures adopted during the depression to protect farmers and small retailers were retained after the war. The weaknesses in coal mining, particularly in the Walloon region in the south, were a constant preoccupation, a drain on resources, and a cause of high energy costs (Milward 1992).

During the 1950s the attention of Belgian governments was largely focused on non-economic issues. Economic policy, such as it was, put priority on the balance of payments, then price stability, then employment (Bismans 1992). There were some limited measures to encourage private investment and productivity growth, and public investment was low. The lack of government initiatives owed much to its chronic deficit, the Belgian public sector being the only net dissaver in Western Europe during the 1950s (Camu 1960).

Belgian governments did try to encourage good relations between employers and unions. Yet, despite the so-called Social Pact of 1944, industrial relations after the war were far from peaceful (Pasture 1993). Strike activity in Belgium was as high during the late 1940s and 1950s as it had been in the 1930s, though there were some signs of improvement.

The Dutch had much greater success on international markets in the 1950s, due in part to the devaluation of 1949 and in part to their low labour costs.

Although wage restraint remained central to Dutch government policy in the 1950s, wages, in fact, grew faster in the Netherlands than elsewhere in northwestern Europe (van Ark and De Jong 1996). That Dutch labour costs were still well below those in neighbouring countries in 1960 was due to the extraordinarily slow rate of growth in real wages during the 1930s and 1940s. There was wage restraint in the 1950s only in so far as Dutch workers did not catch up faster.

Low labour costs and booming export markets made for high profits. The tax structure encouraged firms to reinvest these profits, though entrepreneurs needed little encouragement during this period (Dercksen 1986). Over 22 per cent of national product was being invested in the Netherlands during the 1950s, as against only 17 per cent in Belgium.

This investment expanded and diversified Dutch industry. The modernization of industry was a central goal of government policy, the theme of eight memoranda published between 1949 and 1963. These memoranda laid out desired industrial investments by sector, but they were only indicative and, unlike the French case, had few government resources behind them. Industrial policy during the 1950s was

> a beautiful concept, a good propaganda machine, a number of measures that above all tried to improve the industrial climate, but the government did not really bother itself with industry. (van Zanden and Griffiths 1989, p. 246)

The government's major contribution to economic growth in the 1950s was probably its own high rate of investment in schools, infrastructure and utilities.

THE GOLDEN 1960s (AND EARLY 1970s)

Economic growth in both countries accelerated in the 1960s. The boom in world trade, of which growth in trade within the embryonic European Union played a part, provided ample opportunities for Belgian and Dutch industry. In the Netherlands the increase in the growth rate was small; in Belgium it was so large as to be one of the defining features of the country's post-war history. Yet, while the reasons for the speed-up in Belgian productivity growth deserve careful attention, behind the smaller Dutch acceleration was a major change in the nature of its growth.

The difference between the two countries' experience in the 1960s shows up most clearly in the ratio of capital to output. Both economies had long been relatively capital intensive, though Belgium, with its concentration in metalworking, had a significantly higher capital–output ratio in the 1950s – about 4 to 1, as against 3 to 1 in the Netherlands (similar ratios had prevailed in the 1920s). During the 1960s the positions were reversed, so that in 1973 the Belgian ratio was 3 to 1, while the Dutch ratio was 3.4 to 1. Both countries invested more in the 1960s, with the Dutch having to accumulate more and more capital to sustain rapid growth of output, while the Belgians were getting more and more output from the capital they invested.

The Dutch case is the more straightforward. Investment was increasingly channelled into capital-intensive industries, something that had probably already begun in the late 1950s. Major public investments in infrastructure, notably around the port of Rotterdam, facilitated private investments in oil refining, chemicals and distribution. The discovery and exploitation of the Groningen gas fields from 1963 itself absorbed an enormous amount of capital, and the initially low price of gas stimulated a variety of energy- and capital-intensive industrial activities, such as hot-house farming, metallurgy and chemicals.

Another reason for the increase in the Dutch capital–output ratio was the rapid rise in labour costs during the 1960s. Dutch wages grew faster than wages elsewhere in northwestern Europe during the 1960s. They also grew faster than labour productivity, squeezing profits in the open sector of the economy. Firms tried to substitute capital for increasingly expensive labour, and labour-intensive industries such as textiles fell on hard times (Den Hartog and Tjan 1976). Employment in the manufacturing sector had already begun to decline by 1965, so that almost all of the growth in the labour force during the 1960s went into the service sector.

The way in which Dutch labour costs rose had important sectoral effects. Although the government withdrew from the wage negotiation process during the 1960s, bargaining remained highly centralized. The tight labour market permitted the powerful union movement to negotiate large increases from employers in sectors with high productivity growth, notably metal manufacturing, then to apply them to sectors with lower productivity growth (Driehuis 1975). This led to inflationary pressures, which were reinforced by the introduction of wage indexation in the late 1960s. Indexation quickly translated foreign and domestic price rises into higher labour costs.

Despite cost pressures, the Dutch share in world exports increased during the 1960s. To maintain their competitiveness Dutch firms had to keep down export prices, which they tried to compensate for by charging higher prices on the domestic market. Foreign firms were able to penetrate the Dutch market quite easily, leading to a wave of mergers in manufacturing and services as Dutch firms sought not only to obtain economies of scale and attract new capital, but also to diversify production and find new markets. The process of concentration was supported by the government, which provided grants to declining industries, such as ship-building and coal mining, on the condition that the firms find new partners.

In Belgium the investment rate increased by more than in the Netherlands. Investment also moved toward capital-intensive activities, such as oil refining and chemicals, and was increasingly oriented to saving labour as wages rose. But much more significant in Belgium was the improvement in the efficiency with which capital and labour were used: here Belgium did much better in the 1960s than might have been expected (Dowrick and Nguyen 1989). Belgian performance on international markets also improved. Where in the 1950s it had lost market shares, during the 1960s these were maintained (NBB 1988). Growth in the early 1960s accelerated first in the open sector but remained more or less balanced until around 1967. The same is true of the growth in labour productivity. By contrast, in the late 1960s and early 1970s the growth of both output and labour productivity in the open sector was exceptionally high, so that the golden 1960s and early 1970s stand out as a prolonged open sector investment boom. Capital formation in the sheltered sector also increased, but much more gradually, and only reached its peak rate in the mid-1970s.

The initial impulses for the acceleration in Belgian growth around 1960 came both from home and abroad. During the first years of the 1960s almost all of the growth in Belgian exports went to its partners in the newly formed European Economic Community. This did not increase the already high rate of export growth, but it had profound effects on the nature of Belgian industry. Studies of the gains from integration show that the direct effects of tariff reductions were not large (Van Meershaeghe 1992). But the prospects of the large European market and the suppression of barriers gave a new dynamism to the Belgian economy. One indication is the noticeable improvement in Belgian performance against other EEC members in the important German market, where all of them faced similar tariff changes (Kervyn de Lettenhove 1968).

The changes in Belgian industrial structure during the 1960s were subtle, but profound. The distribution of output across major industries did not change markedly, leading some to argue that the rapid growth of demand during the 1960s boom retarded necessary shifts in specialization (Van der Wee 1985). But important changes did take place within sectors (Kervyn de Lettenhove 1968). Many traditional Belgian products lost market share, even within the EEC. Producers of both linen and cotton yarn, long-standing Belgian specialities, suffered (though spinners of wool benefited from the rise in carpet manufacture). At the same time new specialities, such as plastics, soap, plywood and automobiles, developed within traditional sectors (NBB 1969).

The development of new products was often associated with direct investment by foreign firms. Between 1960 and 1972 foreign direct investment accounted for one-third of gross investment and half of net investment in manufacturing, although the net inflow of capital was much less since foreign firms often raised funds in Belgium (Van Rijckeghem 1982). For a country with few indigenous multinationals, US and European firms were important conduits for new technologies and new forms of organization (Vanden Houte and Veugelers 1989). Both by direct competition with Belgian firms and by example, they probably improved the performance of domestic firms (Kervyn de Lettenhove 1968; Weber 1983). The multinationals' effects were strongest toward the latter part of the period when the stock of foreign direct investment had become large enough to make a difference to aggregate output growth. Foreign investment was disproportionately concentrated in Flanders and helped output and incomes in the hitherto impoverished north of the country to surpass those in the older industrial areas of Wallonia.

Both inward and domestic investment may have been stimulated by the Expansion Laws of 1959, which provided loan guarantees, interest subsidies, tax relief and other benefits to investors. Originally intended as temporary measures to help get the economy out of recession, they were repeatedly prolonged until the late 1970s. Much of the aid went to foreign firms, particularly those setting up in Flanders. Far from backing 'national champions', Belgium, if anything, bent over backward to attract firms from abroad. But the significance of the Expansion Laws has been questioned. The aid given was not large enough to have significantly increased the rate of investment (Gilot 1987). It was also given unselectively and tended to favour capital-intensive projects, often ones undertaken by existing firms in traditional industries (Van den Broeke 1984).

The turnabout in Belgian economic performance around 1960 also owes something to the renunciation of a variety of anti-competitive policies. Fiscal pressures and the impatience of Belgium's partners in the European Coal and Steel Community led to the decision, in November 1959, to let the coal mining industry in Wallonia run down (Milward 1992). Subsidies and restrictive agreements employed in the 1950s to limit the effects of Dutch competition within Benelux were wound up (Boekestijn 1990). Other restrictions were lifted in the service sector. After 1961, small shopkeepers lost much of their protection from the competition of supermarkets and large-scale retailers (van Waterschoot and Deleeck 1992). From 1962, commercial banks were no longer required to keep 65 per cent of their assets in government securities. These decisions were taken individually and for different reasons, but together they represented a move toward liberalization of the economy.

Industrial relations improved noticeably in the 1960s, with a marked falling-off in strike activity. Increased cooperation between employers and unions was consecrated in 'social programming', another innovation made around 1960 (Dancet 1988). This involved biannual consultations between employers' organizations and trade unions. A national agreement first established certain norms, often minimal, for changes in wages and other benefits. These norms then guided negotiations at the sectoral and firm level. The government was not a formal partner in these negotiations but was expected to legislate in accordance with their outcomes. Whether social programming fostered the acceleration of economic growth, or faster growth simply made it easier to reach agreements, remains an open question. It was certainly the case that the programmed social progress of the late 1960s involved significant extensions of the social security system that would be a major factor in the rising public sector deficits of the late 1970s and early 1980s. When conditions did become more difficult in the 1970s the system singularly failed to deliver agreements that were consistent with economic conditions.

THE LEADEN 1970s AND 1980s

In Belgium and the Netherlands, as almost everywhere else in Europe, economic growth slowed markedly from the mid-1970s and has remained slower ever since. As in other countries, the possibilities for making easy gains through catching up to the US had largely been exhausted. And the increasing preponderance of services, in which the rates of productivity growth tended to be low, slowed down the overall rate of growth. For small countries heavily dependent on exports, the deceleration in growth of world income and trade was a major drag on output and employment (Mehta and Sneessens 1990). Even the recovery of world demand in the late 1980s was only a faint echo of the golden 1960s. The world had changed and, not surprisingly, businessmen, trade union leaders and policy makers took many years to realize that this was so. During the 1970s, expectations of a return to faster growth in sales and wages, and policies directed toward restoring such growth, led to rising unemployment, persistent inflationary pressures and a marked deterioration in the public finances. By around 1980 it had become clear that major changes were needed to adapt to slower growth, changes that were hurried on by the second oil shock in 1979 and by the sharp contraction of the world economy in the early 1980s. The ways in which Belgium and the Netherlands got into difficulty, then tried to get out of it, during the 1980s have left them in different states today, with the Dutch economy distinctly the healthier of the two.

THE 1970s: GROWTH ON CREDIT

The slowdown in the growth after 1973 led to major sectoral imbalances in both Belgium and the Netherlands. As one would expect, the sectors open to trade took the brunt of the shock (Kremers 1986). Exporters, whose profits had already been falling since the late 1960s, saw them squeezed mercilessly from several directions. As heavy users of oil and gas, Belgian and Dutch manufacturers were especially hard hit by the 1973 oil shock. Nominal wages continued to rise rapidly in both countries, first on the basis of previous collective agreements, then as unions sought to compensate for accelerating inflation. In Belgium the long-standing practice of adjusting wages to changes in the consumer price index created further cost pressures. In the Netherlands efforts at wage moderation were partly offset by increases in the legal minimum wage. Rising wages also increased the prices that exporters had to pay for inputs from the sheltered sector. Suppliers of business services, notably banks and utilities – electricity, water and telephone companies – were often able to pass on higher labour costs in the form of higher prices. Exporters were generally unable to do so, faced as they were with the slowdown in the growth of world trade. Open sector difficulties caused both countries' trade balances to move into deficit during the 1970s. In Belgium the deterioration in the current account was continuous; in the Netherlands it took place mainly after 1976. The Dutch payments position was stronger thanks to its exports of natural gas, which cushioned the effects of the oil shock.

The upward pressures on wages were more severe and more prolonged in Belgium than in the Netherlands. Some workers with jobs, especially those in the sheltered sector, made handsome gains during the 1970s. By 1980 average earnings in some service sector occupations were far higher in Belgium than in neighbouring countries. In manufacturing Belgian earnings also tended to be higher but the differences were much smaller (Petit 1986). This wage explosion took place despite increased government intervention in the labour market after the breakdown, in 1975, of the system of national collective agreements between employers and trade unions. In the Netherlands, too, wages rose rapidly in the early 1970s, but their subsequent growth seems to have been moderated more by rising unemployment than was the case in Belgium.

Pressures on firms' labour costs were even greater than the rise in nominal wages indicates. A large gap opened up between what it cost firms to hire labour and what the workers actually received, the result of increasing social security charges and higher income taxes. The late 1960s and 1970s saw major extensions of social security benefits and coverage. When unemployment began to rise during the 1970s, the increased costs of the system were met in part by higher charges and in part by higher taxes. Rising direct and indirect labour costs made firms increasingly reluctant to take on workers. Employment security legislation making it difficult to discharge workers reinforced this reluctance in the uncertain conditions of the 1970s.

While labour costs rose, real interest rates remained low. Although nominal interest rates increased, concern for unemployment during the early to mid-1970s kept monetary policy expansionary. Although from 1976 the Belgian central bank had to become more restrictive in order to maintain the value of the franc relative to the guilder and the mark, the Dutch central bank was able to continue an expansionary policy, thanks to the strength of the guilder. Low, even negative, real interest rates led households and firms, as well as governments, to take on more debt during the 1970s. Indeed, it has been argued that the relative prosperity of the years from 1973 to 1979 was bought on credit (van Zanden and Griffiths 1989, p. 260).

Despite low real interest rates, the growth of investment in both Belgium and the Netherlands fell off sharply from the giddy days of the 1960s. Investment in housing was maintained to some extent by low real interest rates and by households' efforts to protect their savings against inflation. But business investment, especially in the open sectors, was limited. Due to uncertainties about the growth of world demand and to rising labour costs, such investment as took place was oriented more to saving labour than to increasing capacity.

Slower growth of investment in the 1970s, together with its labour-saving bias, made it difficult to employ the growing numbers in the working-age groups.

In both countries, but especially in the Netherlands where population growth remained high by European standards, the large cohorts of young people born after the war were entering the labour force. More women, particularly married women, were looking for work during the 1970s, though it is a matter of interpretation whether this was an effect of the slower growth in incomes or a development that had deeper social and cultural causes. In any case, more job seekers were competing for a slowly growing number of jobs, with the result that unemployment started edging upward.

Rising unemployment was a major factor behind the deterioration of the public finances that took place in both Belgium and the Netherlands during the 1970s. Deficits rose as the governments took in less tax revenue and paid out more in unemployment benefit. The deficits were swelled further by the costs of trying to keep unemployment from becoming even worse. Public sector employment was maintained and even increased, and state-owned industries were encouraged to take on workers. Governments also became increasingly involved in keeping private firms in business (Buyst 1993; Leonard and Van Audenrode 1993). The Belgian government was particularly lavish in dispensing subsidies to save jobs: between 1975 and 1984, state aid to enterprises grew by around 10 per cent per annum. The Dutch government was also increasingly drawn into industrial subsidies but was somewhat more restrained in their use.

The Dutch and Belgian governments experimented with a wide range of policies during the 1970s but their room for manoeuvre was running out by the end of the decade. Despite their efforts, unemployment continued to rise and so strain their finances. Rising levels of public indebtedness were disquieting but still manageable as long as real interest rates remained low but this could not last. Increasing concern about inflation and mounting trade deficits, exacerbated by the second oil shock in 1979, made it necessary to tighten monetary policy (Wellink 1989). When monetary stringency in the US pushed up interest rates even further and led to a depression in world trade, the situation became untenable. In both Belgium and the Netherlands, rising interest rates created a 'snowball effect' whereby, unless drastic measures were taken, the national debt would keep rising simply because the government would have to borrow in order to pay the interest on it.

THE 1980s AND 1990s: ADJUSTING TO SLOWER GROWTH

After some hesitant measures, both the Belgian and Dutch governments acted forcefully in 1982 to bring their own finances under control and to reduce labour costs so as to restore business profits and investment. Real wages had already been pushed down by the recession. In Belgium they were depressed further when, in 1982, the franc was devalued by 8.5 per cent, the system of wage indexation was temporarily suspended, and the government intervened to prevent increases in public and private sector pay. In the same year the new

Dutch government acted vigorously to cut public spending and begin cutbacks in the social security system. By contrast with Belgium, the Dutch government withdrew from direct intervention in the labour market (except for cutting the salaries of its own civil servants), though it did continue to advocate wage moderation (Hartog and Theeuwes 1993).

The hallmark of Dutch development since the early 1980s has been very slow growth in real wages. This arose from a remarkable consensus between employers' organizations and trade unions, a consensus which also made possible the gradual paring down of the social welfare system. The unions did not go away empty-handed, concentrating instead on securing shorter working hours. But, even though hours worked per person have dropped even further below the levels in other European countries, the slow growth of hourly labour costs restored and maintained Dutch competitiveness. This moderate wage growth has paid off in job creation and falling unemployment.

In Belgium, by contrast, there has been no such consensus on economic policy and income distribution. While it was clear that something had to be done in the early 1980s, unions strongly resisted changes in the system of wage indexation and cutbacks in the social security system. Public spending also proved very difficult to reduce. Once economic conditions improved somewhat in the mid to late 1980s, fiscal discipline was relaxed and wages were pushed up, leading only to further crises in the 1990s. Although the policies of the early 1980s helped restore Belgian competitiveness, this has repeatedly been eroded, bringing the government back into regulation of the labour market. The rate of growth of the public debt has slowed, but its level has remained stubbornly high at 120–140 per cent of GDP. Unemployment has also remained high.

In both countries the policies adopted in the early 1980s sought to stimulate investment and growth by restoring business profits. (Government investment was very low during these years and has remained so ever since.) Profits did rise but initially were often used to reduce corporate debt rather than to modernize or expand capacity. Only from the late 1980s, with the renewed expansion of the world economy, did investment spending recover, albeit at rates well below those of the golden 1960s. Productivity growth rates in the two countries not only failed to recover; they continued to fall in the late 1980s and 1990s.

CONCLUSION: RETROSPECT AND PROSPECT

Despite differences in policy and economic environment, there was surprisingly little difference between Belgium and the Netherlands in overall growth performance during the period after 1973. If anything, Belgium seems to have crept ahead of the Netherlands in per capita income, though this owes something to the large reductions in working hours and to the prevalence of part-time employment in the Netherlands.

However, the overall similarity in growth rates conceals important underlying differences. One, which has been mentioned already, is the contrast between 'jobless growth' in Belgium and the greater creation of employment in the Netherlands. Measured unemployment has fallen to 7 per cent in the Netherlands but remains near 10 per cent in Belgium. 'True' unemployment in Belgium, taking account of discouraged workers, early retirements and a variety of schemes to keep people out of the statistics, may be more than 20 per cent.

A second important difference shows up in sectoral productivity performance. Productivity growth in manufacturing generally outpaces that in the rest of the economy, but in Belgium the gap has been exceptionally large since the early 1970s (Englander and Mittelstädt 1988). Very rapid productivity growth in Belgian manufacturing probably owes much to the fact that since the 1960s it has become largely foreign-owned, which has allowed it to benefit from techniques and methods developed elsewhere. Foreign ownership has also enforced greater discipline on costs, with plants that failed to remain competitive on world markets being quickly closed. Very slow growth in productivity outside manufacturing may be traced in part to inertia in the public sector and in state-owned industries, where entrenched interests have been able to resist rationalization. Privatizations were undertaken only in the 1990s, largely as the result of the government's financial difficulties. Such contrasts in sectoral productivity growth have been less marked in the Netherlands, where deregulation and privatization were undertaken much earlier.

Although Belgium has grown at more or less the same rate as the Netherlands since the 1970s, it may find it more difficult to keep doing so. Its growth has in part been bought by running down assets and building up liabilities. Public investment in infrastructure and education has been one of the major casualties of the government's financial problems. The widespread use of early retirement to deal with industrial decline will have to be paid for in the years to come. With its already high public debt, Belgium will have little room for manoeuvre in dealing with its problems, and persistent social and regional conflicts will make it difficult to arrive at effective solutions.

The prospects for the Netherlands may be brighter, thanks to the decisive steps taken during the 1980s, but some weaknesses remain. As in Belgium, public investment in infrastructure and education has been low since the financial crisis of the 1980s. The policy of wage moderation has helped reduce unemployment but may be in part responsible for the particularly low rates of growth in productivity and average income. The reductions in working hours and the boom in part-time employment may reduce the incentives for human capital formation by individuals and firms. And given the expected increases in labour supply, more public and private investment will be needed to keep employment growing.

REFERENCES

This chapter draws on Cassiers, De Villé and Solar (1996) on Belgium, and van Ark, de Haan and de Jong (1996) on the Netherlands, for which we would like to express our gratitude to our co-authors. These papers contain extensive and up-to-date bibliographies, as do the books by Mommen (1994) on Belgium, and van Zanden and Griffiths (1989) on the Netherlands. We have indicated some useful readings in English with asterisks but it should be noted that much of the important work on post-war growth in these countries has been written in Dutch or French.

Abert, J. G. (1969) *Economic Policy and Planning in the Netherlands, 1950–1965*, New Haven, CT.

Balthazar, H. (1981) 'Bien-être social et politique de concertation, un souhait non accompli', in *L'industrie en Belgique. Deux siècles d'évolution 1780–1980*, Brussels, pp. 243–60.

Baudhuin, F. (1958) *Histoire économique de la Belgique 1945–1956*, Brussels.

Bismans, F. (1992) *Croissance et régulation. La Belgique 1944–1974*, Brussels.

Boekestijn, A. J. (1990), 'The Formulation of Dutch Benelux Policy', in R.T. Griffiths (ed.), *The Netherlands and the Integration of Europe 1945–1957*, Amsterdam, pp. 27–48.

* Buyst, E. (1993) 'The Decline and Rise of a Small Open Economy: The Case of Belgium (1974–1990)', in Erik Aerts et al. (eds), *Studia Historica Economica: Liber Alumnorum Herman Van der Wee*, Leuven, pp. 71–80.

Camu, A. (1960) 'Essai sur l'évolution économique de la Belgique', *La Revue Nouvelle*, Vol. 32, No. 11, pp. 397–418.

Camu, A. (1961) 'Essai sur l'évolution économique de la Belgique II', *La Revue Nouvelle*, Vol. 33, No. 5. pp. 481–500.

Cassiers, I. (1989) *Croissance, crise et régulation en économie ouverte: la Belgique entre les deux guerres*, Brussels.

Cassiers, I. (1993) 'Du "miracle belge" à la croissance lente: l'impact du Plan Marshall et de l'Union Européenne des Paiements', *Bulletin de l'IRES*, Juin.

* Cassiers, I., De Villé, P. and Solar, P. M. (1996) 'Economic Growth in Postwar Belgium', in N. Crafts and G. Toniolo (eds), *Economic Growth in Europe since 1945*, Cambridge: Cambridge University Press, pp. 173–209.

Crafts, N. F. R. (1992) 'Productivity Growth Reconsidered', *Economic Policy*, Vol. 15, pp. 387–426.

* Crafts, N. F. R. and Toniolo, G. (eds) (1996) *Economic Growth in Europe since 1945*, Cambridge: Cambridge University Press.

Daems, H. and Van de Weyer, P. (1993) *L'économie belge sous l'influence*, Brussels.

Dancet, G. (1988) 'From a Workable Social Compromise to Conflict: The Case of Belgium,' in R. Boyer (ed.), *The Search for Labour Market Flexibility*, Oxford: Oxford University Press, pp. 96–118.

De Brabander, G. (1981) 'La création d'un état d'abondance', in *L'industrie en Belgique. Deux siècles d'évolution 1780–1980*, Brussels, pp. 207–42.

de Jong, H. J. and Soete, A. (1996) 'A Comparison of Belgian and Dutch manufacturing Productivity 1937–87', in E. Buyst et al. (eds), *Historical Benchmark Comparisons of Output and Productivity, 1750–1990*, Leuven, pp. 99–129.

den Hartog, H. and Tjan, H. S. (1976) 'Investment, Wages, Prices and Demand for Labour', *De Economist*, Vol. 124, Nos 1–2, pp. 32–55.

Dercksen, W. J. (1986) *Industrialisatiepolitiek rondom de jaren vijftig*, Assen.

Dowrick, S. and Nguyen, D. T. (1989) 'OECD Comparative Economic Growth 1950–85: Catch-Up and Convergence', *American Economic Review*, Vol. 79, pp. 1010–30.

Driehuis, W. (1975) 'Inflation, Wage Bargaining, Wage Policy and Production Structure: Theory and Empirical Results for the Netherlands', *De Economist*, Vol. 123, No. 4, pp. 638–79.

Dupriez, L. H. (1951) 'Pourquoi de hauts niveaux de remunération en Belgique', *Comptes-rendus des travaux de la Société Royale d'Economie Politique de Belgique*, February, pp. 5–23.

Englander, A. S. and Mittelstädt, A. (1988) 'Total Factor Productivity: Macroeconomic and Structural Aspects of the Slowdown', *OECD Economic Studies*, No. 10, pp. 7–56.

Frognier, A.-P. (1988) 'The Mixed Nature of Belgian Cabinets Between Majority Rule and Consociationalism', *European Journal of Political Research*, Vol. 16, pp. 207–28.

Gales, B. P. A. and Sluyterman, K. E. (1992) 'Outward Bound. The Rise of Dutch multinationals', in G. Jones and H. G. Schröter (eds), *The Rise of Multinationals in Continental Europe*, Aldershot.

Gillingham, J. (1995) 'The European Coal and Steel Community: an Object Lesson?', in B. Eichengreen (ed.), *Europe's Postwar Recovery*, Cambridge: Cambridge University Press.

Gilot, A. (1987) 'Les aides publiques aux entreprises privées. Essai d'évaluation', *Bureau de Plan, Planning Paper*, DS 713.

Griffiths, R. T. (1980) 'The Netherlands Central Planning Bureau', in *The Economy and Politics of the Netherlands since 1945*, The Hague.

Griffiths, R. T. (1990) 'Macroeconomic Planning in the Netherlands 1945–1958', in E. Aerts and A. S. Milward (eds), *Economic Planning in the Postwar Period*, Leuven.

Groote, P., Albers, R. and de Jong, H. J. (1996) 'A Standardised Time Series of the Stock of Fixed Capital in the Netherlands 1900–1995', *Research Memorandum*, GD-25 Groningen.

Hartog, J. and Theeuwes, J. (1993) 'Post-war Unemployment in the Netherlands', *European Journal of Political Economy*, Vol. 9, pp. 73–112.

Hogg, R. L. (1986) *Structural Rigidities and Policy Inertia in inter-War Belgium*, Brussels.

Katzenstein, P. J. (1985) *Small States in World Markets: Industrial Policy in Europe*, Ithaca.

Keesing, F. A. G. (1978) *De conjuncturele ontwikkeling van Nederland en de evolutie van de economische overheidspolitiek 1918–1939*, 2nd edn, Nijmegen.

Kervyn de Lettenhove, A. (1968) 'Quelques problèmes actuels de la structure économique de la Belgique', *Reflets et perspectives de la vie économique*, Vol. 7, pp. 17–30.

Kindleberger, C. P. (1987) 'Belgium after World War II: An Experiment in Supply Side Economics', in A. Steinherr and D. Weiserbs (eds), *Employment and Growth: Issues for the 1980s*, Dordrecht, pp. 167–84. Reprinted in C. P. Kindleberger (1987) *Marshall Plan Days*, Boston, pp. 230–44.

Kremers, J. J. M. (1986) 'The Dutch Disease in the Netherlands', in J. P. Neary and S. van Wijnbergen (eds), *Natural Resources and the Macroeconomy*, Oxford: Oxford University Press.

Kurgan-van Hentenryk, G. (1993) 'La Belgique et le plan Marshall ou les paradoxes des relations belgo-américaines', *Revue belge de philologie et d'histoire*, Vol. 71, pp. 290–453.

* Lamfalussy, A. (1961) *Investment and Growth in Mature Economies*, London.

Leonard, J. and Van Audenrode, M. (1993) 'Corporatism Run Amok: Job Stability and Industrial Policy in Belgium and the United States', *Economic Policy*, Vol. 17, pp. 355–400.

Lijphart, A. (1981) 'Introduction: The Belgian Example of Cultural Coexistence in Comparative Perspective', in A. Lijphart (ed.), *Conflict and Coexistence in Belgium: The Dynamics of a Culturally Divided Society*, Berkeley, CA, pp. 1–12.

Maddison, A. (1991) *Dynamic Forces in Capitalist Development*, Oxford: Oxford University Press.

Maddison, A. (1995) *Monitoring the World Economy, 1820–1992*, Paris: OECD.

Mehta, F. and Sneessens, H. R. (1990) 'Belgian Unemployment: The Story of a Small Open Economy Caught in a Worldwide Recession', in J. Drèze et al. (eds), *Europe's Unemployment Problem,* Cambridge, MA, pp. 120–55.
* Milward, A. S. (1992) *The European Rescue of the Nation-State,* London.
* Mommen, A. (1994) *The Belgian Economy in the Twentieth Century,* London.
NBB (National Bank of Belgium) (1969) 'De buitenlandse handel van de Belgisch–Luxemburgse Economische Unie van 1958 to 1968', *Tijdschrift voor Documentatie en Voorlichting,* Vol. 44, pt II, No. 6, pp. 655–91.
NBB (1988) 'L'évolution structurelle de l'économie belge', (extrait du *Bulletin de la Banque Nationale de Belgique,* Juillet–Août 1987, Novembre 1987 et Novembre 1988).
* Pasture, P. T. (1993) 'The April 1944 "Social Pact" in Belgium and its Significance for the Post-War Welfare State', *Journal of Contemporary History,* Vol. 28, pp. 695–714.
Petit, P. (1986) *Slow Growth and the Service Economy,* London.
Tinbergen, J. (1954) 'The Significance of the Marshall Plan for the Netherlands Economy', in *Road to Recovery: The Marshall Plan, its Importance for the Netherlands and European Cooperation,* Ministry of Finance, The Hague.
* van Ark, B., de Haan, J. and de Jong, H. J. (1996) 'Characteristics of Economic growth in the Netherlands during the Postwar Period', in N. F. R. Crafts and G. Toniolo (eds), *Economic Growth in Europe since 1945,* Cambridge: Cambridge University Press, pp. 290–328.
van Ark, B. and de Jong, H. J. (1996) 'Accounting for Economic Growth in the Netherlands since 1913', *Economic and Social History in the Netherlands,* Vol. 7, pp. 199–242.
van Bochove, C. A. and van Sorge, W. (1989) 'Constant Wealth National Income: Accounting for War Damage with an Application to the Netherlands, 1940–45', *Review of Income and Wealth,* Vol. 35, No. 2, pp. 187–208.
Van den Broeke, C. (1984) 'L'incidence sur l'économie des aides d'expansion économique', *Bulletin de documentation du Ministère des Finances,* pp. 33–73.
Van Den Bulcke, D. (1986) 'Role and Structure of Belgian Multinationals', in K. Macharzina and W. H. Staehle (eds), *European Approaches to International Management,* Berlin, pp. 108–27.
Vanden Houte, P. and Veugelers, R. (1989) 'Buitenlandse ondernemingen in België', *Tijdschrift voor Economie en Management,* Vol. 34, pp. 9–34.
van der Eng, P. (1986) *De Marshall-hulp. Een perspectief voor Nederland 1947–1953,* Houten.
Van der Wee, H. (1985) 'De Belgische economie in de maalstroom van een halve eeuw 1925–1975', in *Gaston Eyskens 80,* Tielt, pp. 59–118.
Van Meershaeghe, M. A. G. (ed.) (1992) *Belgium and EC Membership Evaluated,* London.
Van Meerten, M. A. (1996) *Gross Private Fixed Asset Formation in Belgium, 1910–1954,* PhD thesis, University of Groningen.
* Van Rijckeghem, W. (1982) 'Benelux', in A. Boltho (ed.), *The European Economy: Growth and Crisis,* Oxford: Oxford University Press, pp. 581–609.
van Schaik, A. (1986) *Crisis en protectie onder Colijn,* Amsterdam.
van Waterschoot, W. and Deleeck, T. (1992) 'De Belgische distributierevolutie van 1961 in retrospectief', *Economisch en Sociaal Tijdschrift,* Vol. 46, pp. 389–406.
van Zanden, J. L. and Griffiths, R. T. (1989) *Economische geschiedenis van Nederland in de 20e eeuw,* Utrecht.
Vuchelen, J. (1991) 'Verkiezingen, politieke instabiliteit en het overheidstekort', in J. Vuchelen (ed.), *Verkiezingen en de economie,* Brussels, pp. 77–112.
Weber, M. (1983) 'Sources et développement de la crise industrielle en Belgique (1950–1980)', *Bulletin de documentation du Ministère des Finances,* Vol. 7, pp. 39–112.
Wellink, A. H. E. M. (1989) 'Dutch Monetary Policy in an Integrating Europe', in N. Bub et al. (eds), *Geldwertsicherung und Wirtschaftsstabilität,* Frankfurt, pp. 391–410.

6 The Iberian Economies: Divergence to Convergence?

David Corkill

INTRODUCTION

To the casual observer the economies of the two Iberian neighbours, Spain and Portugal, appear to have followed broadly similar trajectories in the post-war era. Relatively recently they were backward economies isolated from the European mainstream before joining the ranks of the late modernizers during the 1960s. Both countries were governed by authoritarian regimes that traced their origins to the period which witnessed the rise of European fascism. Prompted by the vogue for economic nationalism, the Franco and Salazar dictatorships adopted inward-looking, autarkic economic strategies which they clung to well into the prosperous liberal capitalist era in the non-communist world. Both regimes survived long after fascism's demise and eventually began to integrate their economies, followed later by their political destinies, into Europe. In both cases economic modernization preceded political transformation. When the long-delayed process of catching up with Western Europe did commence from the late 1950s onward, it was characterized both by high growth rates (rating the epithet 'economic miracle' in the Spanish case) and a marked unevenness as agriculture proved to be largely immune to the stimuli that gave such an impulse to the rest of the economy. Growth has not been continuous and has been punctuated with relatively short-lived recessionary troughs. On occasions the slowdown can be attributed to the exhaustion and limitations in the economic model being adopted. A further determining factor is that progress has been intimately related to external growth, especially the stimulus emanating from the European and world markets.

The 'Europeanization' of the Iberian economies began long before their joint accession in January 1986 when they were accorded full member status of the EC. Since joining the Community the two countries have often made common cause in the struggle to close the gap with the advanced European economies and Iberia has emerged as an important sub-region within the broader supranational framework provided by the EC/EU. Both economies have taken remarkable strides forward, but the convergence process is incomplete and major obstacles stand in the way of its realization. Despite the similar paths followed by the two countries, a closer examination of economic policy making reveals divergent interests and conflicting strategies that warn against facile generalizations about recent Iberian economic history.

Table 6.1 *Per capita income: Iberia (EU = 100)*

	1960	*1970*	*1975*	*1980*	*1985*	*1990*	*1992*
Portugal	38.7	48.9	52.2	55.0	52.0	55.7	56.3
Spain	60.3	74.7	81.9	74.2	72.5	77.8	79.9

Source: *Eurostat.*

Although we are dealing with two countries that have undergone dramatic changes in their economic structures, it is important to underline that we are not comparing like with like. Spain is a much larger and more diversified economy with a GDP per head that was 109 per cent greater than Portugal's in 1986. Spain sees itself as close to joining the fast track advanced European countries and is the self-styled leader of the 'southern lobby', promoting its own agenda and distinct interests (relations with the Mediterranean Basin, Latin America, and so on) when holding the rotating EU presidency in 1995. Nevertheless, Spain is still a relatively closed economy (Hudson and Rudcenko 1988) with an export–GDP share standing as low as 23 per cent (1986), while Portugal's economy traditionally has been more open and reliant on overseas markets.

Salazar's attempt to establish a 'Portuguese economic space' or *escudo* area merely served to cushion national producers through its guaranteed markets and artificially cheap raw materials. The strategy did little to prevent Portugal falling further behind the rest of Europe.

THE POST-WAR ERA, 1945–60

Although growth picked up between the end of the Second World War and 1960, the Spanish and Portuguese economies performed comparatively poorly, although, of the two, Portugal managed to grow faster in these years. Despite their neutrality during the global conflict, neither country could avoid import shortages and reduced export opportunities. Certainly, damage during Spain's civil war (1936–9), which was probably more limited than originally thought, did restrict Spain's ability to respond to the opportunities offered by the rapid growth of world trade, particularly in the light of the economic embargo imposed by the United Nations which deprived the Franco regime of Marshall Aid (Lieberman 1995). Although Portugal was a recipient of US aid, average per capita GDP growth in the immediate post-war period (1946–50) was, according to one estimate, 3.2 per cent, well below the European average at 8.1 per cent (Martins 1994). The performance picks up slightly between 1950 and 1960, averaging 3.9 per cent, but is still lacklustre compared to the 7 per cent registered between 1962 and 1973. It is more fruitful to seek the causes of this relative underperformance during the immediate post-war period in the reluctance to abandon some of the policies founded in 1930s economic nationalism. Franco's victorious nationalist forces pursued centralizing, interventionist and nationalist economic policies. This combined with vengeful reprisals against the defeated Republicans (or 'anti-Spain' as the nationalists regarded them) which were visited particularly harshly on the inhabitants of the industrial heartlands in Catalonia and the Basque Country. The civil war and the international ostracism that followed reinforced the belief in self-sufficiency. In this way the regime's ideology and economic philosophy were fused in a vindictive, contradictory and ultimately detrimental and unsuccessful strategy. It has been debated whether alternatives to autarky did exist (Esteban 1976). Undoubtedly autarky was freely chosen, not imposed on the dictatorship by circumstances. In fact, Franco merely accentuated trends that had been dominant in Spanish economic policy making since the late nineteenth century. The protectionist legislation introduced to ensure that the domestic market was reserved for home producers resulted in Spain becoming 'the most closed economy in Western Europe' (Harrison 1992), which clearly held back Spain's capacity to exploit catch-up opportunities and grow at rates commensurate with the rest of the Continent.

The components of the regime's ideology of dominance included a prominence given to the peasant as the embodiment of 'Spanishness' and the repository of values that the dictatorship wished to promote – despite which the peasantry bore much of the poverty that racked the rural economy during the 1940s and early 1950s. Sacrifice and suffering were elevated to the status of virtues to be stoically endured. Indeed, the regime's propagandists extolled the Spanish people's inbred capacity to work long hours and survive hardship (Richards 1995). In this scheme of things, industrialization, based on cheap labour, would be achieved on the back of the sacrifices made by the working population. Evidence that this line of thinking did not transplant easily is provided by the level of repression (exile, imprisonment and shootings) required. In the early post-war phase Franco tried to hermetically seal Spain from the outside world. In isolation a purge could be conducted by a disciplinarian authority in order to cauterize the 'sick patient'. The extent to which the ordinary Spaniard suffered the direct consequences from these policies is evident from the figures for private consumption which fell at an average rate of 8 per cent between 1940 and 1945 compared to 1935 (Richards 1995). In addition, some 200 000 deaths have been attributed to starvation in this dark period. Only the wheat and other foodstuffs imported from pro-Axis Peronist Argentina staved off the spectre of national catastrophe. In the midst of scarcity an officially condoned black economy flourished, managed by the authorities to ensure that food was shared out according to political loyalties rather than need. It encouraged corruption and state interference to control agricultural production and prices.

In line with contemporary thinking Portugal's dictator, António Salazar, also pursued a strategy based on autarky, corporatism and state intervention during the 1930s. The centralized controls and regulatory mechanisms that typified autarkic systems appealed to his conservative instincts which emphasized traditionalism and sought to protect rural and colonial interests from the upheavals normally visited upon societies undergoing modernization and change. To achieve the desired order and stability, the regime used its influence to limit potential conflicts between antagonistic interests through government intervention and bureaucratic regulation. Hence the attractions of corporatism which, in theory, offered to deliver structures that would reduce the potential for class conflict and act as a mechanism for social control. The Second World War encouraged the tendency for state involvement for a variety of reasons. The state attempted to control raw material prices, keep down wages (despite strong inflationary pressures) and enforce mergers and reorganizations in sectors where local firms could not satisfy demand. Often the undesired result was the creation of a tacitly condoned and thriving black market which traded greater volume than the official one in some products (Preston 1990). The war exposed the Iberians' vulnerability to external events and their dependence on the outside world. Against this background Salazar became more receptive to calls for industrial development.

The 1945 Industrial Development and Reorganization Law signalled that this change was under way. Despite being a member of the OEEC (later the OECD) and in 1960 a founder member of EFTA, however, Portugal was unable to take full advantage of the booming conditions that existed in the post-war international economy because conservative interests managed to dilute the demands coming from the industrial modernizers. A series of Five Year Plans (starting 1953) concentrated on infrastructure projects until the 1960s when, under pressure to pay for the cost of expensive colonial wars (beginning in 1961), economic growth and export promotion received priority. Gradually, the structure of Portuguese industry began to diversify. The traditional textiles, clothing, footwear, mining, food and drinks sectors were supplemented after 1945 by newcomers such as chemicals, metallurgical products, paper and pulp, machinery, and so on. However, this did not represent a wholesale conversion to industrialization and a commitment to growth, as attested to by the low wage, poorly skilled, workforce and the large-scale emigration that was a major feature of the two decades after 1950.

Similarly, in Spain, attitudes towards industrialization, while cautious, were not wholly negative. Agricultural incomes were kept deliberately low in order to extract a surplus that could be utilized to promote industrial development. The Franco regime established the *Instituto Nacional de Indústria* (INI) – a pale copy of Italy's IRI – to oversee the drive for self-sufficiency and to promote developments in the chemical, iron and steel, electrical, engineering and other industries. To some, INI laid the foundations for future growth by developing an infrastructure, but others point to the high cost of such projects (Naylon 1987). In fact, industry remained hamstrung by the limited domestic market and an inefficient, hence low income, agriculture.

In any analysis of the decade and a half following the end of the Second World War, one question must be asked: would a more open economy have brought forward the economic take-off in Spain? Certainly the lessons from the opening-out of the French and Italian economies suggest that an acceleration in the growth rate may have been the result. Instead, by comparison with elsewhere, recovery was slow and the immediate post-war decade was characterized by stagnation. Apologists for the regime blamed this predicament on a combination of the ravages inflicted during the three-year civil war, a persistent drought and the economic isolation orchestrated by the United Nations after 1946. In practice, the civil war losses were far from crippling, with much of the industrial plant, located principally in Catalonia and the Basque Country, untouched by the fighting. The regime failed to respond effectively to the chronic structural problems afflicting the agricultural sector and the UN boycott could hardly have been unexpected.

A cluster of factors conspired to limit the potential for growth: the heavy bureaucratic deadweight which slowed down decision making, corrupt practices that permeated the system, Franco's ignorance of economic matters and the prioritization of political survival before economic good sense and rational decisions. As a result, 'the dispassionate advice of Spain's tiny band of professional economists was ignored while the country was run like a military barracks' (Harrison 1992). In addition a notable obstacle to broad-based development came from the straightjacket applied to foreign trade by the import–export licensing system, an overvalued currency and multiple exchange rates. Cut off from the European Recovery Programme (Marshall Aid), Spain relied heavily on credits from Argentina and drip-feed commercial bank credits from the US that signalled the country's gradual shedding of its pariah status. In summary, modest early post-war growth was restrained by long-term structural problems, a reluctance to dismantle policy mechanisms associated with the 1930s (autarky and regulation), an unfavourable external environment and the belief that growth might bring instability and imperil political survival.

A NEW ECONOMIC CLIMATE

The pivotal date in Spain's recent economic evolution is usually identified as 1959 when a Stabilization Plan provided the platform for take-off into an era of sustained economic growth and signalled an end to isolation. While the Plan did mark an important turning point, there had been earlier signs during the 1950s that gradual progress was under way. The labour force began to leave the land in ever increasing numbers, National Income grew steadily and industrial production edged upwards. However, these steady improvements were purchased at a price: higher inflation, a worsening trade balance and the persistence of structural weaknesses which included a predominance of small-scale industrial enterprises – firms with fewer than five workers accounted for

85 per cent of the total in 1958 – low productivity and competitiveness compounded by meagre support provided for exporters (Harrison 1992).

The directional shift during the sub-period 1950–9 is identifiable in the willingness to solicit imported foodstuffs to make up for shortfalls and the import of machinery and raw materials to assist agriculture and the expanding manufacturing base. An important contributory factor to this comparatively modest progress was the availability of small, but crucial, amounts of US aid ($625m between 1951 and 1957) in return for the use of military and naval facilities. In September 1953 Spain signed an agreement with the Eisenhower administration permitting US bases on Spanish soil in return for economic assistance. The inflow helped to offset the trade imbalance, gave a gentle push to living standards and reinforced the arguments set out by the economic liberals. However, these developments took place strictly within the confines imposed by the import substitution model. The US still encountered irksome restrictions on foreign investment, a legacy of the regime's enduring suspicion of anything foreign. This undermined the possibilities of technology / managerial transfer, thereby restraining the technical efficiency of Spanish industry. It needed a quantum leap forward in economic policy to begin to tackle the major organizational and structural problems that persisted.

Only a serious threat to the regime's survival could have engineered such a policy shift. The threat of bankruptcy and imminent economic collapse signalled by a balance of payments crisis and a run on the gold reserves in the late 1950s triggered a response which took the form of a Cabinet reshuffle. Personnel changes brought in new Finance and Trade Ministers, Mariano Navarro Rubio and Alberto Ullastres, who, along with Laureano López Rodó, belonged to the economically liberal Catholic group, *Opus Dei*. At first they lacked a coherent strategy, but external developments soon shaped their thinking. The signing of the Treaty of Rome in 1957 marked the start of a process which Spain would ignore at its peril. While in Paris the French government introduced its stabilization plan to confront mounting inflation and to get ready for obligations implied by the Treaty, such developments convinced the *Opus Dei* technocrats that Spain must look towards Europe for its economic salvation and should introduce market mechanisms (MacKenzie 1973). Franco's instinct for political survival overcame his autarkically minded conservatism, particularly when the prospect was offered that economic progress could be decoupled from political liberalization.

The late 1950s and early 1960s marked the onset of a new 'insertion' phase when the Iberian economies became more closely tied to the European and international economies. Spain returned to the international fold by joining the Organization for European Economic Cooperation, the World Bank (July 1956), and the IMF, before signing a trade agreement with the EEC in 1970. For its part Portugal joined the European Free Trade Association (EFTA) as a founder member in 1958, along with GATT, the IMF and the World Bank (1960). The next milestone on the road to integration came in 1972 when Portugal signed a trade agreement with the European Community. Closer ties were constantly being reinforced by emigration, which conveniently relieved the pressures on the labour market to generate new jobs for migrants from the rural sector, and tourism. Portugal's balance of payments relied increasingly on contributions from emigrant remittances (12.1 per cent of GDP in 1972) and earnings from foreign visitors (tourist numbers reached 4 million in 1972).

The traditional picture often presented of the Portuguese economy under the dictatorship is one of economic immobilism and backwardness. Hammond (1988) writes of 'a stagnant economy dominated by a backward-looking oligarchy' and indicts government policy for preventing development. Machado (1991) categorizes Portugal as the most backward country in Europe, and Gallagher (1983) refers generally to economic stagnation, although he does allow for 'a modest economic boomlet' during the 1960s. This negative picture has been challenged in recent years by Baklanoff (1992) and other revisionists. Nunes, Mata and Valerio (1989) demonstrate that Portugal experienced high growth rates (averaging 5.4 per cent for 1946–73) – with the greater part of this coming after 1959. In addition the economy underwent a profound restructuring. The contention is that Portugal's performance during the late dictatorship deserves to be placed alongside not only the rapidly growing Southern European economies, but also the Asian Tigers. In support of this argument it is pointed out that the economy became more market oriented; integrated more closely into Europe through trade, emigrant remittances and inward investment; and that there was an improvement in income distribution. In this interpretation Portugal was 'poised between industrial Europe and Africa, and between a fading corporatism and an emerging market capitalism' (Baklanoff 1992). Pitcher (1993) tries to reconcile the stagnation and integrationist approaches:

> the regime tried to balance disparate and conflicting interests and placate the fears of the conglomerates. It tried to satisfy those tied to the colonies and those wishing to integrate with Europe, arguing as late as 1972 that integration with Europe and unity with the colonies was both possible and beneficial ... That these positions produced contradictions and divisions which helped to weaken and then bring down the government, it either overlooked or could not avoid. (p. 215)

It is important to acknowledge the extent to which external pressures prompted the change in attitude towards economic development. Closer relations with Europe nudged the economy forward and, crucially, the decision to cling on to the empire, which flew in the face of economic logic, dictated that higher levels of economic growth be achieved. This, more than anything, forced the Portuguese dictatorship into a new, more dynamic phase of development during the 1960s and early 1970s. In broad terms the new phase displayed the following features:

- Attitudes to foreign investment were gradually liberalized. The rules relating to direct foreign investment were relaxed in 1965, although penetration into strategic sectors was still prohibited and nationalist concerns remained strong. Within a short time, inward investment, attracted by low wage costs and tax advantages, began to transform the industrial fabric. Foreign multinationals invested in infrastructure projects such as the Tagus suspension bridge and airport construction. FDI came to dominate the newer sectors, principally the capital intensive, export-oriented industries that generated comparatively little additional employment. It served to reinforce the dualism within the industrial sector between the modern, technologically advanced industries and the traditional sector using old machinery and techniques, exacerbated regional imbalances, and further widened the gap between the primary and secondary sectors.

- In addition, economic growth helped to reinforce financial and industrial concentration. Salazar had granted monopoly concessions to a small number of firms closely linked to the regime. In turn, groups like CUF and *Espírito Santo* established close links with multinational capital in a range of areas including ship-building, synthetic fibres, mining and paper pulp. The conglomerates owned extensive colonial interests – a factor which inclined them to lend support to the regime's resistance to demands for decolonization. Interests both in Africa and Europe were not mutually exclusive and some of the conglomerates continued to invest in both markets, although the tensions and contradictions in such a strategy became increasingly apparent.

FROM ECONOMIC MIRACLE TO OIL CRISIS

Between 1961 and 1973, Spain completed the transition from an agrarian to an industrial economy, although it stopped short of becoming a fully-fledged market economy. Spain's GDP grew at an annual average rate of 7.5 per cent, on the back of a dramatic increase in foreign trade with imports rising thirteenfold and exports up fourteenfold. The proportion of the labour force employed in the rural sector plummeted from over 40 per cent in 1959 to 24.1 per cent by 1973 as 2 million workers abandoned the land. During the same period, agriculture's contribution to GDP dropped almost to single figures (11.4 per cent), while industry continued its inexorable rise from a fraction under 30 per cent to 42.9 per cent (Harrison 1992).

To what can we attribute this remarkable transformation? There is little evidence to suggest that endogenous factors played a significant part. Indeed, controversy exists over the contribution made by the regime's much-vaunted planning mechanisms and the importance to attach to the Stabilization Plan. It has been criticized as being too harsh, and only good fortune prevented a severe downturn as a result. However, the Plan did lay the basis for the era of technocratic development policies which introduced a combination of 'coherence, realism, imagination and ambition' into economic management (Harrison 1992). The three Plans (1964–7, 1968–71, 1972–5) did involve greater state intervention, but at best their influence was probably marginal (Naylon 1987). Faster growth might have been achieved without the Plans and they actually delayed the implementation of much-needed structural reforms. Likewise, protective tariffs remained in place and government officials retained powers to raise wages and preserve jobs – a vital ingredient in the regime's ability to buy labour peace. As in Portugal, employers raised few objections to the state's *dirigiste* role as it ensured the continuation of their privileged status. It is important to put the progress made into perspective: industrialization failed to generate jobs for three-quarters of a million Spaniards who emigrated during the 1960s and a further quarter of a million who were unemployed (Lieberman 1995).

Table 6.2 *Average GDP growth rates 1950–95 (annual percentage change in GDP 1990 prices)*

	Portugal	*Spain*	*EU12*
1950–73	5.4	5.7	na
1973–95	2.4	2.3	2.1
1961–70	6.4	7.3	4.8
1971–80	4.7	3.5	3.0
1981–90	3.0	3.0	2.4
1991	2.1	2.2	1.5
1992	1.1	0.7	1.0
1993	–1.2	–1.1	–0.5
1994	1.1	2.0	1.5
1995	3.0	3.1	2.8

Source: *European Economy* (1995), no. 60.

In seeking to explain the 'economic miracle' it is necessary to focus on exogenous factors which flowed directly from the expansion experienced in the West European and US economies during the 'Golden Age' (1950–73). The following ingredients comprised the formula for success as an industrial latecomer:

- First, as one of the poorest nations in Europe – GDP per capita is estimated to have been only a quarter and labour productivity to have been only a fifth of the US level in 1950 (Maddison 1996) – Spain had a greater catch-up potential than most of Europe.
- Second, after 1959 Spain enjoyed a foreign investment boom as capital, attracted by cheap labour and the geographical proximity to a dynamic

centre, flowed into the country. Foreign direct investment (FDI), which grew from 3.9 million pesetas in 1959 to 105.4 million pesetas in 1973, introduced new technologies and raised productivity levels in industries such as chemicals, metals, motor cars and foodstuffs. However, Spain's export capacity continued to suffer from a lack of international competitiveness and foreign trade was still not regarded as the important motor for economic growth.

- Third, Spain was able to finance the massive import growth essential to her industrial development because of a dramatic surge in earnings from tourism and the strong demand for immigrant labour in northern Europe which furnished the exchequer with emigrant remittances. Between 1960 and 1975, over 6 million Spaniards (around a quarter of the population) left the countryside to find work in the cities and one million went abroad (Hudson and Rudcenko 1988). Tourism became a key corrector of the current account balance with earnings from the sector offsetting up to 85 per cent of the deficit.
- Fourth, the availability of cheap energy supplies, oil especially, underwrote the industrial expansion, but ensured that Spain became heavily dependent on imported energy supplies.
- Finally, the internal market expanded rapidly, as did the stock of local entrepreneurial skills.

Although less dramatic, similar factors lay behind Portugal's progress in this period. Almost imperceptibly the structure of the Portuguese economy began to modernize. From an almost exclusively agrarian economy, Portugal became gradually transformed into an industrial one. Whereas agriculture contributed 7.8 per cent to GNP growth between 1950 and 1960, its contribution slumped to 3.9 per cent in the following decade and was actually negative (–0.3 per cent) between 1970 and 1973 (Martins 1994). Major social changes accompanied this metamorphosis. The movement of people was a particular characteristic. Migrants flocked from the countryside into the towns. Many then joined the ranks of nearly 2 million Portuguese who chose to emigrate between 1946 and 1973. The outflow was particularly strong after 1960 when more than 1 million left the country, motivated both by a desire to avoid being conscripted into Portugal's African wars and to search for employment in the booming economies of northern Europe (Martins 1994).

In part the rural–urban exodus owed something to the modernization process under way in specific regions, such as the Alentejo, where some mechanization occurred, although the structure (*latifúndio/minifúndio*) remained and high prices continued to be paid to producers. In contrast, considerable change took place in the secondary and tertiary sectors, although always tempered by the regime's obsession with sound finance and social stability. Gradually, however, autarkic policies gave way to a strategy combining export promotion with import substitution and industrialization. At first the series of national plans starting in 1953 were 'little more than an organized programme of public investment' bereft of social-economic objectives and were reliant on private initiative to stimulate industrial development (Rollo 1994). As the arguments in support of industrialization slowly gained the upper hand the process took on distinguishable characteristics. First, growth and diversification was concentrated almost exclusively in the coastal belt (the Oporto–Lisbon–Setúbal axis), and, second, the dynamism in the new sectors, such as metallurgical industries, chemicals and petroleum, contrasted with the stagnation in the traditional sectors such as mining, textiles, and so on. Third, protectionism reserved national and colonial markets for domestic producers, although they continued to impose constraints on account of their limited size, and industrial regulation stifled competition by reserving market sectors for favoured national monopolies. Fourth, the regime relied on maintaining low cost factors of production, especially cheap labour and raw materials.

By the late 1960s, when Marcelo Caetano replaced the aged and infirm Salazar, autarky and corporatism were no longer predominant, although a vast, deadweight bureaucracy continued in place. Economic policy prioritized growth of national output, higher living standards and export promotion. The liberalization measures introduced during what became known as the 'Lisbon Spring' have prompted some historians to imply that the progress during the late dictatorship was sustainable and strong enough to underpin the emergence of a modern liberal democracy (Baklanoff 1992). While the view that the Portuguese economy was stagnant for the duration of the dictatorship is no longer tenable, it is unwise to imply that fast growth and a new emphasis on external markets during the late 1960s and early 1970s could have laid the foundations for democratic development. Genuine political reform did not accompany economic liberalization and the factors underlying strong growth led to distortions. Caetano's 'New Industrial Policy' achieved impressive results with the manufacturing sector growing at an annual average rate of 9 per cent during 1968–73. Nevertheless, the signs were appearing that such rapid growth would be unsustainable. Real wages rose sharply, pushed up by emigration, labour militancy and military call-up, although they still remained the lowest in Western Europe. The large monopolies did not dissent from the regime's costly and politically fatal determination to cling on to its empire. The wars against national liberation movements in the African colonies – Angola and Mozambique – absorbed just under half of government expenditure at a time when the economic logic pointed inexorably in the direction of Europe as the priority.

The collapse of the successor regime of Marcelo Caetano (1968–74) ensured that we shall never know whether the metamorphosis into a liberal democracy would have taken place without an abrupt regime shift, but there is ample evidence to cast doubt on such a supposition. The high growth rates registered during the period disguised the strains inherent in the *Caetanista* economic model:

- First, for decades emigration had acted as a safety valve for relieving political and socioeconomic pressures. In the process Portugal earned the distinction as the only country in Europe to suffer a net population decrease during the 1960s. On average around 100 000 people emigrated each year, reaching a peak in 1970–1, when the majority were illegal immigrants. The economy benefited directly from this outflow of course in the form of emigrant remittances which represented around 10 per cent of GDP by the end of the 1960s and helped to cover the balance of trade deficit. Nevertheless, there was a negative side to this windfall: industry experienced labour shortages, particularly among younger skilled workers and agriculture, especially the small, labour-intensive operations, and stagnated because of emigration (Pitcher 1993).
- Second, the determination to hold on to the colonies extracted a heavy price and distorted the development process. Expenditure on defence, which consumed just under 30 per cent of the budget in 1960, rose to over 40 per cent by the early 1970s, three times the proportion spent on promoting development. The wars did, however, necessitate the (reluctant) abandonment of long-held, cherished policies. Portugal needed to borrow abroad, seek foreign investment, dip into the gold and currency reserves and stimulate economic growth. Even the long-neglected colonies were encouraged, for the first time, to develop their economic potential and Lisbon actively promoted settlers with promises of assistance and prosperity.
- Third, efforts to introduce political and economic reforms were emasculated, delayed or blocked. Caetano's failure to overcome the power of the hardliners is apparent in the economic sphere. Although he introduced a group of young technocrats into the government, it is significant that they were not given Cabinet rank and wielded far less influence than the technocrats in the Spanish Cabinet. Another example is provided by the painfully slow and not always successful efforts to dismantle the deadweight of the old bureaucratic corporatist regulations and controls over industry.

Taken at face value, the economy performed well under Caetano. Annual GDP growth averaged 8 per cent between 1968 and 1973. By the early 1970s manufactured goods accounted for more than 60 per cent of exports. But there were clear signs that the economy was overheating. Inflation, which stood at 6.1 per cent in 1968, surged to almost 20 per cent by 1973. The development model pursued by Caetano depended upon a highly favourable external environment. Just how high-risk the strategy was became clear after 1973. The oil crisis derailed the economic strategy as energy prices soared and the cost of imported goods rose considerably. The impact that the crisis and subsequent recession had on the modernization drive is encapsulated in the Sines project. The designation of a growth pole in the western Alentejo symbolized the break with Salazar's policy of 'contained industrialization'. The plan to build a port facility linked to a major industrial complex comprised the centrepiece of a New Industrial Policy (NIP). It represented the new technocratic approach to industrial development under which the state assumed a prominent role as facilitator and provider. The government took responsibility for the infrastructure while private capital was expected to develop the industrial base.

Unfortunately the whole project was badly timed. The oil crisis exposed world overcapacity in steel, petroleum and deep-water port facilities. Sines became a white elephant project, unable to adjust to the new realities and impossible to abandon because of the political consequences and the impact on unemployment that would result (Lewis and Williams 1985). Moreover, the project generated tensions between the once supine private sector and the Lisbon authorities. Despite being awarded the petroleum contract, CUF refused to locate its mineral processing plant at Sines as the planners requested. It was further evidence that the close ties between business and the dictatorship were loosening.

ECONOMIES UNDER TRANSITION AND REVOLUTION

The mid-1970s is a seminal period for the two Iberian nations. Political crisis and transition politics coincided with the international recession which followed the 1973–4 oil crisis to generate a unique set of circumstances. Despite the different political trajectories (Portugal's sharp rupture with the old regime followed by instability and upheaval, contrasting with Spain's smoother, gradual transition from dictatorship to democracy) a number of features are shared in common:

- Economic matters took a back seat while the vital and time-consuming task of moulding a new political order was undertaken. Democratization undoubtedly took precedence over the crucial decisions and structural changes demanded in response to the world economic crisis. It was not surprising that the primacy was given to consolidating democracy by leaders such as Adolfo Suárez and Mário Soares whose skills lay in political negotiation rather than in economic management, but it did constrain economic decision making.
- The oil price rises in 1973–4 could hardly have come at a more inopportune time for the energy dependent Iberian economies. Spain's energy bill jumped by 210 per cent during 1974 and accounted for over 27 per cent of the total import bill in the mid-1970s as the terms of trade deteriorated. Portugal's import bill jumped from $184m in 1973 to $743m in 1977. Needless to say, the impact on the balance of payments was dramatic.
- Coming in the aftermath of sustained high growth rates, the economic recession hit the Iberian economies hard. Spain's average GDP growth, which reached 7 per cent for a decade and a half after 1960, dropped to 1.5 per cent (1981–5), falling below the OECD average. Spanish industry

was particularly affected, registering an average annual growth of only 1.8 per cent in the decade after 1975 against an OECD average of 3 per cent.

- Finally the protracted transition process unfolded against a background of rapidly depleting gold and foreign currency reserves, rising inflation, wage increases above those justified by productivity, and losses posted by smokestack industries such as steel, ship-building and textiles. Sooner or later difficult decisions had to be taken in order to cope with the growing crisis.

Inflation leapt ahead during the Spanish transition process (see Table 6.3), reaching 25 per cent in 1977, well above the 9.8 per cent EC average (Hudson and Rudcenko 1988). The impetus came from rising oil costs and the propensity for importing inflation-prone goods. Wage inflation was another contributory factor, rising almost 7 per cent per annum in the 1960s and 1970s. Nor could the government harness its resources effectively to counter the negative trends, because of the inefficient tax system, characterized by large-scale evasion, and the thriving underground economy. The economic centrepiece of Spain's consensual transition was the Moncloa pacts, a deal brokered by the UCD government and the opposition political parties to impose an upper limit on wage rises in exchange for improved social benefits and other reforms. It explicitly recognized that Spain had to move towards a market economy and reduce public spending, initiate tax reform and boost exports. It was the first serious attempt to tackle the multilayered crisis that had been exacerbated by short-sighted pre-1975 attempts to camouflage the impact through subsidies, wage indexing and price controls (Lieberman 1995). The second oil price hike in 1979 blew the anti-inflation effort off course, boosted unemployment still further (to 2 million by 1982) and stoked a worsening trade deficit.

Table 6.3 *Spain and Portugal: inflation and unemployment (%)*

	Inflation		*Unemployment*	
	Portugal	*Spain*	*Portugal*	*Spain*
1961–70	2.8	7.2	0.5	2.7
1971–80	17.3	15.1	5.1	5.4
1981–90	17.1	9.3	7.0	18.4
1991	11.1	6.3	4.0	16.4
1992	9.8	6.4	3.9	18.2
1993	6.8	5.1	5.1	21.8
1994	5.6	4.8	6.1	22.4
1995	5.1	4.6	6.0	21.9

Note: Unemployment figures are as percentage of civilian labour force; inflation figures are percentage annual change (private consumption deflator).

Source: *European Economy* (1995), no. 60.

It is often pointed out that what distinguishes the transition processes initiated in the former Soviet bloc after 1990 from the Iberian experience during the 1970s is that the former countries faced the twin challenge of introducing capitalism simultaneously with political democracy. It is true that private capital played an important part in Spain and Portugal prior to the regime changes, but in the latter case it can hardly be claimed that market forces predominated. State-protected private monopolies dominated the modern sectors of the Portuguese economy. Following the overthrow of the dictatorship in 1974, economic controls were tightened and the impact of market forces reduced still further. Price controls, subsidies to industry, the nationalization of land, banks and insurance companies along with major industries such as ship-building, brewing, steel, petroleum refining, and so on, increased the size of the state sector substantially (Baer and Leite 1992). As a result the state accounted for about one-quarter of the value added and one-half of investment. It also actively intervened in an effort to achieve income redistribution through higher wages and controlled prices. In addition, Portugal divested itself of its empire thus giving a severe jolt to sectors that had relied on guaranteed colonial export markets and cheap raw material imports. During the brief revolutionary period dominated by the left (1974–6) the long-term process of opening-up the economy became stalled. The process restarted in the late 1970s as is evidenced by the rise in the export/GDP ratio to 37.2 per cent in 1988 (from 16.9 per cent in 1960) and the import/GDP ratio to 46.4 per cent (from 23.2 per cent in 1960). The geographical distribution of foreign trade also shifted dramatically towards the EEC, with exports rising from under 20 per cent in 1970 to almost three-quarters in 1989, and imports showing a similar increase to 67 per cent in the same year (Baer and Leite 1992). There is ample evidence of growing international specialization in textiles, shoes and clothing, drinks and light machinery in the 1980s and of rising foreign investment which peaked in the late 1980s with the Ford-Volkswagen decision to site the AutoEuropa plant at Palmela near Setúbal.

EUROPEANISM AND ECONOMIC GROWTH 1982–92

The next major turning point came in the 1980s when in Spain the Socialists (PSOE) under Felipe González won power (October 1982) and in Portugal Aníbal Cavaco Silva's centre-right Social Democrats (PSD) established an electoral stranglehold that endured for a decade from 1985. The Iberian economies jointly began a period of expansion during which growth rates outperformed the European average. Both governments inherited formidable problems: neglected and crisis-hit economies with serious structural problems including a bloated public sector, rigid labour laws, an uncompetitive small-scale industrial sector and, in the Spanish case, high unemployment. Although the PSOE and PSD occupied different positions to the left and right of the centre-ground, the policies they pursued were remarkably similar. Ironically, the once revolutionary and Marxist PSOE began to reduce the role of the state, promote pro-private sector measures and encourage multinational capital. They pursued strategies in line with the neo-liberal agenda – sound finance, controls on public spending, an anti-inflation drive, financial liberalization, reductions in the level of state intervention and privatization. Above all, both governments pinned their faith on Europe as a panacea for their economic ills. Little debate took place over the terms of entry which were 'hastily negotiated' (Gooch 1995) and 'punishing' (Harrison 1992), but the Iberians pushed ahead with integration into the EC / EU and made little distinction between support for membership and later acceptance of the Maastricht terms (Hooper 1996).

In the short term a number of factors coalesced to stimulate economic activity:

- The confidence-generating political stability established after a period of uncertainty. There was continuity in macroeconomic policy under four consecutive Socialist administrations (1982–6, 1986–9, 1989–92, 1992–6) and three successive PSD governments (1985–7, 1987–91 and 1991–5).
- Joint accession to the European Community and the positive international climate boosted optimism over future prospects based on greater competition and the influence exerted within the EC. This was compounded by a general agreement within the business community on the need to keep wage costs below the OECD average to stimulate investment and improve productivity.
- Foreign investment poured into the peninsula, prompted partly by the dearth of opportunities elsewhere in the world, and acted as a catalyst for the growth spurt in the late 1980s / early 1990s. From a 1975 low point at $900m, direct foreign investment in Spain soared to $8.1b in 1987. In 1989 Spain came fourth in the world table for foreign investment in volume terms. Foreign investment in Portugal doubled annually during the late 1980s, rising from $163m in 1986 to $3.5b in 1990 (Corkill 1993).
- The key contributions to the achievement of higher growth levels were the buoyant tourist industry, the booming retail sector, strong demand for some agricultural products and rising multinational investment in key industries such as motor car manufacturing.
- Finally, in the Spanish case, success in meeting inflation and monetary targets produced deteriorating relations between the government and the *Unión General de Trabajadores* (UGT), the Socialist-led trade union federation. Clashes over economic policy sparked the resignation of Nicolás Redondo, a critic of González's policies which he claimed favoured the rich.

THE 1980s 'BOOM'

Spain's second 'economic miracle' and Portugal's belated catching-up were both consumer-led. In Spain private consumption had been reined back in the early

1980s, largely attributable to wage moderation and the stagnation in disposable incomes which actually declined by an average of 1.2 per cent between 1981 and 1985. The relative austerity imposed during this period provided the springboard for a consumer-led boom after 1986. But the rapid improvement in living standards can also be traced to the investment programme, bettered only by Japan, during the late Franco period: between 1960 and 1975, investment accounted for 23 per cent of total domestic expenditure and a roughly similar share of GDP (Hudson and Rudcenko 1988). Despite declining in the late 1970s/early 1980s, investment remained high in international terms and received an extra boost in 1986 from EC entry and the Single Market programme. Conditions were created which prompted Carlos Solchaga, Economy Minister, to boast of Spain's 'get rich quick' environment (*Guardian*, 15 April 1995).

Confidence spread through Spain's business sector as rising profits gave a further boost to investment. Much of the new capital was destined for productive areas – investment in machinery and equipment rose 14.5 per cent in 1987 – rather than into speculative construction projects. Strong growth sucked in imports, aided by tariff reductions that were part of EC obligations and the surge in domestic demand. Import expansion was in the order of 15 per cent and 20 per cent in 1986 and 1987 respectively. However, Iberia still had a lot of catching up to do in relation to its European partners. On accession Spanish private consumption per capita ($4000) represented 59 per cent of the EC average – yet it was still almost double Portugal's $1961 (Hudson and Rudcenko 1988). The late 1980s growth surge enabled the Iberian economies to narrow the gap in living standards with their European partners in terms of consumer durables (motor car, telephone and TV ownership) and improvements in health care. Inevitably, there were casualties during the process of insertion into Europe and the drive to improve competitiveness. In general, older industries fared badly, while newer, export-oriented businesses took advantage of the opportunities available in larger markets. Spain's 1984 Industrial Reconstruction Programme (IRP) involved financial restructuring and some cuts in capacity and jobs in steel, engineering, ship-building, and textiles. The regional impact of the rundown was uneven, hitting Asturias, Cantabria and the Basque Country (all Socialist strongholds) disproportionately hard. However, as Salmon (1995) points out, the IRP required injections of substantial sums of public money, which

> amounted to cushioning traditional industries from the full impact of the industrial crisis ... diverting attention away from politically more difficult structural change and delaying the process of international specialization which was taking shape in the world economy. (p. 84)

Although industrial policy embraced a privatization programme, it failed to tackle rigidities in areas such as the land market and labour laws until the mid-1990s. Modifications to the Workers' Statute in 1984 did introduce more flexibility into the labour market and made lay-offs easier. A decade later only 2 per cent of new job contracts were permanent and one-third of all job contracts were temporary (Kennedy 1995). This trend is mirrored in Portugal where the proportion of fixed-term job contracts (around 20 per cent) is one of the highest in the EU (Corkill 1993).

Table 6.4 *Unit labour costs (% change)*

	1961–73	*1974–85*	*1986–90*	*1991*	*1993*
Portugal	3.9	21.0	11.7	15.8	6.3
Spain	7.7	14.3	6.4	6.4	3.7
EU	5.2	10.3	4.0	5.6	2.5

Source: *European Economy* (1994), no. 58.

The high point of the González boom came in 1992, known as the 'Year of Spain' when Barcelona hosted the Olympic Games and Seville was the venue for the World Expo. A severe recession followed which cruelly exposed the weaknesses in the economic structure which had been disguised by the international economic upturn in the late 1980s. However, higher oil prices in the wake of the Gulf conflict, growing competition from Eastern Europe and the financial hangover from the expensive 1992 extravaganza, combined to tip the economy into recession. The crisis revealed that EC entry and the subsequent boom had not transformed ingrained attitudes and practices. Despite the neo-liberal agenda, the state, instead of contracting, increased its size and influence and, according to some calculations, still accounted for as much as 50 per cent of GDP at the beginning of the 1990s (Bruce 1991). State sell-offs proceeded at a snail's pace as González did little to hide his preference for an efficient, market-sensitive INI – defensible at least as a pragmatic approach based on the realization that the Spanish capital market did not have the capacity to absorb substantial privatizations. Tax evasion, fraud and bribes linked to state contracts were rife (Gooch 1995). It exposed the fallacy of Spain's pretension to be in the front rank in the European project.

It is clear that the popularity of both the González and Cavaco administrations rested in substantial measure on their economic achievements. However, a few years on, their attempts to claim credit for the accelerated growth recorded during the late 1980s / early 1990s lack credibility. If we accept the argument that governments have little effect on long-term growth and that EU funds alone cannot account for surges in growth, then other, principally exogenous factors must have been responsible (Lains 1996). In fact, the economic 'boomlet' enjoyed by the Iberian economies is explained by a combination of factors. The endogenous factors make a contribution but are far from decisive and, in any case, originate in the 1970s. In Spain's case the rapid improvement in living standards owed much to the high investment levels in late Francoism, while Portugal's closer commercial links with Europe (dating from the late Salazar era) and the application for accession to the European Community lodged in 1977 established the platform for later growth. Both Cavaco and González laid much store by the political stability enjoyed under their administrations and its positive contribution to the economic climate. However, Lains (1996) argues that, as demonstrated by Italy (as well as France during the Fourth Republic – see Chapter 3), there is no clear relationship between government stability and economic growth. If we compare the decade since EU accession with the 1960s, some startling conclusions can be drawn. Portugal benefited more from its relationship with Europe *before* accession than in the post-1986 period when lavish quantities of structural, regional and cohesion funds were available. Put another way, Portugal's protected (by the state and by low oil prices), insular exporters performed better than their modern counterparts who operate in a less regulated, more open and business-oriented environment. During the 1980s average annual growth was 2.7 per cent, just 0.3 per cent above the Community average. In the first half of the 1990s the average growth rate (at 1985 prices) had slumped to 1.1 per cent, 0.4 per cent below the Community average. Why do the statistics appear not to confirm the apparent realities? Clearly the Iberians found it easier to benefit during the prosperous 1960s than the timetable-dominated 1980s when a demanding reform agenda had to be implemented speedily in a less helpful environment. Moreover, the early phase in the catching-up process is often easier than the later stages when the scope for catch-up is diminishing and competition becomes ever more fierce, particularly when an industrializing economy moves from traditional activities in which it had a comparative advantage to new areas where European and global competition becomes progressively more cut-throat. Perhaps even more surprisingly, the growth rates achieved amid the difficult post-oil crisis years in the 1970s matched those recorded during the so-called boom years in the late 1980s. It might, therefore, be more appropriate to ask why growth in this period was not even stronger.

It is now clear that the economic success was relatively easy to achieve during the period marked at the boundaries by accession to the EC, the Single Act and the Maastricht Treaty. Strong growth among Portugal's major trading partners, high levels of foreign investment, the inflow of structural, regional and other funds from Brussels, falling energy prices and interest rates combined with investor and consumer confidence at home, helped to stimulate economic activity. In addition, Premiers Cavaco and González benefited from an upturn in the economic cycle that followed a decade of stagnation in Spain and, in the Portuguese case, the sharp recession and (with hindsight, oversevere) deflation during 1983–5. It is almost certain that any government of whatever political complexion would have benefited from the cyclical upturn that generated a uniquely favourable set of circumstances. A more technocratic approach to economic management, liberalization, labour law reforms, an ambitious privatization programme and other pro-private sector legislation had a role to play, but would have had much less impact if not accompanied by an economic upswing.

THE 1992–3 DOWNTURN

Spain and Portugal suffered negative GDP growth rates during the recessionary trough in the early 1990s (–1.1 per cent and –1.2 per cent respectively in 1993). The subsequent slow recovery threatened to undermine the convergence effort. Comparison with another of the 'Club of 4' poorer member states, Ireland, illustrates how seriously the Iberians were affected. The Irish barely paused in their race to close the gap with the more prosperous member states: a remarkable 8.6 per cent GDP growth rate in 1990 was followed by a dip to 2.9 per cent in 1991, before strong growth recommenced, reaching 6 per cent in 1994. The European Commission identified four significant factors which have their origins in the 1980s, to explain the Iberian slowdown (European Commission 1995):

- First, closer integration with Europe, symbolized by the peseta's entry into the ERM in June 1989, encouraged large inflows of foreign capital. This forced up the value of the peseta, putting Spain in the novel situation of being a strong currency located at the top of its ERM band. As a result the economy lost competitiveness and the external deficit increased substantially. With hindsight the peseta was clearly overvalued. The temporary boost to confidence by having one of the strongest currencies in Europe gave way to a realization that an economy previously weaned on devaluations to boost competitiveness, could hardly match the stronger European industrial economies in conditions where a real appreciation was under way.
- Second, the Spanish authorities lost control over inflation as high government spending, fuelled by the cost of developing a welfare state and additional layers of regional government, caused the economy to overheat. The government's response – using monetary weapons to fight inflation – pushed up interest rates which buffeted industry and exporters.
- Third, although significant strides had been taken towards liberalizing the economy, the process was far from complete. Rigidities still remained in the labour market and in sectors such as services which were sheltered from competition.
- Finally, growing international competition, sharpened by the recession, exposed longer-term deficiencies such as the slow private sector response to changes in external markets, the failure to innovate and to invest in new technologies and human resources. To these structural weaknesses must be added external factors such as the Gulf War and the impact of

higher oil prices, as well as the competition from emerging markets elsewhere, especially in Eastern Europe.

The 1992–3 crisis revealed the unbalanced character of the late 1980s boom, past overspending and the extent to which the Iberian nations had lost their ability to conduct an independent economic policy. This was brought home starkly by the ERM crisis and the subsequent blow to consumer and investor confidence. In response Spain took steps to ameliorate the state of public finances and remove lingering rigidities in the labour market, as well as revising its convergence programme in June 1994. As a result, industries that previously had operated with the benefit of a cushion provided by government regulation, market sharing, price fixing and public subsidy, faced an uncertain future. In May 1994 the Bank of Spain became independent, the state oil distribution monopoly was terminated and state subsidies cut.

Ultimately the Cavaco and González governments paid a political price for the economic downturn – defeat in general elections held in 1995 (Portugal) and 1996 (Spain). It is arguable to what extent the economic factors per se explain rejection at the polls. Certainly sleaze, clientelism, and *desgaste* (exhaustion) were important contributory factors, but the reversal of the gains made during the expansionary phase is undeniable. In Portugal just over 400 000 jobs disappeared (73 per cent of those generated between 1986 and 1991). There was a 74 per cent increase in the number of jobless between 1992 and 1995 as unemployment affected more than 7 per cent of the active population. Equally influential was the increase in the number of temporary contracts to cover over 11 per cent of those employed (Corkill 1996). Around one and a half million jobs had been generated during the same period in Spain, but 85 per cent were temporary and the service sector accounted for the vast majority of new employment (Kennedy 1995). Ultimately both leaders paid the price for trying to balance the promotion of a pro-business agenda with continued support for outdated, uncompetitive industries.

CONCLUSION: CERTAINTY TURNS INTO DOUBT

Over 50 years after the end of the Second World War the Pyrenees no longer represent a barrier and Iberia is no longer considered an entity separate from the rest of Europe. The old suspicions embodied in the isolationist mentality have disappeared and Spain likes to think of itself as being at the forefront of European developments, while both governments are flatly opposed to the notion of a two-speed Europe. The extent of the transformation can be gauged by the attempts by some commentators to attribute North European characteristics to the Spanish, labelling them 'the Prussians of the South' (Head 1989). In fact, the 'industriousness' and 'business-mindedness' so admired by German companies such as Volkswagen, refers to Catalans, not all Spaniards.

This highlights the regional disparities that remain a distinctive feature of the contemporary Iberian economic landscape. Poorer regions such as Extremadura and the Alentejo lag far behind the richer regions like Madrid, the Basque provinces, Catalonia and La Rioja – all of which benefited from the 1960s boom. These more fortunate regions, with their industrial concentrations, were well placed to benefit when growth returned in the 1980s, although some, like the Basque Country, were hit by the decline in ship-building, while Madrid and Catalonia benefited from strong foreign investment inflows. The structure of the economy has continued to undergo change with heavy industry contracting and the service sector, especially tourism, continuing to advance along with a more export-oriented agriculture.

Twenty years after the death of Franco, Spain faces the realization that combining democracy with economic prosperity is not an easy task. The year 1992 was a 'jamboree year' when Spain was the focus of international attention but critical voices focused on the waste of EU subsidies and overspending, exposing the fact that Spain was trying to have it both ways in 'demanding special terms as an emerging economy, yet trying to be a top table player' (Gooch 1995). Miguel Boyer, a former Minister for the Economy, ruptured the political and business consensus by warning that the Exchange Rate Mechanism was 'a political trap' with a high economic price, and chastised the political establishment for its 'obsession about sitting down on equal terms with Germany' (*Financial Times* 23 January 1996). Euroscepticism has been fuelled by the belated realization that there has been a loss of autonomy and that 'integration' and 'modernization' involves surrendering powers to Brussels and being increasingly at the mercy of decisions taken by foreign multinationals. As elsewhere in the European Union, there is a realization that the targets for convergence are overambitious. A readjustment is overdue as the Iberians develop a more realistic and balanced view of their own national identities and their place in Europe. Above all, it has to be recognized that there are 'latecomer costs'. Despite all the talk of 'convergence' and 'closing the gap' the reality is that some parts of the European Union will inevitably remain richer than others, and that solidarity is strained when jobs, orders and the allocation of resources are at stake – particularly in the context of admitting the countries of Eastern Europe. It is important to recognize that, despite all the progress toward integration and harmonization, contemporary Europe still comprises competing national capitalisms and that, in such circumstances, it may have been unreasonable to expect two relatively poor, non-core countries to adjust and modernize their economic structures in such a short timeframe.

REFERENCES

Baer, W. and Leite, A. P. N. (1992) 'The Peripheral Economy, Its Performance in Isolation and With Integration: The Case of Portugal', *Luso-Brazilian Review*, Vol. 29, No. 2, pp. 1–43.

Baklanoff, E. (1992) 'The Political Economy of Portugal's Later Estado Novo: A Critique of the Stagnation Thesis', *Luso-Brazilian Review*, Vol. 29, No. 1, pp. 1–19.
Bruce, P. (1991) 'State Still Accounts for Half of GDP', *Financial Times*, Supplement, 15 March.
Corkill, D. R. (1993) *The Portuguese Economy Since 1974*, Edinburgh: Edinburgh University Press.
Corkill, D. R. (1996) 'Cavaquismo: An Interpretation'. Paper presented at *Cavaquismo: The Cavaco Silva Decade In Portugal, 1985-95*, conference held at The University of Leeds, February.
Esteban, J. (1976) 'The Economic Policy of Francoism: An Interpretation', in P. Preston (ed.), *Spain In Crisis. The Evolution and Decline of the Franco Regime*, Brighton: Harvester Press.
European Commission (1995) 'The Economic and Financial Situation in Spain', *European Economy*, No. 7, Brussels.
European Economy, various years.
Eurostat, various years.
Gallagher, T. (1983) *Portugal: A Twentieth Century Interpretation*, Manchester: Manchester University Press.
Gooch, A. (1995) 'Economic Miracle that turned sour', *Guardian*, 15 April.
Hammond, R. (1988) *Building Popular Power: Workers and Neighbourhood Movements in The Portuguese Revolution*, New York: Monthly Review Press.
Harrison, J. (1992) 'Spain', in D. Dyker (ed.), *The National Economies Of Europe*, London: Longman, pp. 189–212.
Head, D. (1989) 'Prussians of the South', *International Management*, October, pp. 86–7.
Hooper, J. (1996) 'South Glimpses Hidden Costs of EU Benefits', *Guardian*, 28 March.
Hudson, M. and Rudcenko, S. (1988) *Spain to 1992: Joining Europe's Mainstream*, EIU Special Report No. 1138, EU, Economic Prospects Series.
Kennedy, P. (1995) 'The PSOE's Attitude Towards European Integration and Its Influence over Economic Policy'. Paper delivered at Annual Conference of the Association for Contemporary Iberian Studies, Belfast.
Lains, P. (1996) 'Can Growth Be Promoted? The Portuguese Economy 1968–1995'. Paper presented at *Cavaquismo: the Cavaco Silva Decade in Portugal, 1985–95*, conference held at The University of Leeds, February.
Lewis, J. and Williams, A. (1985) 'The Sines Project: Portugal's Growth Centre Or White Elephant?', *Town Planning Review*, Vol. 56, pp. 339–66.
Lieberman, S. (1995) *Growth and Crisis in the Spanish Economy 1940–93*, Studies in the European Economy, London: Routledge.
Machado, D. (1991) *The Structure of Portuguese Society*, New York: Praeger.
MacKenzie, L. (1973) 'The Political Ideas Of Opus Dei', *Government And Opposition*, Vol. 8, pp. 72–92.
Maddison, A. (1996) 'Macroeconomic accounts for European countries', in B. van Ark and N. F. R. Crafts (eds), *Quantitative Aspects of Post-War European Economic Growth*, Cambridge: Cambridge University Press, pp. 27–83.
Martins, F. (1994) 'As "Mudanças Invisíveis" do Pós-Guerra', in Rosas F. (ed.), *O Estado Novo (1926–74)* Vol. 7, *História de Portugal* (Dir: Jose Matoso), Lisbon: Editorial Estampa, pp. 419–501.
Naylon, J. (1987) 'Iberia', in Clout, H. D. (ed.), *Regional Development in Western Europe*, 3rd edn, London: D. Fulton Publishers.
Nunes, A., Mata E. and Valerio, N. (1989) 'Portugese Economic Growth 1833–1985', *The Journal of European Economic History*, Vol. 18, No. 2, pp. 291–330.
Pitcher, A. M. (1993) *Politics in the Portuguese Empire: The State, Industry and Cotton, 1926–1974*, Oxford: Clarendon Press.

Preston, P. (1990) 'Spain', in A. Graham and A. Seldon (eds), *Governments and Economies In The Postwar World*, London: Routledge, pp. 125–53.

Richards, M. (1995) 'Constructing The Nationalist State: The Economic, Political and Cultural Aspects of Autarky in the First Francoism'. Paper presented at conference on Nationalism and National Identity in Iberia held at The University of Southampton, 22–23 March.

Rollo, F. (1994) 'A Industralização e os Seus Impasses', in F. Rosas (ed.), *O Estado Novo (1926-74)*, Vol. 7, *História de Portugal* (Dir. José Mattoso), Lisbon: Editorial Estampa, pp. 450–71.

Salmon, K. (1995) 'Spain in the World Economy', in R. Gillespie, F. Rodrigo and J. Storey (eds), *Democratic Spain: Reshaping External Relations in a Changing World*, London: Routledge.

7 Scandinavia

Hans Sjögren

INTRODUCTION

In this chapter we focus upon the three largest Scandinavian economies. As there are deep cultural, economic and political links between Denmark, Norway and Sweden, these countries are sometimes viewed as an entity. There is a long history of political and economic union in Scandinavia: for three and a half centuries, until 1814, Norway was a part of Denmark. Thereafter, for nearly a century, Norway was semi-ruled by Sweden, through a coordinated foreign policy and a mutual king (personal union).[1] The countries also share many religious and ethical roots.

There are, however, major variations, in particular relating to the structure of business and industry. This reflects the fact that conditions for economic activity are different. First, populations differ – ranging from nearly 9 million in Sweden, to over 5 million in Denmark and approximately 4.2 million in Norway. The population in all the countries increased by between 20 per cent and 35 per cent from 1945 to 1995, but they still remain relatively small by European standards. Second, the land area varies from 450 000 to 43 000 square kilometres, with Sweden being the largest and Denmark the smallest. Third, whereas Denmark is a flat country with a mild climate, Norway is mountainous with a much harsher climate, and Sweden is a mix of the two. In terms of agricultural area, Norway has only 11 600 square kilometres, compared to 29 000 in Denmark and 28 000 in Sweden. This implies a variety of possibilities for agriculture and forestry in particular. In other words, the variation in geography imparts a certain structure to the Scandinavian economy and business. For example, Norway, just two generations from rural life, retains a nostalgic relationship to decentralized production and institutionally strong municipalities and administrative provinces. This does not mean that industry is underdeveloped, however – the boom in shipping, oil and gas during the 1970s enlarged the basis of the economy considerably. Even so, Norway's industrial structure remains less diversified than Sweden's, such that there is a dualism between modern and traditional culture. This deep-rooted dualism was best illustrated during the three anti-EEC/EU campaigns in 1961/2, 1972 and 1994 (see further below – 'Inside or Outside Europe?').

In policy terms, the Scandinavian combination of state intervention and the play of market forces is well known and the economies are also characterized by extensive social welfare systems. This is something the countries developed as a major feature of social and economic policy after the Second World War.

Recently, however, the model has come under pressure. In this respect, what is (or perhaps was?) the Scandinavian or Swedish model, and how should we explain its successes and failures? To be able to answer these questions, we have to analyse the role of the state, the unions and industrial and financial institutions. In the late 1980s and early 1990s, financial crises exposed substantial problems in both the private and public sectors, which led to the worst economic downturn since the 1930s. The problems not only reflected abnormal cyclical fluctuations but were also related to longer term difficulties in the private sector, principally the slowdown in productivity growth in the 1970s which in turn led to pressure on the welfare system. One key question, therefore, is how we should explain the effects of this transition and the different performance of the economies in recent years?

Industrial transformation and change in Scandinavia reflects the impact of European integration as well as the existence of global competition. How has EC/EU membership affected Denmark's economy and, 20 years later, that of Sweden? From the Scandinavian countries' point of view, what are the pros and cons of the European Union? Why have Norwegians rejected entry on three separate occasions?

THE 1950s TO THE 1990s: AN OVERVIEW

In the period of recovery after the Second World War, along with much of Western Europe, between 1948 and 1954 Denmark and Norway received substantial capital under the Marshall Plan. Sweden, as a neutral non-combatant nation, did not need to undertake a process of reconstruction but none the less was the recipient of small amounts of Marshall Aid. Besides capital flows, efforts were made within the Marshall Plan to reorganise the Danish and Norwegian economies. American advisers visited Denmark and devised plans for more productive methods, at the same time as Danish technicians were sent to the US to receive new ideas about organizing companies more efficiently (Johansen 1987). One important motivation in the Marshall Plan was the opening of the European market to the US: the flow of dollars financed a greater volume of imports from the US to help with reconstruction, so that in due course Europe's recovery would provide markets for US producers. These changes facilitated increased overseas trade activity in Scandinavia which fuelled the post-war boom.

Generally, economic growth in Scandinavia had been equal to or higher than the West European average from the late nineteenth century on. It was markedly superior in the inter-war period, and in addition Sweden benefited from its neutrality during the Second World War. As a consequence, the Scandinavian economies were near the top of the league in terms of productivity and income per capita in Europe. Over the period 1950 to 1973, the annual average rate of growth of per capita GDP in all three economies accelerated to just over

3 per cent[2] (see Table 7.1). This faster growth throughout Scandinavia added markedly to general standards of affluence, but, nevertheless, as it was below the West European average of 4.7 per cent, their leading position was eroded somewhat.

Table 7.1 *Growth of per capita GDP: Denmark, Norway and Sweden vis-a-vis Western European average* (%)

	1870–1913	*1913–50*	*1950–73*	*1973–94*
Denmark	1.6	1.6	3.1	1.6
Norway	1.3	2.1	3.2	2.9
Sweden	1.5	2.1	3.1	1.2
W. Europe (12)*	1.3	1.2	3.8	1.8

*Excludes southern Europe and Ireland.
Source: Maddison (1995), Table 3–2, p. 62.

The higher growth rates between 1950 and 1973 compared to inter-war performance reflected the usual forces. There was, for example, greater accumulation of physical capital – the ratio of investment to GDP was rarely less than 20 per cent per annum. But the major contribution came from 'Total Factor Productivity' (TFP) which explained by far the largest proportion of growth rates – Henrekson et al. (1996) argue that in Sweden TFP was responsible for 70 per cent of the growth rate between 1950 and 1960, and became even more significant in the 1960s and 1970s. The existence of high levels of human capital of course facilitated technological change: a good deal of attention had traditionally been paid to human capital – not only in the sense of formal education, health care, and so on, but also in terms of policies directed toward the retraining and mobility of the labour force, particularly in Sweden.

As elsewhere in Europe, 'catch-up' was at work in all three economies. This was less significant for Sweden than for the other two countries, however, as productivity levels were already among the highest in Europe. For example, Maddison (1996) has Sweden's labour productivity at some 56 per cent of the US level in 1950, compared with 46 per cent in Denmark and 43 per cent in Norway. The European average at that time was 40 per cent.

It was during these years of continuous expansion that the foundations of the welfare state were consolidated and the political consensus about the nature of the 'good society' became complete. Throughout the period there was also an awareness that small, open economies needed to be flexible and competitive in international terms.

However, as in other European countries, the rapid growth of the post-war period was followed by a deceleration consequent upon the two oil price shocks in the 1970s. Sweden in particular has performed poorly – from 1973 to 1995 the average growth rate decreased to 1.6 per cent per annum. This compares with some 2.2 per cent in Denmark and 3.5 per cent in Norway. The deceleration in growth was not as sharp in Norway as in the other countries. This was largely a consequence of the discovery of oil and gas in the North Sea and the export revenues generated by this crucial product from the 1970s onwards. By contrast, Denmark and Sweden suffered severely from the two oil price shocks – although there is some evidence of a deterioration of Sweden's performance prior to 1973. Deep-seated problems affected most industries and households, and eventually led to substantial changes in industrial and fiscal policy. The economies did not recover from this hangover until the mid-1980s, when they all enjoyed a spurt in output growth. This seemed to be the result of a cyclical upturn, however, and the timing was slightly different in each case. Denmark's spurt actually started in 1982 and lasted until 1986; for Norway the timespan was 1983 to 1986, and for Sweden the period really only covered the two years, 1984 and 1985. This improved performance, however, was possible largely because of the existence of spare capacity – it did not reflect an improvement in productivity growth which was negative in Denmark in 1986 and was growing very slowly in Sweden. This period coincided with a reorientation of economic policy from state regulation toward market solutions.

Substantial liberalization of the capital market, in harmony with the international environment, was undertaken in both the EC-member Denmark and the two non-members Norway and Sweden. With more or less continuous deregulation in the 1980s, a very generous supply of credit was facilitated and this in turn added risks to the economic boom: after a jump in annual growth rates to between 4 and 5 per cent in 1984 and 1985, the acceleration ended brutally in the late 1980s, and particularly in the early 1990s. Major financial crises then occurred which threatened the banking systems of Norway and Sweden. The combination of the short boom and financial deregulation had induced the banks into ill-considered and overoptimistic lending operations.

Denmark suffered least, but Norway had some very difficult years in the late 1980s, including price deflation and considerable use of public funds by the state to rescue the banking system. In Sweden the growth rate was negative for a period of three years, and the country experienced the worst depression since the 1930s. One long-term result of the crisis was unemployment rates at considerably higher levels than before (see Table 7.2).

Historically, in terms of unemployment, Denmark has had a different experience compared to Norway and Sweden. With the exception of the 1960s, recorded unemployment in Denmark has on average been almost twice that in Norway and Sweden respectively. These different performances reflect contrasting views of economic policy and the role of the state, especially with regard to the nature of the social security system. Denmark has generally been more reluctant to utilize active public support and intervention in the labour market. By contrast, in addition to direct cash benefits, both Norway and Sweden provided substantial retraining and re-education programmes as well as other social support. The underlying incentive was to maintain the saleability of labour power, at the same time as people were reintegrated into society. However, the effect of these measures, which have been termed 'Active Manpower Policy', introduces problems when comparing unemployment statistics across countries. The labour force engaged in retraining programmes is not gainfully 'employed', but nor do they appear in the officially measured unemployment rate. In other words, since people are involved in various programmes, we have to distinguish between openly unemployed and unemployed *though temporarily occupied* in training programmes. Early retirement also has to be considered, as this amounted to nearly 4 per cent of the Swedish labour force in the mid-1990s. If these latter groups are included in the total rate of unemployment, the differences between Norway and Sweden on the one hand and Denmark on the other, become less significant. Nevertheless, by use of such measures Norway and Sweden had, throughout the 1970s and for most of the 1980s, been able to maintain very low rates of unemployment by European standards. Following the financial crises, however, they moved much closer to the European average and, given existing pressures on public expenditure, it is unlikely that they will see a rapid return to former levels.

Table 7.2 *Rate of unemployment in Denmark, Norway and Sweden 1960–94, % of labour force*

	Denmark	*Norway*	*Sweden*
1951–60	4.3	2.1	1.8
1961–70	1.4	1.9	1.7
1971–80	4.6	1.7	2.4
1981–90	9.1	3.0	2.9
1991	10.5	5.5	2.7
1992	11.2	5.9	4.8
1993	12.2	6.0	8.2
1994	12.1	5.4	8.0

Sources: Derived from Maddison (1991) p. 262. *European Economy* various years.

The inflation rate, measured as changes in consumer prices, has been rather similar in all the Scandinavian economies. Although sometimes more rapid economic growth is accompanied by rapid inflation, by the use of highly articulated incomes policies, governments were able to keep down inflation rates during the long boom after the Second World War. The Bretton Woods system of fixed exchange rates with the dollar as the anti-inflationary anchor certainly helped to maintain relatively low inflation rates until the early 1970s, but as a result of international factors such as the inflationary financing of the Vietnam War and the oil price hikes, both wholesale and consumer prices began to increase sharply in the mid-1970s. The long upward trend of prices accelerated from the second half of the decade until the late 1980s, when the inflation rate varied between 5 and 10 per cent per year in all the countries.

Fluctuations in the balance of payments have increased over the post-war period, which is partly the result of growing international dependence at a time when the global economy has become more unstable. In addition, national debt has increased substantially as budget deficits mounted steadily as a result of welfare state commitments. While there is no straight correlation between high debt and a weak economy, the combination of rapid increases in national debt plus larger budget and / or balance of payments deficits indicates potential problems in the future.

The major cause of the various financial problems – inflation, payments difficulties and debt – was the two oil price shocks of the 1970s. Norway was better placed to cope but in Sweden and Denmark oil imports provided about 75 per cent of domestic energy consumption, so the price rise was particularly problematical. In addition, since the international economy was heading downwards, there was little chance to cover the increased foreign outlays by expanding exports. The impact on the balance of payments was very severe with deficits as a percentage of GDP escalating sharply to over 5 per cent for Denmark and in excess of 3 per cent for Sweden.

While the OPEC countries deposited their increased revenues in international banks – approximately $147 billion (50 per cent) of the total – the importing countries had to borrow internationally to cover their payments deficits. Among industrialized countries, the size of the payments deficits and the required borrowings caused by fuel expenditures reflected several factors: geography and climate, the availability of substitutes for oil, the existence of oil reserves of their own, and the liquidity and solvency of the national economy. For Scandinavia the situation varied: in Denmark, with a milder climate and alternative fuel sources, there was a shift towards coal in thermal power stations; in Sweden the rapid development of nuclear power eased the transformation to electricity-based energy, and reduced at the same time long-term dependency on oil; Norway, despite its difficult climate, was in a much better position as a result of North Sea oil and gas. Furthermore, Norway was already less dependent on oil because of extensive hydroelectric sources. In addition to these balance of payments problems, fiscal deficits from the mid-1970s led to greater domestic and international borrowings by the state. These comprised new credits to meet new commitments and to finance rising interest rates on existing loans. National debt in relation to GDP increased rapidly in most Western European countries from the 1970s on and Scandinavia was not totally immune from these trends. In Denmark, the national debt as a proportion of GDP increased by more than three-quarters between 1972 and 1984. The percentage in Sweden rose from 19 per cent to 61 per cent during the same period, while the figure in Norway was steady at around 25 per cent, thanks to revenues derived from the exploitation of oil and gas. Indeed, by the mid-1990s Norway, after years of amortization, had virtually no state debt left.

The problems in the 1970s, however, can only explain part of the continuing difficulties in the 1980s and the 1990s. In Denmark, the shift to the right-wing government in 1982 implied, among other things, the implementation of a fixed exchange rate and a reorientation of the monetary regime. The reining in of public spending and the consolidation of the budget – moves which were to become a feature of economic policy throughout Western Europe in the 1990s – allowed interest rates to fall quickly. This is often put forward as an explanation for the stronger growth performance of the Danish economy thereafter, but the price has been higher unemployment.

In Sweden, developments took the opposite course. For the left-wing government that returned to power in 1982, devaluation of the currency became the prescription for the economy's difficulties. When the financial crisis burst less than ten years later, the Swedish economy was exposed to substantial structural problems which the effects of devaluations had not and could not solve. After several years of increasing budgetary deficits, related to expensive labour-market policies and an extensive social welfare programme, state indebtedness began to accelerate with serious difficulties in terms of the increasing taxes and the willingness of the electorate to accept the burden.

ECONOMIC STRUCTURE

Economic structure reflects the international comparative advantage of the Scandinavian economies. Thus among the dominant industries in Denmark are fishing and agriculture – particularly dairy farming and food processing. The food industries in the early 1990s accounted for one in five industrial employees, and generated one-third of total industrial production by value. Engineering also enjoys a prominent position in the business structure, reflecting high levels of technical education. Other important segments of manufacturing are chemicals and medicine, porcelain, toys and furniture. Although the share of employment in industry remains substantial from an international perspective, various private and public services have increased their proportions and constituted 67 per cent of employment by 1990 (see Table 7.3). Since this includes a growing financial sector as well as services related to information, human capital and tourism, the change is not all accounted for by a larger public sector.

As with other economies, industry's contribution to employment has contracted sharply. By comparison, industry's share of GDP has not suffered the same fate (it must also be remembered that GDP by 1990 was more than three times larger than 1950). In comparison with Denmark, Norway has seen a faster contraction of the share of employment attributable to industry but the share of GDP which comes from this sector has held up much more strongly. This is partly a function of the very substantial output of the gas and oil sectors. Hence Norway's industrial structure is dualistic in that one sector is export-orientated, based on natural resources and dominated by large firms; while the other part is orientated toward the domestic market and contains mainly specialized, flexible, small and medium-sized enterprises. This pattern was already evident in the 1960s and was reinforced when the oil economy took off in the 1970s. The consequences for the Norwegian economy were even greater than during the transformation of traditional industry back in the nineteenth and early twentieth century (Sejersted 1993, p. 199).

Table 7.3 *Sectoral distribution of employment and value added 1950–90 (%)*

	Agriculture		*Industry*		*Services*	
	1950	*1990*	*1950*	*1990*	*1950*	*1990*
Denmark						
Employment	25.1	6.0	33.3	27.0	41.6	67.0
Value added	10.0	6.3	28.5	27.7	61.5	66.0
Norway						
Employment	29.8	6.4	33.2	24.8	37.0	68.8
Value added	16.0	2.9	39.0	34.7	45.0	62.4
Sweden						
Employment	20.3	4.0	40.8	29.0	38.9	68.0
Value added	9.0	3.4	29.8	32.2	61.2	64.4

Note: Agriculture includes forestry and fisheries; industry includes mining, public utilities and construction; services includes public and private sector services.

Sources:
Figures for 1950 are derived from Maddison (1991) p. 248.
Figures for 1990 are from OECD Country Surveys.

The discovery of oil and natural gas also produced a substantial upswing for petrochemicals during the following decade when very large investments were made to develop the industry (about NKr 380 billion over the period 1983–93). Although some of these investments were funded domestically, from the Norwegian security market, the majority of the capital was imported and raised by private firms involved in the industrial activities. There remains considerable state financial interest in the oil and natural gas industries. When the Western European shipping and ship-building industry lost its primacy in the late 1970s, this sector also suffered severely in Norway, which had traditionally been one of the most important shipping nations. Without the help from investment by the oil and petrochemical industries, as well as the industry's own ability to diversify into the construction of oil rigs and production platforms, ship-building would hardly have survived the 1980s. Similar problems hit engineering, but this too has recovered. Particularly important new branches are the electrochemical and electrometallurgical industries. Thus

Norway is the world's largest exporter of magnesium and furosilicum and the world's second largest exporter of aluminium. At the same time, traditional activities belonging to a rurally based economy are still important in Norway: fishing and timber remain significant even if their contribution has become proportionately smaller in recent years.

In Sweden, mining, forestry and the manufacturing industry have historically been dominant branches. Since the late nineteenth century a handful of multinational firms, largely in engineering, have dominated the industrial sector. The Swedish business structure is nevertheless diverse and contains, to a higher degree than the other Scandinavian countries, a group of globally based concerns. Within the manufacturing industry, iron, steel and other metals are important. In addition the plastic, rubber and mineral industries play a significant role. An even more traditional sector is the forestry, wood and pulp industry. As in other European countries, after the Second World War, new sectors have been added: the motor and pharmaceutical industries, as well as industries related to the environment and retailing, have expanded in Sweden. The latter are based not on technical innovation but on new distribution and marketing techniques.

Structurally, the shift from a rural to an industrial economy, and recently to a service society, shows up in the Swedish case as well. The number of people occupied in agriculture as a proportion of total employment decreased from over 20 per cent in 1950 to 4 per cent by 1990. During the same period the share of employment in the service sector rose from less than 40 per cent to nearly 70 per cent. The service sector's contribution to GDP was nearly two-thirds of the total by the 1990s.

This shift can also be illustrated by figures showing the differential contributions to the *growth* of GDP coming from manufacturing and services. From 1950 to 1973 the annual increase in manufacturing output was between 4 and 5 per cent whereas this fell to 1.4 per cent on average after 1973. By comparison, the growth of output from the services sector had been 3.5–4.5 per cent and decelerated much less to around 2.5 per cent per annum. In comparison with other OECD countries, the Scandinavian countries have been doing worse than the average, particularly since 1973.

INTERNATIONAL TRADE

As relatively small economies international trade is extremely important for Scandinavia and the post-war period has been marked by increasing openness: all three economies have high ratios of exports to GDP – over 25 per cent in the case of Denmark and Sweden and more than 33 per cent for Norway. This openness reflects the traditionally liberal attitudes to international trade and payments which have been a feature of all three countries. As suggested above, geography has shaped the profile of the industrial structure, but in addition has influenced export orientation: for Norway it has been natural to seek its trading partners in the Anglo-American world, while continental Europe and specifically the UK have been the most important customers for Denmark. As for Sweden, the proximity of Eastern Europe and Russia led to the early establishment of trade and other links with these areas. These developments were interrupted by the communist revolution in Russia in 1917 and the occupation of Eastern and Central Europe after 1945, so in the early post-war period Sweden had to develop stronger relationships in Western Europe and in North America.

In terms of balance of payments performance there is some similarity: after having had a relatively strong negative balance until 1978, Norway moved into export surplus in the latter part of the period as oil and gas revenues began to come on-stream. The other two countries, too, have improved their trade balance, from a deficit in the 1970s to a surplus. One reason is simply the falling real price of oil and other raw materials, but also various policy changes have led to this positive development.

INTERNATIONAL BUSINESS

Since the industrial breakthrough in the nineteenth century, Scandinavian business has been international and an established part of the European network of entrepreneurs, innovators and bankers. In 1995, four Swedish and two Norwegian firms were among the world's 100 largest businesses, measured by number of employees. Ranked by profits and sales, Scandinavian representation declines to three large firms. Some have explained this international profile with country-specific causes, such as access to local natural resources, a strong emphasis on human capital and an early system of technical education. Others have stressed the liberalization movement in the middle of the nineteenth century, which provided valuable institutions as a platform for high economic growth during the following century (Myhrman 1994).

The climate for domestic business generally changed sharply from the late 1960s onwards: many industries failed to compete with more productive international firms. Thus textiles and the shipping industry experienced severe losses due to increasing efficiency and lower wages in similar industries in Iberia, Japan and South Asia. Hence there was a growing recognition that the internationalization of business was a necessary outcome. In relation to total world GDP the share of Scandinavian international business activity is quite impressive (Olsson 1993a, pp. 99, 107). For example, in terms of global foreign direct investment (FDI), in the early 1990s Sweden accounted for 4 per cent while the contribution to world trade was less than 2 per cent. Internationalization took place in two waves: before and after 1977 (see Tables 7.4 and 7.5).

Table 7.4 *Swedish outward and inward foreign direct investment 1961–90* ($US billions)

	Outward	*Inward*
1961–65	342	87
1966–70	703	662
1971–75	1 556	368
1976–80	2 864	507
1981–85	5 115	848
1986–90	21 332	5 107

Source: Olsson (1993a), p. 108.

During the first period the yearly net outflow of capital in the form of FDI increased eightfold in constant prices. After some years of stagnation, the yearly growth in the value of FDI increased to almost 30 per cent between 1979 and 1988. The second wave also reflected the global trend of liberalization of foreign exchange controls. This allowed the actors not only to invest in financial and real assets abroad, but also to take advantage of profits abroad through an increasing capital inflow back home. Figures on Norway exhibit the same pattern and reflect efforts made by the government since 1981 to encourage domestic industry to become more international (Hodne 1993, p. 135–6). The volume of foreign direct investment in relation to gross capital formation was doubled between 1986 and 1990 (from 14 to 29 per cent). Investments were concentrated geographically, largely in Denmark, Sweden, the UK and the Netherlands, but the total EC/EU area represented nearly half of all investments.

Figures for Denmark also show how rapidly the economy is becoming internationalized: there has been an acceleration in the number of new foreign establishments throughout the twentieth century (see Table 7.5).

Table 7.5 *Number of foreign establishments in Denmark and average number of employees*

	No. establishments abroad	*Av. no. employees per estab.*
1900–50	16	371
1951–64	54	165
1965–75	112	83
1976–83	165	38
1984–86	136	34
1987–89	208	36
Total	691	53

Source: Pedersen et al. (1993), p. 44.

Taking a period of 90 years, nearly half of all foreign establishments (344) occurred between 1984 and 1989. Some of them, however, were the result of mergers and acquisitions (137 out of 636). As for the number of persons employed per establishment, there has been a strong tendency toward fewer people, reflecting the almost universal trend to 'downsizing'. Also, in the early years it was more common to establish large production plants in comparison with service-based activities today. The directions of international operations have, in the Danish case, reflected the geographical position of the country (see Table 7.6). This means a bias in the foreign establishments towards neighbours such as the UK, Germany and Sweden.

Table 7.6 *Foreign establishments in Denmark identified by host country, 1991 (%)*

UK	16
Germany	14
Sweden	11
USA	9
Norway	8
France	6
Other	36

Source: Pedersen et al. (1993).

To some extent, the process of internationalization of large firms has been one of the barriers to further enlargement of the public sector – in Sweden particularly. The state loses control over the firms' activities and tax revenues when markets become globalized and activities are located overseas. Potential tax revenue disappears from the home country as value added and the supply of jobs migrates. Among the 20 largest Swedish firms, more than half of their employees work outside the country (Olsson 1993b). Since there is not the same level of foreign direct investment coming into Sweden, the net result for employment is negative. In a situation where they are faced with high levels of taxes and other social costs (largely associated with the welfare system), many international firms decided to locate their new plants in countries with a friendlier business climate.

If the major firms leave the home country, the economy comes to rely more on small and medium-sized firms. In this respect, there is a high proportion of smaller firms in Denmark – above the European average (see Table 7.7). In Sweden, however, the situation is the opposite, with a very dominant large-firm sector and a tiny sector of small and medium-sized enterprises.

There is a metaphor for the Swedish business structure, which uses the idea of a 'schnapps glass': with a wide top, a thin neck and a small base. Such a dominant large-firm sector is, even from an international perspective, quite unusual. Taking into account the effects of global competition, such an asymmetric formation might be a disadvantage: financial problems in only one or two major firms mean difficulties for the whole economy. Also, the main political focus tends to remain on the performance of large firms even though their contribution to the creation of employment and tax revenues diminishes. While domestic manufacturing employment decreased by approximately 100 000 in Sweden between 1960 and 1986, employment in *foreign* branches of the Swedish multinationals increased by 150 000 (Swedenborg 1992, p. 92). If we add the number of people occupied in other Swedish affiliates overseas, the multinationals in 1986 employed nearly as many abroad as in Sweden. With regard to sales, the domestic market halved in importance for the multinationals between 1965 and 1986, from 47 to 23 per cent of total sales, which illustrates an ongoing shift towards further globalization and how dramatically international dependency has increased for the Scandinavian countries.

Table 7.7 *Percentage distribution of business sector employment by enterprise size, 1991*

	Enterprise size (no. of employees)				
	1–19	*20–199*	*200–499*	*500+*	*Total*
Denmark*	40	23	17	20	100
Norway	41	30	10	19	100
Sweden	18	17	7	58	100
France	29	21	16	34	100
Germany	26	19	18	37	100
UK**	33	16	17	34	100

* Private economy except extractive industries.
** 1–19 includes sole proprietorships.
Sources: OECD *Economic Survey* Denmark, August 1994, p. 62; Statistik sentralbyrå, *Statistics Norway*, SCB, Företagarregistret.

PUBLIC AND PRIVATE SECTOR

In the first three decades after the Second World War the demands on the public sector were almost insatiable. In Norway, local and central government spending accounted for nearly 50 per cent of GDP by 1980, compared with 26 per cent in 1950 (Hodne 1983, p. 227; see also Table 7.8). Denmark and Sweden faced the same problem even more acutely – by 1980 public expenditure in relation to GDP rose to 56 per cent in Denmark and over 62 per cent in Sweden. The driving force in this expansion was essentially transfer payments, as can be seen in sections A and B of Table 7.8. In each case public consumption, that is, exhaustive spending, takes a smaller share of total spending by 1980 compared with 1960. Nevertheless, the expansion of public consumption – spending on goods and services – is also very strong in every case. In 1993, during the recession, government expenditures – exhaustive spending plus transfer payments – in Sweden peaked at 73 per cent of GDP.

Table 7.8 *Expansion of the public sector in Scandinavia 1960–85*

	1960	*1965*	*1970*	*1975*	*1980*	*1985*
A. Total public expenditure (% of GDP)						
Denmark	24.8	29.9	40.2	48.2	56.2	50.9
Norway	29.9	34.2	41.0	46.6	48.9	48.1
Sweden	31.1	36.1	43.7	49.3	62.1	64.5
B. Public consumption (% of GDP)						
Denmark	13.3	16.3	20.0	24.6	26.8	25.3
Norway	12.9	15.0	16.9	19.3	18.8	18.6
Sweden	15.8	17.8	21.6	23.8	28.9	27.4
C. Share of public sector employment in total employment (%)						
Denmark	–	13.2*	16.8	23.6	28.3	
Norway	12.0	13.9	16.4	19.2	21.9	
Sweden	12.8	15.3	20.6	25.5	30.7	

*1966.
Sources: OECD *Historical Statistics;* OECD *National Accounts;* Mjöset (1986).

In the early post-war period, the labour force was still moving from agriculture to the industrial sectors, a common pattern of structural adjustment. The new ingredient in Scandinavia, however, was the expanding public sector, which recruited people from both the agrarian and industrial spheres. Later still, surplus labour from the declining parts of manufacturing industries, such as textiles, was absorbed by the growing public sector, although some people also had to join the long-term unemployed. While a major part of the new generation of Swedes became civil servants from the 1960s onwards, industrial jobs were taken mainly by immigrants. In the 1950s and 1960s, workers in the expanding manufacturing industries were, especially in the Swedish case, recruited from Finland, the Baltic countries and the former Yugoslavia.

As to civil servants in general, during the 1960s, personnel in government services, and so on, expanded very rapidly – for example, in Denmark this rose from 12 to 20 per cent of the labour force and reached nearly 30 per cent by 1980. Hence it comes as no surprise that the expanding public sector was already being questioned by social commentators in Denmark by the 1970s. It was not until the return of right of centre governments in 1982 that real efforts were made to reduce the size and growth of the state – after a standstill in employment between 1983 and 1985 it was increasing again by 1986. By mid-decade, it was obvious in all three Scandinavian countries that 'a clash between a slow-growing economy and an expanding public sector had become inevitable' (*The Economist* 18–24 February 1994, p. 6). The serious consequences of the structural problems were illustrated by the recession of the early 1990s when industrial production in Sweden fell by 17–18 per cent. This strongly affected the labour market but, compared to 30 years before, the public sector was already overlarge and could not absorb the newly unemployed. A rapid rise in unemployment increased the pressure on social security programmes. Benefit spending and a fall in tax revenues implied further difficulties for the public purse, causing widening deficits. In Sweden, public spending on social protection in the 1980s was 33 per cent of GDP – fully twice as much as in the US (15 per cent).

A solid and large public sector presupposes a strong private economy, and at the same time the content of the public sector influences the scale and the scope of the private one. One critical issue for how vigorous the public sector can be, however, is the level and rate of growth of productivity in the private economy. Looking at Scandinavia, the high rate of growth of 4 per cent per annum was interrupted in the mid-1970s (see Table 7.9), and productivity growth thereafter fell to under 2 per cent in Denmark and Sweden in the 1980s. In Norway, as might be expected, however, the downward trend was less marked.

Table 7.9 *Annual percentage increase in productivity in the private sector 1960–88*

	1960–73	*1973–9*	*1979–88*
Denmark	4.3	2.6	1.5
Norway	4.2	3.9	3.0
Sweden	3.9	1.4	1.6
OECD average	4.4	2.3	2.2

Source: OECD (in Korpi 1992, p. 145).

Falling productivity was not confined to Scandinavia: the development was observed in the whole industrialized world. The oil price shocks implied an international fall in the utilization of capacity. As opposed to the first decades after the Second World War, many economies were not able to make full use of productive potential. The issue of whether Scandinavia, especially Denmark and Sweden, were doing much worse than other OECD countries has been the subject of intense discussion among scholars (see, for example, Korpi 1992). Depending on the statistical methods and the years of measurement chosen, the results differ. There has also been a political dimension to the discussion;

namely, attitudes toward a continuous transfer of resources to an expanding public sector and a more developed welfare system, and whether this could be seen as a cause of a lower level of profits in the private sector and a lower level of growth for the economy in general.

KEYNESIANISM TO NEO-LIBERALISM

In the mid-1940s the Scandinavian economies had adopted Keynesianism as the major policy framework.[3] Indeed, in the 1930s, before Keynes's ideas were widespread, there was a consensus among economists and politicians about the long-term benefits of state intervention in various economic sectors to keep up employment and reduce fluctuations in the economy. By encouraging the public sector, investing in infrastructure and giving subsidies to housing, new jobs were created. The introduction of a more or less planned economy in Scandinavia took place at the same time as Social Democracy was established as the dominant political ideology. Hence economic achievements after the Second World War do not stem from pure socialism nor from economic liberalism. The mix of state plans and market forces was essentially reformed capitalism, with roots in both traditions. By the 1970s some institutional changes, especially in relation to resource allocation, labour and industrial policies (particularly nationalization), carried the stamp of Marxist ideas. But later, in the 1980s, the middle way in economic policy was re-established.

The term 'mixed economy' is best used to characterize the regime. Within this framework, the function of the private sector is to obey the institutional rules that constitute the market, which in turn is conditioned by overriding macroeconomic goals decided by the government. In order to keep control over the mixed economy, the political system regulated the market very heavily. Although low interest rate policy from the inter-war years was given up, a fiscal policy of high income taxes, higher duties and compulsory savings was established. To direct the flow of credit and investments, restrictions were imposed on the capital market: until the early 1980s, there were, for example, restrictions on bank borrowing, bond issues and foreign loans.

Governments directed support to certain favoured sectors – mainly housing, infrastructure and the industrial sector. This so-called '*kredittsosialisme*' (Sejersted 1993, p. 190) prescribes extensive public support to industry even when this is financially insolvent. Most public institutions identified with left-of-centre policies with the implied objective of protecting the decreasing numbers of jobs. However, in many cases, industrial and financial policy was counterproductive, as the state was simply throwing good money after bad and disguising the seriousness of the situation.

In some cases, the content and timing of policy were exactly right: thus efforts were made in the 1960s, especially by Norway, to attract large industries to invest in the country. This policy was successful and led, for example, to the establishment of an aluminium industry on a large scale (Sejersted 1993, p. 191). Low energy costs, through extensive hydroelectric power, was the most important determinant in foreign investors' choice of Norway.

For many years the Scandinavian version of Keynesianism went hand in hand with the picture of the perfect welfare state. Economic growth in the 1950s and 1960s gave the illusion of an ever faithful couple and outside observers frequently looked to Scandinavia as *the* model of welfare capitalism. However, the 'marriage' broke down during the recession from the mid-1970s when budget and balance of payments deficits began to expand. Governments in Denmark and Sweden were forced to devalue their currencies; for example, Sweden had to depreciate the krona four times between 1976 and 1982. Finally, with a timelag of between five and ten years, the Scandinavian countries adopted the new economic policies coming from the US and the UK, that is, 'Reaganomics' and 'Thatcherism'. The impact of neo-liberalism and monetarism on government decision making was evident from the mid-1980s. Denmark was the first country fully to adopt the new liberal policies and, as suggested above, benefited from this reorientation quite rapidly as the consolidation of the budget allowed interest rates and inflation to fall sharply and this stimulated the economy such that 200 000 new jobs were created in the private sector and unemployment fell in 1983.

Although Denmark was the first Scandinavian country to adopt the new liberalism, in the first half of the 1980s constraints were lifted from capital markets in both Norway and Sweden. At the same time, new financial instruments were introduced in order to cover budget deficits and to pave the way for open-market operations by the central banks. The operations of the central bank in the market determined the development of short-term and long-term interest rates. The shift in Sweden was initiated and implemented by the Social Democrats and it was clearly a break with traditional policy. The strategy was heavily criticized by trade unions and the left-wing factions within the party. In the mid-1990s, after strong pressure from the left, there was a decision to move away from a reliance on monetary policy alone. Instead, the government started to use a combination of fiscal and monetary policies through taxes and inflation targets.

As indicated above, the shift toward liberalism embraced sectors other than the financial. Various types of controls were lifted from the transport, building and housing sectors. Monopolies were broken up and replaced by a competitive environment. The adoption of 'Thatcherism' also meant privatization of state-owned companies, although the state maintained considerable influence in the private enterprises that followed. In Sweden, state monopolies in the railways, telecommunications and energy were abolished in the late 1980s and 1990s. Except for railways, Norway followed suit. In Denmark, telecommunications were liberalized while the energy sector was partially deregulated.

Deregulation and privatization have certainly changed the structure of the Scandinavian economy. The state has more or less waived the right to maintain central collective services in society, but has also deprived itself of revenues from these organizations and firms. It is too early to evaluate the results and long-term implications of the new regime as teething problems have to be dealt with before matters of distribution of resources (equity), democracy (active participation through private ownership) and relative efficiency (profits) can be resolved satisfactorily.

The liberalization movement was temporarily interrupted in the late 1980s and early 1990s when the Scandinavian countries were hit by a deep recession and a major crisis in the financial system. Since the 1930s the authorities' approach to the banking system in Scandinavia had been one of very close control and tight rules on capital flows. After an attempt at deregulation in the 1970s, the authorities reinstituted the traditional approach, and then in 1984/5 a second wave of deregulation occurred. The banks shifted rapidly into new lines of business – expanding consumer credit and pushing for market share – without the same critical attitude to credit quality. The long tradition of regulation of the capital market made for a vacuum of competence when the rules were relaxed and the deregulation process had been so fast that education and training lagged behind in most institutions. The result was that bad loans and losses escalated rapidly and the central bank, as a lender of last resort, had to step in and rescue the banking system in both Norway and Sweden (and, incidentally, Finland). The cumulative cost to the public purse was very considerable: in Norway, in the years 1988–92, some 3 per cent of GDP (NKr 21 billion) was expended in rescue operations, while in Sweden 5.2 per cent of GDP (SKr 74 billion) was spent in 1991–3. Since many financially distressed firms went into bankruptcy, the question of the nature of public help in liquidity crises was a key issue in the debate. Negative consequences could not be prevented, however, and for the first time since the 1930s, Sweden experienced three years of falling GDP. Crucially, this did not lead to a reversal of the deregulation and privatization begun in the 1980s, so that by the mid-1990s many central elements in the mixed economy had been replaced by market-oriented functions. In sum, the question of whether a strong, generous Scandinavian welfare system was sustainable had to be asked.

END OF THE SWEDISH MODEL AND THE SCANDINAVIAN WELFARE SYSTEM?

The Swedish model was essentially a pragmatic model, not a theoretical model. Its main characteristics were a strong belief in social engineering, a corporatist state, and economic growth and political stability through the hegemony of a powerful Social Democratic Party. After the Great Depression, many argued that the market left to its own devices could not secure growth and full employment and that these required a stronger state role in the economy.

Substantial elements of the new regime were interventionist social measures, including housing programmes and active labour market policies. The economic parts of the model were informed by a Keynesian approach to macro management. The Stockholm School of economists – most prominently Ohlin, Myrdal, Lundberg and Lindahl – had in the early 1930s anticipated some of the ideas Keynes was to put forward, so that academic and political opinion was predisposed to Keynesianism. Hence this approach was very influential in the formulation of policy.

A key feature of the model was stable party government operating with a bias towards consensus, and although the operation of the model coincides with a long period of Social Democratic hegemony (1945–76), the essential principles were supported by most non-socialist parties. In addition, the existence of a nexus of neo-corporatist institutions was important for the introduction and implementation of new ideas, both inside and outside Parliament. A further basic feature was the pragmatic trade-off between capitalist and socialist values. This phenomenon involved accepting a strong relationship between the financial/industrial elite and the major political parties. There was consensus among most institutions, including the unions, that the economy as a whole would benefit from a solidaristic wage policy and extended social security.

In the 1980s, however, the Swedish model was questioned for the first time since the Second World War. This was the result of the overloading of government, tensions between private and public sectors and the effects of the internationalization of the economy. For example, the model abandoned the original Rehn–Meidner commitment, made in the late 1940s, to tight monetary policy and failed to keep down effective demand arising from private consumption and, in particular, public expenditure during the booms (see Lundberg 1985). A secular trend of steadily growing public expenditure was not a feature of the original Keynesian theory – instead, higher expenditure during recessions should have been offset by lower expenditure during booms so that over the economic cycle the budget was balanced. But this did not happen. Hence the pace of the increasing budget deficit led to urgent calls for some form of action.

The extensive welfare state was possible because of large revenues from the private sector. After having rationalized industry in the 1920s and 1930s, Swedes enjoyed a higher per capita income than many other European countries. In addition, as a result of war-time neutrality, a large part of Sweden's industrial structure was intact, and although the authorities feared an international slump, a substantial downturn never occurred; hence Swedish firms quickly reached a prominent position in the industrialized world.

In the middle of the 1960s, the Swedish model had reached its zenith. The government took advantage of the long boom to implement further reforms to the framework of the welfare system: the state decided it was capable of financing further rapid growth of the public sector. Unfortunately, however, it was becoming clear that there was a substantial difference in productivity growth between those sectors of the economy subject to external competition and the sheltered, largely public, sector. Henrekson et al. (1996) demonstrate that productivity grew at twice the rate in the competitive sector, but this was not reflected in the wage policy; hence costs rose sharply and as a consequence taxation started to take a progressively larger proportion of GDP.

Given the slowdown of productivity growth from the mid-1970s, the norms of wage determination previously regarded as satisfactory disappeared. The incompatibility between a less productive competitive trading sector and growing expenditure in the public sector required action. In spite of this, trade unions kept imposing burdens upon the system by demanding higher salaries and increased social expenditure. The losses in the industrial sector became even higher. The process hit labour-intensive industries, such as textiles, iron and steel and shipping, especially. The trade unions, supported by the government, seemed to assume that organized capitalism was capable of carrying indefinitely increasing burdens in the form of private consumption (wages) and extra public consumption. In the absence of substantial productivity growth, these demands imposed intolerable burdens on the real economy.

In addition, the general institutional setting as well as tax policy, did not encourage small and medium-sized firms to emerge and grow – instead the system was heavily biased toward investment within existing large firms which had the effect of ossifying competition.

Obviously, one reason for the breakdown of the model was the low incentive to increase productivity. Instead of changing wage policy, negotiators in the labour market simply pushed for high increases. Given the egalitarian aspirations which had been a feature of Swedish society, these wage increases would be generalized throughout the economy. However, a solidaristic wage policy and egalitarianism were only possible as long as consensus reigned and individuals were prepared to pay higher taxes. Until the early 1970s everyone seemed to benefit from better social, health and educational services, but by the early 1980s negative effects had begun to appear. As the marginal tax rate for persons in the upper income groups approached 100 per cent, they became reluctant to contribute to a continually growing public sector. Even ordinary workers faced marginal rates of tax of 60–90 per cent.

The egalitarian spirit, a crucial feature of the model, seemed to be dissipating. The difficulties of maintaining wage policies while striving for common goals and social provision in many areas of life were reflected in growing suspicions of politicians and a stronger emphasis on individual choice and spending. The free-rider problem was obvious as there was a strong temptation to cheat the state in one way or another – thus informal markets and tax evasion went hand in hand with lower incentives to search for a job, given how much was received through the extensive social security system. As a result the model was becoming counterproductive because it had lost its central driving features – consensus and collective responsibility.

In the early 1990s, the welfare system was struggling to fulfil some of the basic needs without considerably increasing foreign debt. To begin with, the recession in the 1970s had led to substantial budget deficits in both Denmark and Sweden. After the recovery, the main structural problems remained but the short-lived strong economic boom of the mid-1980s gave the illusion that the difficulties had blown over: in 1986 and 1987 budgets in Sweden were balanced, the economy was flourishing due to the devaluations in the early 1980s and in addition a return to growing prosperity seemed assured as there was an expectation of steadily increasing values in all kinds of assets (asset price inflation). By the 1990s it became clear that this was simply an illusion, and the ensuing financial crisis forced a major rethink.

There were numerous examples where substantial real resources in the public sector were combined with free provision at the point of consumption, which very often led to inefficiency and overallocation. For example, in Sweden the state's subsidy to housing disguised the real costs from the business and household sector. Between 1985 and 1990, costs in the building and construction sector exceeded the rise in consumer prices by about 100 per cent. The normal market signals would have implied less expenditure on housing, yet subsidies enabled individuals to afford larger accommodation than ever before (Larsson and Sjögren 1995, p. 183). Even in 1985, before the boom in the real estate market, room-space per capita was greater in Sweden than in the other Nordic countries, which are already well endowed by European standards. In 1988 the gross rent and construction subsidy in Sweden was over 2 per cent of GDP. The net subsidy (subtracting housing taxes) was +1.49 per cent of GDP in Sweden, whereas by comparison it was –2.44 per cent in the UK, –0.19 per cent in France, –0.03 per cent in Germany and –0.16 per cent in Denmark. These subsidies had the effect of distorting investment decisions as well as adding to the problems of controlling the budget deficit.

THE LABOUR MARKET

An active labour market policy was a key element in the Swedish model. Public expenditure for these policies was much higher than in any other country in the 1980s and only 10 per cent of the budget for the labour market went as cash support to the unemployed. The rest was spent on vocational training, education and encouragement of mobility. This reduced the dangers of structural unemployment and facilitated the shift of resources out of industrial production and trade. However, the goal of full employment was also maintained thanks to a simultaneous rise in public sector employment. This also helped to absorb the growing number of female workers. Thus the supply of female labour increased during the post-war period and reached exceptional levels in international terms in the early 1990s.

The high levels of female participation in the labour market partly reflected the emphasis on gender equality in Scandinavia. However, it was not a sudden change; rather an evolution during the whole post-war period which has mainly been embraced in the public sector. The proportion of women in the labour force has almost doubled since 1950 in both Norway and Sweden (see Table 7.10).

Table 7.10 *Women in the total labour force 1950–90 (%)*

	1950	*1960*	*1970*	*1980*	*1990*
Denmark	32	30	36	43*	46
Norway	24	23	28	41	45
Sweden	26	29	35	46**	48

* 1979 – No registration was done in 1980.
** 1981.
Sources: *Statistical Yearbook*, various years, SOS; *Yearbook of Nordic Statistics*, 1985 and 1995; Hodne (1983), p. 184; Johansen (1987), p. 189; *Studia Historica Jyväskylensia*, No. 27, 1983, p. 41.

Better opportunities for women to participate in the labour force are the result of many factors, such as rapid economic growth; a growing public sector; extensive child care services coordinated, run and subsidized by municipalities, and a movement toward equal incomes between men and women. Although the following quotation is a flippant illustration of increased female participation in Sweden, it catches the core of what critics of this transformation would argue:

> A large fraction of women work in the public sector to take care of the children of other women who work in the public sector to take care of the parents of the women who are looking after their children (*The Economist*, 18–24 February, 1994, p. 44).

By contrast, male participation in the labour market has declined somewhat; for example, because of child care. Sweden implemented a generous combination of parental leave, all-day child care and all-day school attendance, and this has resulted in lower participation. There is also a considerable gap between contractual and actual hours worked in Sweden compared to elsewhere (see Table 7.11). This is a result of several factors: the rules for sick leave have been generous and include time off to care for sick children; leave is also allowed for other family reasons, for example, to take care of close relatives; leave is granted for immigrants to study Swedish; and time off is allowed for education and trade union activity. The comparison for paid parental leave is also instructive – in 1987 this was 276 days in Sweden, 150 days in Norway and 70 days in Denmark (in Japan there were no allowances at all).

Table 7.11 *Contractual and actual hours worked by full-time employees in manufacturing (1990)*

	Contractual working hours per annum (A)	*Sick leave*	*Other leave*	*Actual working hours* (B)*	*B/A %*
Denmark	1 679	104	9	1 635	97
Norway	1 725	152	36	1 650	96
Finland	1 716	136	37	1 608	94
Germany	1 623	136	16	1 538	95
UK	1 778	96	18	1 664	94
Sweden	1 808	216	180	1 472	81

* Includes overtime hours.
Source: OECD *Economic Survey of Sweden*, January 1994, p. 89.

One reason for the original success of the Swedish model related to the size of the economy. Since the population was small and homogeneous, the implementation of rules set by the government was relatively easy. Neo-corporatist institutions, together with an extensive and organized bureaucracy, guaranteed that various asymmetries were efficiently adjusted to changes in the environment. However, when the long tradition of government by Social Democrats was overturned in 1976, some parts of the machinery were beginning to break down. The stability in Parliament, which was characteristic of the 'Golden Age', turned into a period of confrontation and unpredictability. Domestic instability was accompanied by growing international influences – mainly, but not exclusively, European. However, as well as the forces of competition, there were major domestic reasons for internationalization: as suggested above, because of tax policy and rigidities in the labour market, large firms felt less loyal to Sweden. To get cheaper labour and get away from a negative business climate, they increased foreign investment. Another reason for overseas investment, in Western Europe as a whole, was to surmount the common external tariff of the European Community.

To sum up, the Swedish model could be defined and interpreted in at least three ways. Using a strict definition, the model embraced the efforts to establish a solidaristic wage policy, where centralized wage negotiations between the two actors representing employees and employers was essential. From the political side, the incentive was to avoid open class conflict, which, in the event of success, would benefit both private and public interests. The economic ideas of full employment, high economic growth and price stability had been the inspiration for the model, but from the mid-1970s it became progressively more difficult to attain these objectives. When central negotiations were abandoned by the representatives of employees and employers in the 1980s, the Swedish model, at least in this operational form, had apparently come to an end.

If we consider the welfare state as the crucial element of the Swedish model, we may come to a different conclusion. It emerged during the recession in 1930s as a successful method to bring people back to work, by subsidizing investment in housing and infrastructure. During the post-war period, it continued as a giant project where the unemployed and women could more easily get access to the labour market and where many services in society became nationalized and channelled within an expanding bureaucracy. In this definition the Swedish model is not distinguished by a special wage policy but by the range and size of the public sector: in this case all the Scandinavian countries would qualify, given their comparatively high levels of state expenditure and employment in the public sector. Thus, in the sense of viewing the level of welfare as an indication of the persistence of the model, the Swedish version of the mixed economy is still alive, if under threat, in the late 1990s.

If by the Swedish model we mean a specific approach of 'compromise thinking' and a middle way between socialism and capitalism, we will get a similar answer. The tradition of compromise goes back a long way in the history of Scandinavia and has not disappeared, although it has recently been undermined by European integration and the globalization of industry and services. To maintain relations with the opposition and obtain mutual advantages has been a common objective in the behaviour of parliament, trade unions and industrial leaders during the post-war period. This could be interpreted as a form of corporatism where the state is centralized but still open, the bureaucracy professional but not authoritarian, and where policies are differentiated but have a central coordination (Rothstein 1991, p. 149). In this respect the Swedish model has sometimes been viewed as a nearly ideal-typical case of corporatism. The corporatist style, however, is not limited to Sweden: the mutually supportive process of state building and economic development after the Second World War in both Denmark and Norway is distinguished by various elements of corporatism. However, the role of the state is less obvious in Denmark: it exerts a lower degree of social control, has less use of public bureaucracy in the administration of benefits, more private schools, more private charity and generally less public intervention (Knudsen and Rothstein 1994, p. 216). By contrast, in Sweden, labour market policy has been characterized as a form of paternalistic corporatism, where it has been legitimate to force people to move from the countryside to the cities, then from areas with high unemployment to regions with better prospects. In the case of Norway, corporatism is certainly evident in the links between the state and the industry; that is, a rather strong central government role in major industries (Sejersted 1993, p. 199 ff.). What makes it so fruitful is the combination of a strong middle class, robust democratic institutions, powerful local networks and access to flexible specialization. Within this context the term 'corporatism' takes on a wider meaning, which makes it difficult to distinguish the expression from the concept of industrial capitalism. A comprehensive term for Scandinavian-type arrangements might be a 'combination', that is, 'corporative capitalism'.

This last perspective may suggest that in all three countries it is still relevant to talk about a Swedish/Scandinavian model, but it also seems clear that except for Norway the model is under severe strain.

INSIDE OR OUTSIDE EUROPE?

This issue has proved one of the most difficult and divisive in all the societies in Scandinavia. In 1973, Denmark became a full member of the European Community. The main argument for doing so was that the Danes' largest market – the UK – had decided to join. The same motivation had been at work in 1959 when Denmark was a signatory of the EFTA agreement because the UK was the leading player. Later, when the UK negotiated entry to the European Community, Denmark followed suit. However, this time the question was wider and more complex: first, a relatively large part of Danish trade was with non-EC countries; second, the Danish tax structure was different from the EC average; third, labour market problems were different.

Since 1973 moves toward deeper integration have evoked more scepticism in Denmark than in other EC countries: debates about the role of the Community institutions have split the political parties and these divisions have sometimes produced contradictory outcomes. Constitutionally, for example, this scepticism has led to the establishment of a unique committee in the Danish Parliament, where the decisions of the EU Council of Ministers have to be confirmed. Yet, at the same time, Denmark has dutifully incorporated more EC/EU directives into national laws than any other member. Similarly, while wishing to maintain close relationships with the European Union, Danes showed a reluctant frame of mind by voting narrowly against the Maastricht Treaty.

Whatever the doubts, Denmark has been, and still is, an active member of the Union – as is Sweden, having joined in 1995. However, Norway decided, after its latest referendum in 1994, to stay outside, thereby confirming the earlier decision of 1972. Why is opinion and political strategy in Norway so different from Denmark and Sweden? What have been the main arguments in Norway compared to Denmark and Sweden for opting or rejecting membership of the Union? Do Denmark and Sweden, because of their geographical position, have stronger links to continental Europe than Norway? Does it matter if a country is out of or in the EU, as long as it is prosperous like Norway or Switzerland?

A major issue in the debate in Norway and Sweden related to defence policy. This matter has to be seen in the context of developments in Eastern Europe and the geographical proximity to the former USSR. Concerns about strategic security were among the main arguments in the Norwegian debate, although these concerns did not succeed in bringing the country into the Union. Norway, a stalwart and long-time member of NATO, foresees a continuous disengagement by the US in Europe, and fears that this withdrawal will hurt economies on the periphery which are militarily and strategically important. US withdrawal would leave a vacuum which Western Europe would need to fill, yet there was and is a reluctance in the European Union to take on this mantle. Hence Norway's membership of the EU may only have accelerated US withdrawal without putting any real alternative in place. But in any case political unions are generally not very popular in Norway, after having experienced rule by its immediate neighbours until the early twentieth century. Norwegians therefore opted for continued independence instead of being incorporated in something open-ended and unpredictable.

In Sweden, with a history of 150 years of neutrality, defence and strategic issues never played a decisive role in the debate. After the Second World War, Sweden chose to go its own way in defence matters. In the early days of the Cold War, Swedish governments attempted to construct a neutral Scandinavian defence union. However, when Norway, and later Denmark, chose membership of NATO, this proposal had to be abandoned. Sweden therefore continued with a policy of non-alignment in times of peace, meaning neutrality in case of war. This did not mean disengagement in international affairs: on the contrary, during the whole post-war period, Sweden has been a major contributor of finance and personnel to conduct peace negotiations and/or action under the flag of the United Nations. However, membership of the EU may suggest a reorientation of this policy. Whether this will mean a total withdrawal from neutrality and a replacement of traditional security policy is still an open question, but a question which may increase in importance when integration problems in Europe and the relationship to non-European countries are on the agenda.

The argument in Sweden for joining the EU related principally to economic and commercial matters. In addition the decision was taken during one of the worst depressions in modern Swedish history: the years 1991–3 saw three successive falls in the GDP, and unemployment, having been considerably below the OECD average for most of the 1980s, jumped to over 9 per cent – exceeding the OECD average by nearly 2 percentage points – from 1993 onward (OECD *Economic Survey of Sweden* 1996, Annex Table 21). There was a clear need to increase investment, to calm markets and to keep up employment, so the key issue was to bring down interest rates as well as the state budget and national debt. It seemed to be possible that in such a situation in future, a helping hand from 'big brothers' in Europe might provide a safety net – at least, that might be the perception that brought marginal voters in Sweden to say 'Yes', while a similar group of people in a now more prosperous Norway said 'No'.

The result of the Norwegian and Swedish referenda also revealed a distinction between urban and rural areas. The polarization of voters was most evident in the case of Norway, where the northern parts in general voted 'No' and the southern parts said 'Yes'. Thus, since the major cities are located in the southern parts of both Norway and Sweden, the results partly revealed the difference in mentality between the rural and urban populations. Also, the distance to Brussels seemed to be positively correlated with interest in being a member of the EU; that is, the closer one lived to Brussels the more likely one was to vote 'Yes'.

The question of being inside or outside mainstream Europe as represented by the EU, remains a matter of major political debate in all the Scandinavian countries. Close results in referenda and elections, with marginal decisions by voters on either the 'Yes' side or the 'No' side reveal the general uncertainties shared by people in all three countries. This situation partly reflects geographical location – on the periphery of Europe – and the similarity of political / cultural roots, but other factors play a role. Some have been suspicious that, by being high income countries, they would be particularly welcome contributors to the solution of southern Europe's expensive social and economic problems. Many also believed that the tradition in Scandinavia of an open and democratic society might be compromised. More recently the question of EMU and the Single Currency has split both the Danes and the Swedes. In Sweden, election of members to the EU Parliament in 1995 showed some resistance to what is going on in Brussels. In a low turn-out, half of the votes were given to members that were against the EU. Clearly many Scandinavians were of the view that it would be better to stay outside. In contrast to this view there is an acknowledged need to be involved in international decision making. Such ambivalence has been evident in other policy areas in these small, open economies.[4] The question therefore has to be asked, are the Danes and the Swedes really committed to the EU? Particularly when, to be on the safe side, links are being developed further with the other Nordic countries through the Nordic Council and the Nordic Ministry Board.

In general, then, there are reasons both to stay inside and to be outside the European Union: as long as Denmark and Sweden perceive some tangible political and economic benefits – not only for government, but also for other actors such as business in these countries – they will remain persuadable with regard to further union. On the other hand, since both Norway and Iceland remain outside, there is no complete *Nordic* representation. In Scandinavia a rather schizophrenic view has weakened the political outcome: human and economic sources are divided between, on the one hand, Nordic cooperation without any strong international influence, and, on the other hand, an EU membership which lacks the leverage a solid Nordic bloc and full representation would bring. Scandinavian indecision is not unique, of course – other members of the European Union have similar doubts and equivocations, most obviously the UK; hence the argument for looser approaches to collaboration is shared with other countries.

Until there is greater consensus about defence issues, the labour market, welfare, foreign and monetary policy, the pros and cons of membership will remain actively debated and a residual scepticism will remain. Attitudes might become more favourable if the European Union could be persuaded on key issues to take a more obviously Scandinavian point of view. But even if that were to happen, given that these economies are small and very open, their cultural, social and economic linkages to non-EU countries will continue to play a significant role in the future.

NOTES

1. Other Nordic countries such as Iceland and Finland have been parts of Denmark and Sweden respectively, but we exclude them here for reasons of space.
2. In the case of Denmark, this disguises a slow start with growth at just over 2.5 per cent between 1950 and 1957, followed by a sharp acceleration to nearly 4.5 per cent between 1958 and 1973.
3. Some scholars stress that Keynesianism was evident in Swedish economic policy already in the 1930s, while 'fiscal policy pursued in Denmark had considerably more points of similarity with fiscal policy in Great Britain than with the Swedish policy of the 1930s' (Topp 1985, p. 339).
4. The ambiguity which characterizes attitudes in Scandinavia to international organizations can be found in other policy areas. For example, Denmark's membership of NATO had a conditional clause, saying that no military bases or nuclear weapons should be placed in the country. In the 1980s, an additional sentence was added forbidding the stationing of medium-range missiles. At the same time, the government decided to act for a Nordic Nuclear Free Zone.

REFERENCES

The Economist (1994) *Special Survey on the Nordic Countries*, 18–24 February.

European Economy, various years.

Henrekson, M., Jonung, L. and Stymne, J. (1996) 'Economic Growth and the Swedish Model' in Crafts, N. F. R., and Toniolo, G. (eds) *Economic Growth in Europe Since 1945*, Cambridge: Cambridge University Press.

Hodne, F. (1983) *The Norwegian Economy 1920–1980*, London: Croom Helm.

Hodne, F. (1993) 'The multinational companies of Norway', in G. Jones and H. G. Schörter (eds), *The Rise of Multinationals in Continental Europe*, London: Edward Elgar.

Johansen, H. C. (1987) *The Danish Economy in the Twentieth Century*, London: Croom Helm.

Knudsen, T. and Rothstein, B. (1994) 'State Building in Scandinavia', *Comparative Politics*, January, pp. 203–20.

Korpi, W. (1992) *Halkar Sverige efter? Sveriges ekonomiska tillväxt i jämförande belysning*, Stockholm: Carlssons Förlag.

Larsson, M. and Sjögren, H. (1995) *Vögen till och från bankkrisen, Svenska banksystemets förnådring 1969–94*, Stockholm: Carlssons Förlag.

Lundberg, E. (1985) 'The Rise and Fall of the Swedish Model', *Journal of Economic Literature*, Vol. 23, pp. 1–36.

Maddison, A. (1991) *Dynamic Forces in Capitalist Development*, Oxford: Oxford University Press.

Maddison, A. (1995) *Monitoring the World Economy*, Paris: OECD.

Maddison, A. (1996) 'Macroeconomic accounts for European countries', in B. van Ark and N. F. R. Crafts (eds) *Quantitive Aspects of Post-war European Growth*, Cambridge: Cambridge University Press.

Mjöset, L. (1986) (ed.) *Norden dagen derpå, De Nordiske Ökonomisk-politiske modellene og deres problemer*, p. 8, 70–80-talet, Oslo: Universitetsförlaget.

Myhrman, J. (1994) *Hur sverige bleu rikt*, Stockholm: SNS Förlag.

OECD (1996) *Historical Statistics 1960–94*, Paris: OECD.

OECD *Economic Survey for Denmark*, various years, Paris: OECD.

OECD *Economic Survey for Norway*, various years, Paris: OECD.

OECD *Economic Survey for Sweden*, various years, Paris: OECD.

OECD *National Accounts*, various years, Paris: OECD.

Olsson, U. (1993a) 'Securing the markets, Swedish multinationals in a historical perspective', in G. Jones and H. G. Schörter (eds), *The Rise of Multinationals in Continental Europe*, London: Edward Elgar.

Olsson, U. (1993b) 'Industrilandet', in *Äventyret Sverige, En ekonomisk och social historia*, Utbildningsradion och Bra Böcker.

Pedersen, T., Schultz, P. and Vestergaard, H. (1993) *Danske virksomheders etableringer i udlandet*, Copengagen: Handelshojskolens Förlag.

Rothstein, B. (1991) 'State Structure and Variations in Corporatism: The Swedish Case', *Scandinavian Political Studies*, Vol. 14, No. 2, pp. 139–71.

SOS *Statistical Yearbook*, various years.

Sejersted, F. (1993) *Demokratisk kapitalisme*, Oslo: Universitetsforlaget.

Statistik Sentralbyrå (1994) *Statistics Norway*, Oslo: SCB.

Studia Historica Jyväskylensia (1983) Historica IV, Fredrag vid det XVIII Nordiska historikermtet, No. 27 Jyväskyl 1981, Jyväskyln Yliopisto, Jyväskyl.

Swedenborg, B. (1992) 'Svenska multinationella företag', in *Sveriges Industri*, Industriförbundet.

Topp, N.-H. (1985) 'Influence of the Public Sector on Activity in Denmark 1919–39' *Scandinavian Economic History Review*, Vol. XLIII, No. 3, pp. 339–56.

Yearbook of Nordic Statistics, various years.

8 The Visegrad Countries of Eastern Europe

Nigel J. Swain

INTRODUCTION

This chapter is, of necessity, different from the others in this volume. First, we must consider not only issues of growth and stagnation, but also failure, decay and final collapse. For the events of 1989 brought to a clear end the socialist experiment, or at least, a particular type of socialist experiment, in Central and Eastern Europe. Second, the role of politics takes on more importance, because, in the case of the countries which we now call the Visegrad Four (Poland, Hungary, the Czech Republic and Slovakia), it was not governments pursuing policies to *influence* the economy, but rather planners who thought that they could *dictate* the pattern of output and the path of economic change. Third, because the cycles of growth, stagnation, decay and collapse were dictated primarily by problems encountered in trying to plan and only secondarily by developments in the international economy, the periodization is different (see Table 8.1).

Table 8.1 *Growth rates in Central Eastern Europe (annual percentage change of net material product*)*

	Czechoslovakia	*Hungary*	*Poland*
1951–55	8.1	5.7	8.6
1956–60	7.0	6.0	6.6
1961–65	1.9	4.5	6.2
1966–70	6.9	6.7	5.9
1971–75	5.7	6.3	9.7
1976–80	3.7	2.8	1.2
1981–85	1.8	1.4	–0.8
1986–90	1.0	–0.5	–0.5

*Net material product is based on Stalinist methods of National Income accounting which were mainly distinguished by the omission of Services. If the latter were included there is little doubt that the above figures would be considerably smaller.
Source: M. Lavigne (1995).

Recovery after the Second World War was relatively rapid. Under the forced socialist industrialization of the 1950s very high levels of growth were achieved. But these high rates of growth were based on extensive rather than intensive utilization of the factors of production, that is, by the simple expedient of increasing inputs rather than increasing the efficiency with which those inputs were utilized. Over the 1960s growth continued but the pace of advance declined and productivity failed to improve. Growth rates appeared to recover in the first half of the 1970s when the economies resolutely refused to adjust to the consequences of the oil shock in 1973/74. But they faltered in the later 1970s when politicians were finally obliged to recognize the new realities of the second oil shock. From 1979 on, the economies stagnated or declined with the final outcome being political revolution, privatization, market reform and 'shock therapy'. Initially the economies experienced even deeper recession, but it now appears that recovery is under way.

PRIOR TO 1945

In 1945, Czechoslovakia, Hungary and Poland were all young states which had handled their independent status with only modest success. They were all 'successor states' created after the First World War from the break-up of earlier empires. Indeed, Czechoslovakia was an entirely new country, the result of a last-minute notion to unite Bohemia and Moravia, the industrial powerhouses of the Austro-Hungarian Empire, with Slovakia, a backward agricultural area, and Ruthenia – both of which had been part of historic Hungary. Poland was a country with a glorious history as a medieval power, but for much of the nineteenth century was partitioned by Russia, Prussia and Austria-Hungary. Twentieth-century Poland had to be re-created out of three regions with very different experiences of nineteenth-century nation building and economic development. Finally, although Hungary as a political entity was not new, Hungary as a wholly independent country within the boundaries bequeathed by the Trianon peace settlement of 1919 certainly was.

In the aftermath of the First World War all three struggled to adjust their economies to new geo-political realities, to halt inflation and to create stable currencies. All witnessed a degree of prosperity in the late 1920s which was then shattered by the Great Depression and all were subsequently incorporated into Nazi Germany's 'economic space' in the latter part of the 1930s. By the mid to late 1930s only Czechoslovakia qualified as an industrial nation with 25.6 per cent of the labour force in agriculture and 28.3 per cent in mining and industry. By contrast, Hungary, with 50.8 per cent in agriculture and 23.0 per cent in industry, and Poland, with 65 per cent and 18.6 per cent respectively, were categorized as 'agricultural with significant processing facilities' (Spulber 1957 pp. 5, 21–2). Within Czechoslovakia it was only the Czech lands of

Bohemia and Moravia that were industrialized. Little was done in the inter-war period to industrialize Slovakia.

In 1945, therefore, all three countries faced the task of post-war reconstruction, just as Western Europe, but they had no tried and tested consensual economic or political structures to fall back on. Even Czechoslovakia, the most advanced, faced the need for deeper industrialization if it was to catch up with the more developed West. Poland, in addition, had 'shifted' westwards, ceding to the USSR about 46 per cent of its 1937 eastern territories and receiving territories that comprised 33 per cent of its new domain, encompassing land and materials but few people, which had been German for centuries (Landau and Tomaszewski 1985, p. 185). The problem of reconstruction and the manifest failure of inter-war economic and political institutions created a demand for new approaches to which socialist and communist politicians could appeal.

POST-WAR RECONSTRUCTION AND THE ORIGINS OF THE STALINIST SYSTEM

The key features of the Stalinist economic system which came to dominate Eastern Europe after 1945 were extensive nationalization and the creation of infrastructure for a command economy; that is, a planning office with separate ministries taking responsibility for the enterprises under their control. The imposition of the system was not uniform, however. Generally speaking, there were three categories of experience. For example, in the Balkan countries, Yugoslavia and Bulgaria, there was extensive popular support for socialists and communists so that revolutions were 'home made'. Hence nationalization followed hard on the termination of hostilities. In Czechoslovakia and Hungary, on the other hand, the USSR's immediate post-war requirements were no more than the existence of 'friendly' – not overtly anti-Soviet – states. As a result, large-scale nationalization did not take place until the latter part of the decade, after the 'Iron Curtain' had descended upon Europe. The situation in Poland was different again, because of the Soviet Union's outstanding territorial claims. Here Stalin had a need for a 'loyal' rather than a merely 'friendly' state, so he intervened immediately to ensure that a client regime was imposed.

Poland suffered most from the devastation of war. The loss of life alone was among the highest of the combatant nations: estimates put it somewhere between 5 and 6 million; that is, approximately 20 per cent of the pre-war population.[1] In addition, some 38 per cent of the capital stock had been destroyed while the territories newly acquired from Germany had been devastated by some of the heaviest fighting in the last months of the war (Myant 1982, p. 22). Athough as an Allied power Poland had no reparations payments to make, nevertheless the economy suffered from 'reparations related' problems. Much plant was removed by the USSR from the new western territories as 'war booty', and the Poles were required to deliver coal to the Soviet Union at disadvantageous prices as occupier of former German lands (Landau and Tomaszewski 1985, p. 195; Brus 1986a, p. 575; Radice 1986, pp. 516–17). In recompense, Poland received $480 million in aid from the United Nations Relief and Rehabilitation Administration (UNRRA) (Nötel 1986, p. 521). It is extremely difficult to make comparisons between pre- and post-war Poland because of its different territorial structure and an absence of accurate data, but by 1946 industrial production was probably at about 70 per cent of its 1938 figure (Landau and Tomaszewski 1985, p. 199). By 1948 national income and industrial production were more or less above pre-war levels (Brus 1986a, p. 626).

The first reform measure undertaken by post-war governments in all three countries related to agriculture. In all three countries, land reform in the inter-war years had promised more than it had delivered. In Poland, expropriation of land from Polish nobles and larger farmers accounted for some 24 per cent of the land distributed, the bulk (76 per cent) being taken from German owners (Brus 1986a, p. 586). Large-scale nationalization in Poland followed the cessation of hostilities and the Nationalization Act of 1946, which related to all enterprises employing more than 50 in any one shift, gave legal form to what was already a reality (Brus 1986a, p. 603). Nevertheless, at this early date it is clear that even in Poland the intention was not to import the Stalinist model wholesale. Thus an act promoting private industry passed in 1946 waived the 50-employee limit for *newly created* enterprises (Brus 1986a, p. 604). As international tension increased, however, the authorities began to attack the private sector in trade and took control of the cooperative sector. In 1948 the government took over enterprises with fewer than 50 employees and reorganized the banking system along Soviet lines. In early 1949 the State Commission for Economic Planning absorbed the Polish Central Planning Board (created in 1947) and introduced Soviet planning methods (Brus 1986a, pp. 610–14). Hence the necessary features for the socialist experiment were all in place by 1950.

By contrast, Czechoslovakia had been less of a battleground, so that war damage was less severe. In addition, as an ally of the victorious powers, the country faced no reparations burden. Indeed, post-war settlements made it the beneficiary of $70 million in reparations from Hungary (Brus 1986a, p. 572) and it also benefited from UNRRA aid, although to a smaller extent ($260 million) than Poland. Czechoslovakia also experienced major population movements: in revenge for the Nazi occupation some 2.5–3 million Sudeten Germans and 100 000 Hungarians were expelled (counterbalanced by 63 000 ethnic Slovaks from Hungary (Radice 1986, p. 510). Despite this loss of well educated 'human capital' economic recovery was relatively speedy. National income and industrial production had achieved pre-war levels by 1948 (Brus 1986a, p. 626).

Whereas Czechoslovak land reform in the inter-war years had been more radical than in Poland, it had been implemented very slowly. Hence the land reforms of 1947 were presented as the completion of unfinished business. In

1948 more restrictive reform was introduced which set aside more land for cooperative and state farming. The main source of land expropriated for distribution was owned by Germans (and to a smaller extent Hungarians) and comprised over 70 per cent of the total (Brus 1986a, pp. 586–91). Nationalization in the industrial and commercial sectors took place in two distinct phases. The 1945 Nationalization Act was limited to the confiscation of collaborators' property and to 'key industries'; that is, mines, electricity, banks and private insurance, enterprises employing over 500, and 'vital' industries employing over 150 (Brus 1986a, pp. 602–3). As Europe fragmented, however, Czechoslovakia, under pressure from Moscow, refused Marshall Aid and further nationalization took place after the communist seizure of power in February 1948. State ownership was extended to all industrial enterprises with a capacity to employ over 50 and all wholesale and foreign trade. Banking reforms resulted in the creation of a single domestic bank for the Czech lands and Slovakia and other single-purpose banks along Soviet lines. In 1949 a new State Planning Commission was established and authoritarian Soviet-style planning introduced.

In all three countries, the introduction of command planning and the creation of the Council for Mutual Economic Assistance (Comecon) in 1949 was associated with a growing reorientation of trade away from the West. This was particularly true of Czechoslovakia: thus, while only 18 per cent of its exports went to the region in 1945, by 1950 the figure was 54 per cent (Brus 1986a, p. 583). This was associated with a clear shift in industrial strategy to conform to the requirements of the socialist bloc. 'The geographical reorientation was closely tied with a shift away from the pre-war structure of exporting consumer goods and raw materials such as coal towards exporting machinery' (Myant 1989a, p. 17).

Unlike Czechoslovakia, Hungary suffered severe war damage because it was bitterly fought over in 1944/5. The level of damage was estimated by Hungaria Lloyds to be five times the annual income of the pre-war years (Swain 1992, p. 35). As an ally of the Axis powers, Hungary was obliged to pay reparations: $200 million to the Soviet Union, $30 million to Czechoslovakia, and $70 million to Yugoslavia. In addition, all German property in Hungary was ceded initially to the Soviet Union (Swain 1992, p. 35). In the demoralization of defeat and disgrace Hungary proved incapable of controlling her currency: before it was finally stabilized by the introduction of the forint in August 1946, Hungary underwent 'the wildest inflation experienced in history' (Nötel 1986, p. 538). The exchange rate of the pengo, which, in 1938, had been 5.30 to the dollar, became, by 31 July 1946, 4.60×10^{30} to the dollar. Despite the turmoil, however, recovery was rapid and by 1949 national income and industrial production had reached their pre-war levels (Brus 1986a, p. 626).

In Hungary the inter-war land reform had been least radical because of the political power of the landed nobility. The post-war reform, therefore, was the most drastic in the region, and, unlike Poland and Czechoslovakia, it was at the expense of the local landed class. Only 10 per cent of the land came from collaborators and war criminals, the rest came from estates above the legal limit (Brus 1986a, p. 586). Hungarian nationalization in 1946 was limited to mining, and only to the mining businesses themselves, not the conglomerate companies that owned the mines. By the end of the year, however, the government took control of four of the biggest iron, steel and engineering companies because Hungary could not meet its reparations obligations and, after Hungary's Moscow-inspired rejection of Marshall Aid, the communists nationalized the banks in late 1947. This was the beginning of a sweeping new programme of nationalization which eventually, in December 1949, had been extended to encompass all companies with ten or more employees (Swain 1992).

The other two facets of Soviet-style planning had also been imposed at this time – the Ministry of Industry was reorganized according to a sectoral branch structure and the National Planning Office (1947) was transformed from that of advice giver and coordinator to overall supervisor of the entire economic system (Swain 1992, pp. 40–1).

1950s: THE 'HEROIC' ERA OF STALINISM AND EARLY REFORM

As Table 8.2 suggests, all three countries by the end of the 1940s achieved significant economic growth, but the growth was not smooth, and various distortions emerged. Socialist planners always prioritized investment over consumption, heavy industry over light industry, and industry in general over agriculture and services. The First Five Year Plans of all three countries reflected these priorities. Furthermore, following a decision by the Communist International (Comintern) in November 1949 in all three countries, the plans were amended (see Table 8.3) to accentuate this bias as international tension increased and Stalin warned his allies to prepare for a third world war.

Table 8.2 *Gross industrial output in the early 1950s: annual increase %*

	1950	*1951*	*1952*	*1953*	*1954*	*1955*	*1956*
Czechoslovakia	15	15	18	10	4	11	10
Hungary	35	30	24	11	3	8	–14
Poland	26	24	20	18	11	11	10

Source: Economic Commission for Europe (1972).

A directive from the Comintern in 1949 had also started campaigns to collectivize agriculture in all three countries, thereby reversing the post-war commitment to private farming, and by 1953 40 per cent of agricultural land in Czechoslovakia, 26 per cent in Hungary, but only 7 per cent in Poland was collectivized[2] (Brus 1986a, p. 9). Agriculture was to prove an enduring problem for all the economies of the Soviet bloc.

Table 8.3 *Revisions in 1950 to First Five Year Plans**

	Planned increase in NMP %	*Amended planned increase %*
Czechoslovakia	148	170
Hungary	163	230
Poland*	170–80	212

* Poland for the Six Year Plan
Source: W. Brus (1986b), p. 19 of *The Economic History of Eastern Europe 1919–75* Vol. III, edited by M. C. Kaser.

The excessive emphasis on investment and heavy industry impacted adversely on living standards, which fell everywhere: if in each case the index of real wages in 1950 was 100, then by 1953 in Czechoslovakia the index was 95, in Poland it was 92, and in Hungary a mere 85 (Brus 1986a, p. 34). The system shook in 1953 following the death of Stalin: riots in Plzen (Pilsen) and Berlin prompted the Soviet leadership to encourage its satellites to restore equilibrium and adopt what became known as the 'New Course'. This policy retained the essence of the Stalinist model and simply aimed at restoring balance and redirecting resources towards consumption, agriculture and services. The effects of the New Course were most pronounced in Hungary where the distortions had been greatest, and least apparent in Poland. Living standards and real wages increased, conditions of employment were improved (in some cases, forced labour camps were abolished) and resources were switched from industry to agriculture where there was a relaxation of collectivization (Brus 1986b, pp. 56–7).

The effects proved to be temporary only, and by 1955 earlier distortions re-emerged. When the political climate relaxed a second time in the spring of 1956, the consequences were quite different. In Czechoslovakia it was a year of no great significance; in Poland it was a year of political crisis; but in Hungary 1956 was a year of revolution.

The reasons for these differences were largely political. In Czechoslovakia the Stalinist leadership remained in place and unchallenged, except for minor student disturbances. In Poland, the rehabilitation of the major political figure – Gomulka – triggered a crisis from which emerged a 'national' form of communism, committed to relaxing the stranglehold the Soviet Union had held on Polish life since 1944 (Swain and Swain 1993, p. 95). In Hungary the party was split and the politically popular Imre Nagy was pushed by internal pressure to policies far more radical than those of Poland's Gomulka. As a result, reform communism and the notion of separate national forms of communism were perceived as a threat to Soviet hegemony and brutally crushed by military intervention.[3]

The political experiences of 1956 emphasized the need for economic reform. In Czechoslovakia, a package was put together and introduced in 1958. Its key invention was the 'association', that is, multi-enterprise bodies which stood between the ministry and the enterprise (Myant 1989a, p. 82). This increased managerial 'discretion', but did not give managers real autonomy in that they continued to respond to orders rather than market signals. In Poland, a reform which was radical in relation to the role it initially gave to workers' councils was discussed, but much more modest measures were introduced – Autonomous Workers' Councils – only to be placed under the control of the enterprise trade union in 1957, finally to be emasculated within 'the conference of workers' self-management' in 1958. Polish reforms also introduced 'associations' similar to those in Czechoslovakia. One element of post-1956 change in Poland was radical, although it was a non-reform, in that the authorities decided *not* to collectivize agriculture: henceforth Poland was characterized by private peasant farming on dispersed small-scale holdings, the average size of which scarcely increased between 1945 and 1995. In Hungary, reform remained stuck at the discussion stage – radical notions, including roles for the newly created workers' councils, were put forward but were ignored (Swain 1992, pp. 87–8).

Although these reforms had little impact on the running of the economy, they were indicative of a desire to introduce greater flexibility. At the end of the decade, however, Khrushchev decided that the goal of the Eastern Bloc countries was to catch up and overtake the West economically, and he encouraged his allies to revamp their plans with this aim in view. Hungary committed itself to meet the targets of its post-1956 Three Year Plan a year early and revised upwards its targets for the Second Five Year Plan to begin in 1961. Czechoslovakia, buoyed up by the overfulfilment of the Second Five Year Plan, increased its already ambitious targets for the Third Plan (Myant 1989a, p. 90). In Poland, the new investment programme determined in the spring of 1958 was accelerated (Landau and Tomaszewski 1985, p. 253).

THE 1960s: FAILING TO CATCH THE WEST AND RENEWED REFORM

The 1960s began with optimism and the ambitious aim of overtaking the West, but it is now remembered as the decade when the authorities finally recognized that there were deep problems with the Stalinist model. The following decade was spent searching for measures to address them. These included:

- attempting to breath life into Comecon to achieve 'a socialist division of labour'

- switching the emphasis away from heavy industry in favour of 'modern' sectors such as chemicals, petrochemicals and the electro-mechanical and electronics industries (Sobell 1984, p. 116)
- reforming the economic mechanism to find ways of achieving faster productivity growth.

This latter goal was pursued more thoroughly in Czechoslovakia and Hungary than in Poland, where labour shortages were less acute and additional labour inputs could continue to fuel extensive growth.

Czechoslovak experience in the 1960s revolved around two key events: the negative economic growth recorded early in the decade (1963) and the Soviet invasion of 1968. The proximate cause of the first of these events was overinvestment under the ambitious Third Five Year Plan (Myant 1989a, pp. 97–106). The balance of payments was too weak to import the resources needed for the investment programme; partly because poor agricultural performance meant foreign exchange went on food imports, but mainly because it simply could not sell its exports in Western markets. Indeed, by this time the pattern of foreign trade had turned around completely and Czechoslovakia had the lowest share of trade with advanced capitalist countries of any Comecon nation (Myant 1989a, p. 99). The problem was how to find a way to make enterprises more interested in a *qualitative* improvement in performance rather than simply adding new resources (Sik 1967, p. 47 and passim; Myant 1989a, p. 124). In 1965 the authorities accepted the need for 'fundamental change' in the system of management. The central feature which began to be put into operation in 1967 was that enterprises were freed from binding Plan targets, although the degree of direct intervention remained considerable. Price reforms in 1966/7 were inflationary, however, and occasioned further controls and subsidies. Economists saw the solution as extending the reform and creating the basis for socialist pluralism, but in the seven months of 1968 prior to the Soviet invasion, little progress on economic reform was made and policy statements were imprecise. After the invasion, the reforms remained in place until April 1969 when Premier Alexander Dubcek was summarily removed and the so-called Prague Spring brought to an abrupt end.

Hungary's history of the 1960s is similarly a history of reform. In the early years it introduced its variant of 'associations'; for the rest of the decade it prepared for and successfully introduced its New Economic Mechanism, the most radical proposal introduced in the region. They hoped to stimulate the economy which was not growing compared to the 1950s, and to deal with the problem of foreign debt. Investment plans continued to be overfulfilled, yet productivity was not improving, implying that capital was being used less and less efficiently. Despite recognizing the problem as early as 1964, the New Economic Mechanism was not introduced until 1968, when all elements were introduced at a stroke (Swain 1992, pp. 97–9).

The Hungarian approach was different in that, in principle, it abolished entirely central planning in the form of quantitative indicators emanating from the Planning Office and the central allocation of materials. In effect there was an attempt to introduce a set of 'quasi-markets' where enterprises were to exercise genuine autonomy and maximize profit subject to prices set by the authorities rather than quantitative targets: planning was achieved by modifying tax rates and other financial indicators, rather than by issuing instructions. The state, however, retained close controls over investment, isolated the domestic economy from the world market, and baulked at the extension of market forces to allocation of capital (Swain 1992, pp. 99–107).

The Polish economy did not experience the same constraints on 'extensive' development in the 1960s as elsewhere. Economic growth faltered in 1962, but continued at a higher rate thereafter, before beginning to slide again at the end of the decade. Hence reform in Poland was restricted to minor adjustments to the existing structure of associations. More significant was the decision to embark on investment in new sectors of the economy. While the Czechoslovak leadership, in the main, had been pursuing cautious balanced growth since the mid-1950s, and the Hungarian Party had been chastened by the events of 1956, Poland's leaders were more insular and were prepared to fund growth at the expense of current living standards. The 1968 Party Congress initiated a new 'programme of selective development' toward products more saleable on world markets and the mobilization of intensive growth (Brus 1986d, p. 195). Its implementation was obstructed, however, by entrenched interests in the traditional sectors (Landau and Tomaszewski 1985, p. 259), and some questioned the underlying premise of paying for the required imports by exporting meat and producing animal feed domestically (Myant 1982, pp. 59–60). In the event agricultural production rose by only 9.5 per cent in the whole Plan period rather than the anticipated 17 per cent, and there were meat shortages from 1967 onwards (Brus 1986d, p. 196). The consequences of these policies got the 1970s off to an explosive start.

THE 1970s: GROWING ON BORROWED MONEY AND TIME

If Polish economic development differed from that of Hungary and Czechoslovakia in the 1960s, it diverged even more radically in the 1970s. While it is true that all Central and Eastern European economies continued to grow in the 1970s despite the oil shocks, Poland, buttressed by political faith, cheap Soviet energy and plentiful Western credits, experienced its fastest growth since the early 1950s. Not surprisingly, events in Poland dominate the decade. Elsewhere it was a grey period politically and economically, when socialist economic integration within Comecon developed further and there was belated recognition that the economic realities occasioned by the oil shocks could not be ignored. Furthermore, the indebtedness to the West was increasing at a worrying rate (see Table 8.4).

Table 8.4 *Indebtedness in Eastern Europe 1971–90 (gross debt) ($US billions)*

	Czechoslovakia	*Hungary*	*Poland*
1971	0.4	1.5	1.1
1972	0.6	1.9	1.2
1973	0.7	2.3	2.6
1974	1.0	3.1	5.2
1975	1.0	3.9	8.4
1976	1.7	4.5	12.1
1977	2.4	5.2	14.9
1978	3.0	7.6	18.6
1979	3.8	8.3	23.7
1980	6.9	9.1	24.1
1982	5.8	10.2	26.3
1984	4.7	11.0	26.9
1986	5.6	16.9	33.5
1988	7.3	19.6	39.2
1989	7.9	20.4	40.8
1990	8.1	21.3	48.5
1989 $Per head	757	4261	2843

Sources: Economic Commission for Europe (1990) pp. 332, 416; D. Cohen (1991).

In Poland, the decade began in crisis. In July 1970 the government and trade unions had been discussing a new incentive scheme which, despite a decade when real wages had stagnated, gave little scope for increasing income (Brus 1986d, p. 197). In December 1970 the government announced a 40 per cent increase in food prices. The outcome was a series of strikes and the shooting of strikers in the Baltic ports. This removed Gomulka from power and replaced him with Gierek, who had no clear economic policy (Myant 1982, p. 87) other than withdrawing the price increases and the proposed new incentive scheme. However, having secured a breathing space in the form of a Soviet loan, he revised the 1971–5 Plan to reflect a greater emphasis on consumption (Myant 1982, p. 87). This apparent success led the regime to increase Plan targets in 1973, and the amended targets were soon surpassed (Myant 1989a, p. 87).

Unfortunately, the motor of this growth was Western credit. Poland benefited from the relaxed political climate and recession in the OECD economies. Thus Western governments were happy to see banks lend to Poland so that their economies might benefit via Polish demand for industrial equipment. Although some of the loans financed consumption (real wages rose by some 40 per cent between 1970 and 1975), much was directed towards investment in sectors where Poland was hoping to win Western markets. Unfortunately, these hopes were not realized. By 1975 exports to the West covered only 60 per cent of imports and foreign banks became reluctant to lend. Furthermore, meat shortages continued and Poland remained dependent on imported grain. Clearly farm prices needed to increase to stimulate domestic production. The problem of 1970 re-emerged and history repeated itself: in June it was announced that food prices would increase by between 30 and 100 per cent, and meat prices rise by 69 per cent. Strikes broke out again, arrests were made, and the price rises were immediately withdrawn.

Despite attempts after 1976 to check imports and shift resources away from investment to consumption, high levels of investment continued and foreign debt increased inexorably. In agriculture the authorities abolished the system of compulsory purchases, which the previous regime had retained despite uncollectivized agriculture, and introduced measures which singled out, for government credits and subsidies, farmers who contracted to sell to the state. Mid-decade policies switched to favour cooperatives and 'collectivization by stealth', but this was later reversed with a lifting of the bans on the sale of agricultural machinery and state land to private farmers, and, in 1977, the granting of pension and national insurance rights to all private farmers.

In Hungary, the 1970s were characterized by a retreat from reform followed by its reintroduction in conjunction with severe deflationary measures. It had always been intended by all but hardliners that there would be a second stage to the New Economic Mechanism, addressing the need to create some sort of capital market, to break up monopolies, and to make enterprises more sensitive to world market prices (Swain 1992, pp. 115–16). However, such plans were shelved and the New Economic Mechanism itself came under attack. Re-centralizers had gained clear supremacy by 1972. Subsequently, privileged enterprises were created (accounting for nearly two-thirds of industry's fixed capital, one-half of total production and three-fifths of exports), to which the full rigours of market discipline no longer applied. The Party Congress in 1975 wanted a return to old ways as it pressed for continued growth and warned of the dangers of 'petty bourgeois attitudes' (Swain 1992, pp. 116–20). Measures extending central control over labour and investment continued into 1976. But the government had already been forced to modify its hostility to the private sector in agriculture following a meat crisis in 1975 (Swain 1981, pp. 244–7). By 1978, the government was obliged once again to rethink economic policy. The years 1979–81 were years of falling domestic consumption and industrial restructuring geared toward exporting to the West, with a view to renewed growth in 1983 (Swain 1992, p. 132).

In Czechoslovakia, after the suppression of the Prague Spring, compulsory indicators were reimposed in 1971, and in 1973 the old system of material balances was reintroduced (Myant 1989a, p. 183), although re-centralization did not return completely to the status quo ante (Brus 1986d, pp. 207–16). Official commentators viewed the 1970s as a success: equilibrium was restored and growth rates in national income and living standards attained acceptable levels. Such optimism ignored the fact that in the second half of the 1970s there was a significant slowing down and results were more or less consistently below plans. Furthermore, Czechoslovakia was losing its supremacy as exporter of machinery to the Comecon bloc (Myant 1989a, pp. 187–91).

1980s: CONTINUED FAILURE AND COLLAPSE

The 1980s opened with yet deeper crisis and the birth of Solidarity in Poland, and ended with the collapse of 'actually existing socialism'.[4] In between, the sharp slowdown in the latter half of the decade brought economic reform on to the agenda again everywhere; and, as in the 1960s, although every country talked about it, only Hungary acted radically. All economies more or less stagnated throughout the decade, until the ultimate demise of the system. One new element in this decade was the creation, in Poland and Hungary, of significant private sectors; but these two countries also experienced spiralling debt (see Table 8.4).

At the beginning of the 1980s Poland was facing an impossible task of servicing and repaying its huge debts as well as satisfying domestic demand. There were shortages of everything, especially food (Myant 1982, p. 111). The economic case for increasing food prices was incontrovertible: demand outstripped supply and production costs were covered by a subsidy approaching 5 per cent of national income (Myant 1982, p. 112). This time, rather than directly increasing prices, the government restricted cuts of meat selling at much higher prices to 'commercial shops'. This expedient had worked successfully in 1979, but this time it resulted in strikes. Individual managements gave in to demands for wage increases, but government attempts to contain the strikes were defeated and, by August, they spread to the Baltic shipyards where there were calls for the formation of independent trade unions (Myant 1982, pp. 113–15). A year and a quarter later, after Poland had announced that it could not meet its obligations to its creditors, and the 6 per cent drop in production for 1980 had doubled to 12 per cent for 1981 (despite Soviet loans equalling $4.2 billion (Myant 1982, p. 127)), martial law was declared in December 1981.

If martial law did nothing else, it finally provided a context in which prices could be increased – by 76 per cent in 1982 – producing a 25 per cent drop in average living standards. The Soviet Union stepped in to aid Poland as Western credits dried up. This culminated in an agreement signed in May 1984 on 'The Long Term Programme for the Development of Economic and Technical Cooperation between the USSR and Poland' (Kolankiewicz and Lewis 1988, pp. 109–10, 185; Brus 1989, p. 257; Myant 1989b, p. 1). More promising however was the post-1982 emergence, in the private sector, of a generation of well qualified young entrepreneurs. A new element in this was the 'Polonia' companies whereby the state encouraged emigré Poles to return and found private companies. Between 1981 and 1989 the number of private firms almost doubled, increasing from 460 333 to 857 430, and the number of Polonia companies increased eighteenfold from 46 to 841 (Gomulka and Jasinski 1994, p. 219). The Communist Party remained ambivalent about private agriculture, however. While a constitutional amendment passed in July 1983 'protected' private farming, it gave no guarantee of continuing private ownership of the land (Kolankiewicz and Lewis 1988, p. 127). In this atmosphere of crisis and distrust, the government looked for additional support, especially since a new round of reforms in 1987, which prefigured Hungarian-style autonomy rather than managerial discretion, was likely to have negative consequences for the population. In August 1988, the Party tried to work toward an 'Anti-Crisis Pact' with the 'constructive opposition' – Solidarity was re-legitimized in early 1989 and in elections in June won a landslide victory of the restricted number of seats available to it. It then took the lead in coalition with the socialists to introduce market reform (Swain and Swain 1993, pp. 192–3).

In Hungary, the 1980s also began badly. A severe liquidity crisis in 1981–2 (which resulted in Hungary joining the IMF and the World Bank) meant that renewed growth anticipated in 1983 failed to materialize. Nevertheless, reform continued. Within the state sector, from 1981 onwards, the focus was on restraint and financial realism (price reform in 1980 was complemented by a single exchange rate in 1981, the extension of foreign trade rights and the granting to enterprises the right to issue bonds in 1982). Other institutional changes were introduced: the break-up of 'trusts', the creation of a single Ministry of Industry, and competition for enterprise directorships. Discussions took place about 'socialist holding companies' taking over property rights (then held by Ministries) and placing them on a commercial footing. This implied the creation of a form of capital market and the government rejected the notion out of hand (Swain 1992, pp. 133–40).

Nevertheless, the floodgates were opening. In 1985 enterprises were given ownership rights over their assets and in 1986 bankruptcy was made possible. In 1987 commercial-type banking was introduced and the reform of Company Law in 1988 allowed for private individuals and companies to own shares in another company (Swain 1992). Despite these changes, the macroeconomy was running out of control and a stabilization plan, very similar to that of 1979, was introduced in 1987 (Swain 1992, p. 144). By 1989, Hungary's gross debt was $20.4 billion, in per capita terms the highest in the region, standing at 63.2 per cent of GDP (Swain 1992, p. 147). Unlike Poland, the majority of this debt was borrowed from commercial banks and was on variable interest rate terms (ECE 1990, p. 208). Another strand of reform related to the private or non-socialist (that is, neither state nor traditional cooperative) sector: new measures in 1982 created a variety of new business forms which increased rapidly and some 600

Small Cooperatives and 30 000 Work Partnerships existed by 1985. The most common form (over 20 000) was the Enterprise Economic Work Partnership (EEWP), however, and this illustrates an important feature of Hungary's 'private sector' in the 1980s: its incorporation within the socialist economy. The EEWPs were a peculiar creation by which a group of workers undertook, in their place of work but outside normal working hours, to do the same jobs they usually did, but on a sub-contracted, profit maximizing, team basis rather than in fulfilment of an employment contract.[5]

The Czechoslovak authorities, faced with growing disequilibrium at the end of the 1970s, drew up a modest plan for the first half of the 1980s and tried to increase exports to non-socialist markets 1980. The only area where there was a significant increase, however, was in raw materials such as wood and cellulose (Myant 1989a, pp. 191–2). Worried by the increasingly hostile world environment and the brief cessation of all credits to the East following the announcement of martial law in Poland, the leadership resolved to eliminate hard currency debt (Myant 1989a, pp. 192–4). In the second half of the decade, in the climate of Gorbachev reformism, the authorities approved 'the most revolutionary change in the management of economic processes since 1948'. This turned out to be a diluted version of the ideas of the mid-1960s and Czechoslovakia's long-term comparative decline could not be arrested. In 1960 Czechoslovak per capita GNP had been 90 per cent that of Austria; by 1985, it stood at 60 per cent of that level (Wightman and Rutland 1991, p. 42).

THE EARLY 1990s: TRANSITION

The general pattern of economic development in the early 1990s is given in Table 8.5. All countries suffered a severe drop in output at the beginning of the decade, from which they had recovered by mid-decade, Poland being in advance of the other countries by about a year. Inflation is more of a problem in Poland and Hungary than in the former Czechoslovakia, but all, except the Czech Republic, suffer from high unemployment, which has been associated with an increase in the role of the 'grey economy' (ECE 1995, p. 119). This has made for difficulties in gauging accurately the extent of the recovery in output. Poland and especially Hungary, whose mainly commercial borrowings have not been forgiven, have large levels of inherited debt, and only Slovakia has a positive current account and trade balance.

The main tasks that the economic reformers in Eastern Europe set themselves were, first, to stabilize the economies, to establish equilibrium; and, second, to create private owners of economic assets. Private ownership and real markets would, it was expected, automatically set the economies on the course of restructuring, finding comparative advantage and enjoying the benefits of economic growth in the world economy.

Table 8.5 *Selected economic indicators for the Visegrad Four, 1989–95 (percentage change or $US billions)*

	1989	*1990*	*1991*	*1992*	*1993*	*1994*	*1995 (est.)*
Czech Republic[1]							
GDP at constant prices	1.4	–0.4	–14.2	–6.4	–0.9	2.6	5.2
Consumer prices(av.)	2.3	10.8	56.7	11.1	20.8	10.0	9.1
Wages (annual av.)[2]	3.2	4.5	16.7	19.6	23.8	15.7	17.0
Current account[3]	0.4	–1.1	0.4	0.6	0.1	–0.1	–1.9
External debt (end year)[4]	6.8	7.7	8.3	3.5	2.3	1.8	–0.7
Unemployment rate	0	0.8	4.1	2.6	3.5	3.2	2.9
Hungary							
GDP at constant prices	0.7	–3.5	–11.9	–3.0	–0.8	2.9	2.0
Consumer prices (av.)	17.0	28.9	35.0	23.0	22.5	18.8	28.2
Wages (annual av.)[2]	na	22.9	25.6	25.9	24.7	21.5	18.0
Current account	–1.4	0.1	0.3	0.3	–3.5	–3.9	–2.5
External debt (end year)	19.2	20.2	18.7	17.1	17.9	21.8	19.6
Unemployment rate	0.3	2.5	8.0	12.7	12.6	10.9	10.4
Poland							
GDP at constant prices	0.2	–11.6	–7.0	2.6	3.8	6.0	7.0
Consumer prices (av.)	251.1	585.8	70.3	43.0	35.3	32.2	27.8
Wages (annual av.)[2]	291.8	398.0	70.6	38.9	31.3	38.6	na
Current account balance	–1.8	0.7	–2.2	–0.3	–2.3	–1.1	–2.4
External debt (end year)	40.2	48.9	48.3	48.2	48.7	40.9	39.4
Unemployment rate	0.1	6.1	11.8	13.6	15.7	16.0	14.9
Slovakia[1]							
GDP at constant prices	1.4	–0.4	–14.5	–6.4	–4.1	–4.8	6.6
Consumer prices (av.)	2.3	10.8	61.2	10.1	23.2	13.5	9.9
Wages (annual av.)[2]	3.2	4.5	16.5	20.2	16.8	17.4	15.3
Current account balance	0.4	–1.1	0.4	0.2	–0.4	0.7	0.3
External debt (end year)	na	na	na	na	3.2	2.6	1.5
Unemployment rate	0	1.5	11.8	10.3	14.4	14.8	13.1

[1] After 1991 figures relate to the Czech and Slovak Republics respectively.
[2] For Czech Republic 'wages in industry', for Hungary 'gross monthly earnings per employee in manufacturing', for Poland 'wages and salaries', for Slovakia 'average wages in industry'.
[3] Excludes trade with Slovakia and incorporates only trade in convertible currencies.
[4] For 1995 first three quarters of year only.

Source: *Economics of Transition*, Vol. 4, No. 1, 1996, pp. 282–94.

Stabilization Policies

It has become conventional to divide the countries of Central and Eastern Europe into those which adopted 'shock therapy' and those that adopted 'gradual reform'. This distinction has been criticized as unhelpful (Islam 1993, p. 186) and is as much a matter of political rhetoric as policies actually pursued. 'Shock therapy' in Poland was really a political idea that filled a temporary vacuum (that is, to fill a policy gap and impress the West (Myant 1993 p. 85)) and was quickly abandoned in the face of popular disquiet. In Czechoslovakia it was even more of a public relations exercise, since it was combined all along with less publicized measures to cushion the shock, while in Hungary there was no 'shock therapy' because it was deemed unnecessary.

Poland's 'therapy' was introduced at the end of 1989, when a highly restrictive budget was implemented. Inflation was reduced after the first few months, but remained consistently higher than forecast, and the fall in output was much worse than expected. Frightened by the severity of the recession, at the year's end the restrictive policy was abandoned in a controlled relaxation of fiscal and monetary policy. Real wages were to increase, but there were no new policies for stimulating investment or exports (Myant 1993, pp. 87–90). Despite an agreement on debt reduction, economic disappointment continued in 1991 and labour unrest began to increase. Selected help to branches of the economy, especially agriculture and the coal industry, was inevitable (Myant 1993, pp. 110–13).

Although there were calls for a new industrial policy in 1991 and 1992, little was done: the authorities remained interventionist, but responded to tactical political considerations rather than a longer-term strategy. The politicization of economic life was reflected in generous subsidies and cheap loans to farmers and huge sums allocated to rescue the state-owned bank affiliated to the Peasant Party (in this respect Poland was not very different from other economies such as France, Sweden and Norway).

Currency convertibility, announced as part of shock therapy, was followed in June 1995 by full convertibility of the zloty for current and capital account transactions. Given the inflation of the 1980s and 1990s, the zloty was re-denominated in the ratio of 10 000 : 1 in January 1995. Poland thus far appears to have effected the transition better than the other countries and is consolidating its position by joining or applying to join the major institutions of the Western bloc. Poland became a member of the OECD in July 1996 and is a candidate for membership of both the EU and NATO. This is indicative of a desire to underpin the economic and political reforms.

Hungary enjoyed something of a head start over its neighbours. As noted above, in the final years of communist rule the government had introduced Western-style banking and taxation, and generous conditions for foreign investors, including full repatriation of profits. Consumer subsidies had for years been smaller than elsewhere in the region so that by the time the Antall government came to power, many of the most painful measures had been taken, and the population was well used to price increases. The government felt no need to introduce full exchange rate convertibility at a stroke since, for all important business purposes, the forint was de facto convertible (BRC 1992).[6] Nevertheless, an austerity package was introduced in July 1990.

Hungary's great success has been in attracting foreign direct investment (FDI), a consequence perhaps more related to the optimistic expectations of Western financial institutions than an economy that actually operated along market lines. Disappointment caused by reality not matching these expectations might explain Hungary's falling, though still dominant, share of FDI in 1994/5. Between 1990 and 1993 Hungary received around half of all investment directed at Eastern European countries, while in 1994 it fell to around one-third and the Czech Republic was beginning to catch up (ECE 1995, p. 151). By the end of 1991 external economic relations were favourable and the currency stable, but with unemployment above 6 per cent there were signs that the government was shifting from its free market commitment towards greater intervention. Between 1991 and mid-1993 the authorities pursued a 'strong forint' policy, but, with continued inflation, the resulting real appreciation of the currency produced a deteriorating trade balance. The policy was abandoned in favour of adjusting the real exchange rate by devaluing the nominal rate by small amounts at discrete intervals (ECE 1995, p. 175). There were fears that the incoming socialist government in 1994 would be more interventionist, but the liberal coalition partners succeeded in defeating moves to extend union influence. In 1995 the authorities made a concerted effort to cut the public sector deficit and introduced wage controls and an import surcharge. Hungary is still to show the sort of growth recovery seen in Poland but, like its larger neighbour, is interested in membership of the various Western alliances. Hungary became a member of the OECD in March 1996 and is a candidate for entry to the EU in the medium-term future.

In Czechoslovakia, the new leadership initially saw the need to 'keep the core of the economy functioning with the aid of a plan'. This became known as the 'minimal plan' (Myant 1993, p. 169) but it was soon abandoned as a result of the radicalism of President Vaclav Klaus. The idea of a national strategy was not lost, however. In May 1990, the decision was taken to eliminate almost all food subsidies followed by full price liberalization in 1991. The koruna was substantially devalued and made convertible. But these policies were reinforced by direct interventionist measures. Thus inflation was attacked via wage control, direct credit limits, and a 15 per cent ceiling on price rises (Myant 1993, pp. 190–1). The exchange rate was supported by a 20 per cent import surcharge (gradually reduced to 10 per cent). Trade unions also accepted a 'General Agreement' which included wage indexation, a minimum wage, job creation and protection policies signed with the government in January 1991 (Myant 1993, pp. 196–7). Subsidies on housing and public transport were also retained. In 1991, in response to protest from farmers and industrialists, increased support was given to agriculture and the Czech Ministry of Industry began a more proactive industrial policy, while the banks wrote off pre-November 1989 debt (Myant 1993, pp. 218–19). As the United Nations noted:

> Examples of ... industrial policies applied extensively in the Czech Republic and clearly at odds with the strong liberal rhetoric of government declarations include the transfer of the equivalent of $815 million from the National Property Fund to indebted state enterprise before their privatization, deliberate delays to bankruptcy decisions, continued subsidies to fuel and energy prices, or the zero-interest loan of $22 million to the beleaguered national airlines CSA. (ECE 1995, p. 198)

The Czech Republic was the first of the nations of Central and Eastern Europe to join the OECD, in December 1995, and is part of the group that awaits full EU and NATO membership.

Czechslovakia split into two separate countries in January 1993 and, as Table 8.5 suggests, the newly independent Slovakia did not fare as badly as some expected. Slovakia had experienced significant industrialization only in the socialist years, and this was reflected in its economic structure, as Myant (1989a) observes:

> Unfortunately the basis for this (Slovak industrialization) had to be the priority sectors of the time, creating a bias towards steel, heavy engineering and petrochemicals, and an emphasis on branch factories of predominantly Czech enterprises. (p. 261)

Despite this, Slovakia achieved significant growth and a positive trade balance with both the Czech Republic and the rest of the world. The explanation for this success would appear not to be related to any inherent dynamism within the Slovak economy, but to the continuance of another feature of the socialist years: cheap Russian raw materials. Slovakia's success was based on 20–30 per cent of the country's largest firms, which all benefited from cheap Russian inputs. By mid-1996 there were signs that this price advantage would not continue (*Transition* 2, 19, pp. 53–4). Slovakia had not joined the OECD by the end of 1996 and there were growing doubts about whether its 'progress' toward a liberal democracy is sufficiently well founded for it to join the EU with the other candidate members.

Privatization

Privatization should not be confused with the growth of the private sector, which has developed rapidly in all former communist countries:

> The bulk of new firms everywhere, and of private sector jobs everywhere, with the possible exceptions of Czechoslovakia and Hungary, have emerged *de novo*, and primarily in the small-scale service, construction, transport, and retail firms. (Estrin 1994, p. 13)

They plugged a significant gap in the economic structures of the centrally planned economies which were characterized by 'gigantism' – a few large near-monopolies and very few small companies. In Hungary, for example, almost 70 per cent of companies employed over 240 people and under 5 per cent employed between 5 and 33, compared with the UK and Japan where the ratios were almost exactly the reverse (Newberry 1990).

By 1994, although there are severe problems concerning the accuracy of the data, the private sector accounted for a substantial percentage of GDP in all four countries: 70 per cent in Hungary, 62 per cent in the Czech Republic, 58 per cent in Slovakia, and 48 per cent (in 1993) in Poland.[7] But when measured as a share of employment, the relative positions are not the same. In 1993 Poland had the largest private sector with 59 per cent of employment, followed by Hungary (53 per cent), the Czech Republic (47 per cent), and Slovakia (28 per cent) (ECE 1995, pp. 72, 83–4). This would appear to confirm the impression of Poland as a country with a large but immature small-scale private sector, compared with Hungary, where the sector is numerically smaller but plays a much more significant role in the economy. As in Poland, the private sectors of the Czech Republic and Slovakia show signs of immaturity. It appears to be generally true that the bulk of the private sector is made up of the self-employed. Of Hungary's approximately 728 000 active (as opposed to registered) economic units in July 1996, some 444 000 were sole traders, a further 100 000 were partnerships, and around 95 000 were limited liability companies (Figyelõ 1996, p. 29). By 1993, Poland had almost 2 million private firms, twice as many as 1989 and all but about 100 000 were unincorporated (Gomulka and Jasinksi 1994, p. 219).

Privatization proper in Eastern Europe confronts two fundamental problems. On the one hand, there is the issue of efficiency versus equity, and, on the other, there is the question of whether to define equity in terms of historic owners or current operators. Yet even selling enterprises is not a simple task. Valuation of assets in a non-market economy is inherently problematic, and, given the extent of international uncompetitiveness in the economy and low levels of incomes and savings within the population, there are likely to be few domestic buyers. The variety of schemes adopted for the free or low-cost distribution of shares to citizens, former owners or the workforce, posed the efficiency / equity problem in a concrete form via the issue of corporate governance. Thus workers and managers are able to combine to use their inside knowledge of the operation to take advantage of less knowledgeable 'outsiders' such as shareholders or creditors. Privatization to the population at large, however, might simply create weak owners if ownership becomes concentrated into investment funds which are run mainly by banks, and the banks remain predominantly state owned, which is the case in the Czech Republic. Priorities in privatization strategy are illustrated in Table 8.6. In the event, however, realities have been more uniform than this table suggests. In all countries, what could not be sold commercially to foreign companies has been distributed on beneficial terms, either to managers or to workers, or to the population at large.

Table 8.6 *Alternative methods of privatization*

To whom	*Existing managers and workers*	*General population*	*Previous owners*	*Foreign/domestic private firms*
Method				
By sale	Employee/management buy-outs: all four countries	Market flotation: no examples	na	Joint ventures (FDI) Hungary
By free distribution	Employee/management take-overs of assets: none of the four	Voucher privatization: Czechoslovakia, Czech Republic, Poland	Czechoslovakia	na

Source: Adapted from S. Estrin (1994), p. 21.

Poland initially favoured 'value for money' and between August and November 1990 a pilot privatization of seven enterprises by public offering of shares was organized. This approach failed – only one enterprise was sold within the original time limit. In June 1991, therefore, a 'mass privatization programme' was approved which was to sell 400 leading enterprises (a quarter of the total). But, in Polish conditions of political uncertainty, rapid progress proved illusory. Privatization became a political football as Polish governments came and went. The programme was finally launched in mid–1995, covering 413 large and medium state enterprises. The government created 15 National Investment Funds which took significant shares in participating companies, with 10–15 per cent of shares going to employees. The population was able to obtain vouchers for a nominal fee which they could use, after November 1996, to buy shares in the investment fund of their choice, or shares directly on the stock exchange. The funds immediately established controlling interests in firms that they were interested in and continued to trade in their shares before the November deadline for obtaining vouchers (*Transition* 1, 14, pp. 10–22). Meanwhile, since the 1990 Privatization Act allowed methods other than 'mass privatization', the programme continued – the most common technique being 'privatization through liquidation'. This term is rather misleading because mainly profitable companies have been affected. The state company is simply dissolved and its former employees, with or without outside investors, take over some or all of the liquidated assets. It has usually been accompanied by far-reaching restructuring, unlike other forms of privatization (Gomulka and Jasinski 1994, p. 229). At the end of 1993, of the 977 privatized enterprise, 98 had been privatized by capital privatization, 707 by liquidation under the

Privatization Act, and 172 as a result of bankruptcy. These techniques continued into 1996, but since the Peasant Party–Socialist Party coalition came into power in 1994, privatization has slowed.

As in stabilization, so too in privatization Hungary had a head start. With the Company Act of 1989 a legal framework had been created for what became known as 'spontaneous privatization' – state companies restructured themselves into state-owned holding companies, with a number of limited liability and partially privately owned subsidiaries (Canning and Hare 1994, pp. 182–5). One of the last acts of the communist government was to create a State Property Agency to oversee privatization and ensure that the underselling of state assets, which had been an integral part of 'spontaneous privatization', did not continue. The incoming administration rejected give-away and cross-ownership methods of privatization and announced its intention to use privatization revenues to service foreign debt. Accepting a slower pace for privatization, the Hungarians contented themselves with the fact that they were at least creating 'real owners'. In the autumn of 1990 a grand privatization programme for 20 prime companies was announced, but it progressed far more slowly than anticipated and a year later not one had been fully completed (Canning and Hare 1994, pp. 188–91).

To rectify this, a policy of 'self-privatization' was introduced for smaller enterprises. The number of private firms in the economy increased very rapidly to about 70 000 at the end of 1992 compared with roughly 15 000 in 1989/90 (Canning and Hare 1994, p. 211). Privatization has contributed significantly to FDI: from 1990 to mid-1993 $5.5 billion of foreign direct investment flowed into Hungary, of which $1 to $1.3 billion was related to privatization (Canning and Hare 1994, pp. 177, 212). The State Property Agency had only privatized some 10 per cent of state-owned assets by the end of 1992. Recognizing the slow progress and the fact that certain companies would remain in the state sector, the government introduced further measures:

- A State Asset Management Company was created as a super holding company for companies of three types: strategic companies, important public service companies and companies whose privatization would take a long time
- legislation was passed to facilitate Employee Share Ownership Plans
- privatization by leasing was introduced
- vouchers to allow investors to buy into privatization cheaply were put on sale.

All has not been plain sailing, however – the socialists who came to power in 1994 initially suspended privatization, and later intervened in the sale of HungarHotels, after which the prospective purchaser withdrew (*Transition* 1, 13, pp. 64–9). In mid-1995 privatization regained momentum with a new law purporting to provide the framework for speedier sell-offs. Policy focused particularly on the utilities and the energy sector (*Transition* 2, 9, pp. 27–9).

Despite the change in strategy the revenue-generating aspect of privatization remained strong. Government sources claim that revenue from privatization in 1995 was 453 billion forints, over half the total revenue between 1990 and 1995, and that 90 per cent of the 1995 revenues were in hard currency (*Observer* 8 September 1996).

Czechoslovakia, and subsequently the Czech Republic, is best known for its 'voucher privatization', although this was by no means the only strategy adopted. Under the procedures adopted in 1991, enterprises were first incorporated with 100 per cent of their shares allocated to either the Federal, Czech or Slovak National Property Funds (Takla 1994, p. 157).

Voucher privatization (used for issuing over 60 per cent of shares by the end of 1992) was generally adopted by financially troubled companies which could not attract outside buyers and, as an experiment in popular capitalism, seemed to be about to fail in January 1992, but for the appearance of the Investment Privatization Funds (Myant 1993, pp. 240–1). These Funds offered to take up vouchers from the general population and invest them on their behalf, which meant that risk-averse individuals were able to spread their investment across a range of companies. The IPFs ultimately became significant owners: they obtained around 70 per cent of shares sold through voucher privatization. The second wave of voucher privatization was begun in October 1993 and privatized some 800 companies. Foreign investors have shown little interest in them because of bureaucratic delays, unresolved debt and unclear ownership structures – the exception being some major deals with Nestlé, Volkswagen, Philip Morris, and Procter and Gamble, where the purchasers were guaranteed a dominant market position (*Transition* 1, 17, pp. 52–5; Takla 1994, p. 171). Not everything has gone smoothly, however, as there was an aura of sleaze surrounding Czech financial affairs generally, and privatization in particular. This was epitomized in November 1994 when the head of the Centre for Coupon Privatization, the chief administrator of the privatization process, was arrested and accused of taking bribes: he had 8 million koruna in cash in his briefcase (*Transition* 1, 3, pp. 36–9).

Stabilization had already been achieved, and privatization was well developed when Slovakia became an independent country in 1993. Under the first voucher privatization, as part of Czechoslovakia, 2.6 million Slovaks participated in the sale of 502 Slovak companies. Furthermore, despite having fewer really desirable enterprises (if the Volkswagen-Skoda deal is excluded), Slovakia attracted slightly more foreign investment per head than the Czech Republic (Myant 1993, p. 249). The first government of Slovakia opposed restitution to former owners (Myant 1993, p. 230), and was lukewarm about voucher privatization, so it delayed the planned second round, preferring 'standard methods'. After electoral defeat, but before leaving office, however, they indicated what 'standard methods' meant in practice by authorizing 40 projects, for which no tenders had been announced, in a bout of wild privatization. The incoming government cancelled some of these schemes, initiated a second round of voucher privatization and accelerated privatization generally, such that the share of the private sector in manufacturing grew from 20.7 per cent in December 1993 to 53.7 per cent a year later. When the previous administration returned to power in the autumn of 1994 they rehabilitated some, sought to cancel others and delayed and reduced the scope of the second voucher privatization. The process was finally ended altogether in 1995 and replaced by 'bond privatization', whereby vouchers were converted into interest-bearing bonds which could be held until maturity in five years. Alternatively they could be exchanged for cash or shares, used to buy health insurance or pensions, or flats from local authorities. Control of privatization was also passed to the National Property Fund, headed by a member of a coalition party, which was authorized to privatize without Cabinet permission and without the need to inform the public of the selling price (*Transition* 1, 8, pp. 44–9).

Although privatization slowed down in Slovakia (ECE 1995, p. 199), it soon became clear that this was less to do with opposition to privatization as such, and more to obtain a breathing space while the government ensured that its political clients were the beneficiaries of 'standard methods'. By 1996, privatization in Slovakia became a game of management buy-outs 'played exclusively by members of the country's industrial lobby as a reward for their past, present and (perhaps) future support' (*Business Central Europe*, 1996, pp. 27–9).

The new owners and former managers do not pay the full value – they make a downpayment of 10–18 per cent and the rest is paid back over a number of years. The redeeming feature of this politicized and blatantly unfair procedure is that the contracts that the new managers have to negotiate with the National Property Fund are tough, and failure to meet the conditions imposed can result in repossession by the Fund. The hope is that, although former managers have become owners as a result of political ties, if they do not introduce good corporate governance they are unlikely to remain owners for long. The danger is that these 'lucrative concentrations of political and economic power ... will stagnate because they are isolated from the competition' (*Business Central Europe*, 1996, p. 29).

Restructuring

The implicit assumption that stabilization and privatization would automatically lead to a more efficient pattern of resource use appears to have been false: 'The fall in output does not seem to have been accompanied by the radical economic restructuring that many expected as part of the reform process' (Berend 1996, citing Bleyer and Gelb 1992, pp. 2–3). Indeed, there is evidence of 'negative structural' change in Hungary and the Czech Republic, involving a move toward an export structure akin to that of developing rather than developed countries. In the Czech Republic, exports of manufactured goods halved and raw materials doubled in the first years of the 1990s (Berend 1996, pp. 359–60). Similarly, Myant (1993, p. 203) reports that the structure of exports shifted to less rather than more sophisticated products, while Slovakia's better than expected performance is based on a continued reliance on its traditional heavy industry products.

The weak link in the chain between stabilization and restructuring is that restructuring may be more difficult to achieve in the deflationary climate stabilization may induce. Thus, as Myant (1993) points out: 'Practically all the evidence ... suggests that [the Balcerowicz programme] failed to stimulate a positive process of adaptation and restructuring' (p. 113). Nor is there necessarily an automatic link between privatization and restructuring – private ownership may be a necessary condition for restructuring but is not a sufficient condition: it also requires market constraints to be binding so that resources do not remain locked into inefficient activities without any incentive to improve performance. This is perhaps best seen in the Czech case where ownership is opaque and the government unwilling to enforce bankruptcy: until autumn 1996 there had been no bankruptcy of a single Czech large state-owned industrial firm. By contrast, in Poland bankruptcy has been more common despite the reluctance of governments to enforce it and their provision of bail-outs for numerous state enterprises (*Transition* 1, 14, pp. 10–22). In Hungary some 30 000 enterprises went bankrupt between the late 1980s and mid-1990s, mostly after the 1992 legislation (*Transition* 2, 15, pp. 38–41).

The absence of real market relations in the Czech Republic is also reflected by other indicators. Thus from 1993 to 1994 Polish banks reduced the share of non-performing loans in their portfolios from 34 per cent to 24 per cent, and in Hungary also the share fell from 29 per cent to 24 per cent. By comparison the share of bad loans held by Czech banks *increased* from 24 per cent to 37 per cent, and this despite the fact that in 1990–1 the non-performing loans of Czech commercial banks had been relieved and consolidated into the *Konsolidacni Banka*. One effect of this rather relaxed approach to losses is that efficiency is likely to suffer: hence labour productivity in the Czech Republic declined 10 per cent during 1992–4, while in Hungary, Poland and Slovakia double-digit gains were recorded (*Transition* 2, 15, p. 40). Hungary and Poland have experienced greater improvements in unit labour costs than the Czech Republic and Slovakia (Bartoldy, 1995b).

ASSESSMENT

This, then, in outline is the history of the Visegrad Four in the 50 or so years from the end of the war until the mid-1990s. It is appropriate in the remainder of this chapter to consider two interrelated problems of a more general nature:

what was the nature of the socialist failure, and why is transition proving so difficult?

Centrally planned economies are necessarily out of equilibrium. This derives from four logically separable aspects of Soviet-style command planning:

- the emphasis on investment rather than consumption
- the bias in favour of heavy industry in the process of industrialization
- the fact that consumer preferences were never incorporated into management incentives
- the wasted potential because prices did not reflect opportunity costs.

The fundamental problem, as noted by Boltho (1971), is that:

> [P]rices ... [do not] reflect opportunity costs. Production costs, whether marginal or average, are only imperfectly incorporated in them and demand factors have almost no influence on them at all ... [F]or a rational price structure to become effective, the first need is for a radical reform of the ... planning system. (pp. 65, 67)

But nowhere was this achieved, and the hierarchical principle informed the behaviour of economic agents throughout the period. Enterprise managers looked not to the market, to customers, to suppliers, to external auditors or shareholders, but to their superiors. The underlying principle was of hierarchical subordination, minimal autonomy, and minimal personal responsibility. Despite four generations of increasingly radical reform, none established the sort of system under which rational prices could develop or where 'soft budget constraints' could be replaced by hard ones. The phrase 'soft budget constraints', as developed by Kornai (1980) in his work on the economics of shortage in relation to centrally planned economies, has been criticized by some economists (see Hare 1989, pp. 70–9), but nevertheless it retains sociological validity. Even in the fourth generation 'market socialist' economies of the former Yugoslavia and, latterly, Hungary, where markets determined many prices and enterprises were de facto owners of their own assets, power relations between unsupervised individuals within institutions where there were no private owners ensured that, when the crunch came, market discipline was not imposed.

The history of socialist Eastern Europe, then, is not a history of the failure of factor inputs, of the failure to create capital, to mobilize labour, or even to improve human capital. Eastern Europe was rather successful at mobilizing resources toward a clear, simple goal such as recovery and reconstruction, and had an impressive record of educating and training; indeed, of creating the middle class (with the exception of its entrepreneurial component) that these countries had lacked between the wars. It is rather a history of inflexibility or sluggishness in prioritizing or responding to many potentially conflicting goals once recovery had been achieved. The crucial incentive to innovate and change was always lacking because preservation of hierarchy became the ultimate criterion by which any modification would be judged.

Unlike Western Europe, where, as has been suggested in this volume, the engine of growth was advances in total factor productivity and catch-up, in Eastern Europe productivity gains were low throughout the period. Kaser (1994) suggests that in the case of the USSR, during the whole of its 70-plus years history, the only time when any positive gains in total factor productivity were achieved was during Khrushchev's reforms between 1957 and 1965. No systematic work has yet been published in English on all of the Central and Eastern European economies in the socialist years, but Myant (1989a) concludes that

> there is some evidence of secular decline at least from 1966 onwards and the impression is unmistakable that the slowdown in overall growth rates was due to worse use of inputs rather than just an absolute restriction on the latter. (p. 223)

Certainly the evidence from Table 8.7 indicates that total factor productivity was making only a small contribution to growth rates in Hungary and Czechoslovakia from the 1960s onward.

Table 8.7 *Annual average percentage growth rates in National Income and Total Factor Productivity in Czechoslovakia and Hungary, 1961–84*[*]

	1961–70	*1971–5*	*1976–80*	*1981–4*
Czechoslovakia				
National Income	4.4	5.7	3.6	1.5
TFP	1.1	1.5	0.6	0.0
Hungary				
National Income	5.4	6.2	2.8	2.1
TFP	1.4	1.6	0.4	0.3

[*]Data is not presented for Poland, although Myant (1989a) suggests the situation was no better there.
Source: Myant (1989a), p. 223.

This was clearly a consequence of the inability of the planning system given its autarkic leanings and inappropriate incentive structures to take advantage of what would clearly have been major catch-up opportunities vis-a-vis the US economy and the rest of Western Europe.

As the United Nations' Economic Commission for Europe (1990, p. 94) noted, the situation did not improve in the latter half of the 1980s. Indeed, it was a persistent feature in official reports on Eastern European economies.

> Between the 1950s and the 1960s the input intensity of total output appears to have increased: while the growth of output slowed down in the 1960s, employment rose

> at an unchanged rate and the growth of capital stock accelerated. Thus the growth of labour productivity slowed down and in the 1960s output per unit of capital stock (capital productivity) ceased to rise. (ECE 1972, pp. 15–16)

> As early as the end of the 1960s and especially by the mid-1970s, it had become obvious that further development on extensive lines was increasingly impracticable. (ECE 1984, p. 109)

At the microeconomic level, the productivity failure in relation to labour was reflected in the perceived shortage of labour. Despite the judgement of Western observers that socialist enterprises were overmanned, management, responding to its non-market signals, always experienced a shortage of staff. Czechoslovakia went so far as to import North Vietnamese guest workers to fill the gaps. The failure of capital productivity is best reflected in the problems enterprises encountered in bringing new, Western investments on-stream. Winiecki (1988) summarized the barriers to technical change thus:

> At every stage of the innovation process, delays because of shortages and quality problems with inputs mean that the minimum efficient production scale is reached too late, the product is more costly to produce than anticipated, and has a shorter presence on world markets than anticipated. (pp. 176–7)

A full study of the diffusion of computer numerically controlled (CNC) technologies in Hungary concluded that their impact 'should have been marked' when it was 'only marginal' because of shortages of components, machinery standing idle for excessive periods, shortage of high-quality inputs and a reluctance to scrap older machinery (Hare and Oakey 1993, p. 140). Poland's all-or-nothing debt-led gamble on Western technology in the 1970s resulted in similar failures (Myant 1982, p. 108).

These productivity problems and the competitive disadvantage which was their consequence were serious enough but they were compounded by the far-reaching technological change which accompanied the adjustment of the OECD economies to the oil shocks of the 1970s. Freeman (1987, p. 14) referred to this as a change of techno-economic paradigm, a change 'so far-reaching that it has a major influence on the behaviour of the entire economy'. Berend (1996) refers to a 'fifth industrial revolution'. But whatever the terminology, at a period when microchips came with everything from aerospace to everyday consumer items, the computer industries of Central and Eastern Europe remained generations behind the leaders (Lee and Swain, 1994) and other industries failed to incorporate them into their products. Central and Eastern European industry was not simply lagging, it seemed to have missed a whole technological revolution.

Eastern Europe's competitiveness problem, therefore, was not small-scale. Despite the apparent successes of the early years it had failed to overcome the historical backwardness of the region. By the 1970s even the most developed country, Czechoslovakia, was falling behind its rivals. Hare and Hughes (1991) argue that, by the end of the 1980s, measuring manufactured output in world rather than domestic prices, 19 per cent of Czechoslovak industry, 24 per cent of Hungarian industry and a similar proportion of Polish industry was producing *negative value added*, that is to say the cost of the inputs was greater than the value of the output, while only between 7 per cent and 22 per cent of industry in the three countries was capable of making a profit.

The scale of the competitiveness problem is not the only reason for the failure of the socialist economies, it is also at the core of why transition has proved so difficult. Market relations could not be fully enforced, despite the rhetoric of 'shock therapy', because whole sectors of the economy would have collapsed as they did in East Germany and unemployment would have reached politically unacceptable levels without the cushion of fiscal transfers which East Germans received from West Germany. The alternative was continued subsidies to industry, but this places pressure on government budget deficits and, unless restructuring takes place, subsidies simply maintain an uncompetitive industrial structure, which is resistant to change, because the cosy hierarchical links of the past are maintained. Uncompetitiveness is compounded by 'institutional inertia': it is one thing to preach the necessity of replacing soft budget constraints with hard ones, but it is quite another thing to convince individuals who have spent all their working lives in hierarchical institutions, watching their backs and avoiding risks, that they have to change their ways. The institutional power relations and behavioural patterns that underpinned such 'soft budget constraints' are difficult to break. Enforcing bankruptcy in order to accomplish restructuring exacerbates the unemployment problem which adds to pressure on budget deficits, at least in the short run.

In a fledgling democracy, it may be difficult and dangerous to reduce budget deficits rapidly to levels acceptable to the foreign exchange or international bond markets because the population, including an articulate new middle class, is reluctant to forgo the relatively generous social and welfare benefits provided by 40 years of socialism. The Visegrad Four are certainly in transition toward a market economy, but the ultimate success of their transition to liberal democracy depends on how well they restructure their economies, and ironically this has been the least satisfactory aspect of the transition to date.

NOTES

1. The USSR suffered the greatest loss in absolute terms: numbers in excess of 20 million perished; that is, about 11 per cent of the population.
2. The ratios of state farm land were more or less the same in each country, between 12 and 14 per cent (Brus 1986b, p. 9).
3. For a brief account of Hungary 1956, see Swain and Swain (1993). For a much fuller account, see Lomax (1976) or Litván et al. (1996).
4. For a brief account of Solidarity see Swain and Swain (1993). For a fuller account see Myant (1982).

5. For a fuller account of the EEWPs, see Swain (1992, pp. 136–8, 177–83).
6. The Blue Ribbon Commission argues that Hungary's de facto convertibility was greater than the declared convertibility of Czechoslovakia (BRC 1992, pp. 31–2).
7. For a lucid general discussion of data problems for the transition economies, see Bartoldy (1995a, pp. 272–6).

REFERENCES

Bartoldy, K. (1995a) 'The interpretation of economic indicators: some caveats', *Economics of Transition*, Vol. 3, No. 2, pp. 272–6.

Bartoldy, K. (1995b) 'Productivity, employment and cost competitiveness', *Economics of Transition*, Vol. 3, No. 4, p. 520.

Berend, I. T. (1996) *Central and Eastern Europe 1944–1993: Detour from the Periphery to the Periphery*, Cambridge: Cambridge University Press.

Bleyer, M. I. and Gelb, A. (1992) 'Persistent Economic Decline in Central and Eastern Europe. What are the lessons?', *Transition*. The Newsletter about Reforming Economies, World Bank, Vol. 3, No. 7, July–August.

Boltho, A. (1971) *Foreign Trade Criteria in Socialist Economies*, Cambridge: Cambridge University Press.

BRC (1992) Blue Ribbon Commission, *Forint Convertibility*, Policy Study No. 1, Indianapolis and Budapest.

Brus, W. (1986a) 'Postwar Reconstruction and Socio-Economic Transformation', in M. C. Kaser and E. A. Radice (eds), *The Economic History of Eastern Europe 1919-1975, Volume II: Inter-war Policy, the War and Reconstruction*, Oxford: Clarendon Press, pp. 564–641.

Brus, W. (1986b) '1950–1953: The Peak of Stalinism, The Thaw and the New Course', in M. C. Kaser (ed.), *The Economic History of Eastern Europe 1919–1975, Volume III: Institutional Change within a Planned Economy*, Oxford: Clarendon Press.

Brus, W. (1986c) '1957–65: In search of balanced development', in M. C. Kaser (ed.), *The Economic History of Eastern Europe 1919–1975, Volume III: Institutional Change within a Planned Economy*, Oxford: Clarendon Press.

Brus, W. (1986d) '1966–75: normalization and conflict', in M. C. Kaser, (ed.), *The Economic History of Eastern Europe 1919–1975, Volume III: Institutional Change within a Planned Economy*, Oxford: Clarendon Press.

Brus, W. (1989) 'Evolution of the Communist Economic System: Scope and Limits', in D. Stark and V. Nee, *Remaking the Economic Institutions of Socialism: China and Eastern Europe*, Stanford: Stanford University Press, pp. 255–77.

Business Central Europe, various.

Canning, A. and Hare, P. (1994) 'The privatization process – economic and political aspects of the Hungarian approach', in S. Estrin (ed.), *Privatization in Central and Eastern Europe*, London: Longman, pp. 176–217.

Cohen, D. (1991) 'The Solvency of Eastern Europe', *European Economy*, Special Edition, No. 2, p. 265.

Economic Commission for Europe (ECE 1972) *Economic Survey of Europe in 1971: The European Economy from the 1950s to the 1970s*, New York: United Nations.

Economic Commission for Europe (ECE 1984) *Economic Survey of Europe in 1983–84*, New York: United Nations.

Economic Commission for Europe (ECE 1990) *Economic Survey of Europe in 1989–90*, New York: United Nations.

Economic Commission for Europe (ECE 1995) *Economic Survey of Europe in 1994–5*, New York: United Nations.

Economics of Transition, Vol. 4, No. 1, 1996, pp. 282–94.

Estrin, S. (1994) 'Economic transition and privatization: the issues', in S. Estrin (ed.), *Privatization in Central and Eastern Europe,* London: Longman, pp. 3–30.

Figyelõ, I. (1996) *Economics Weekly,* Budapest.

Freeman, C. (1987) 'The case for technological determinism', in R. Finnegan et al. (eds), *Information Technology: Social Issues – a Reader,* Sevenoaks: Hodder and Stoughton, pp. 5–18.

Gomulka, S. and Jasinski, P. (1994) 'Privatization in Poland 1989–1993: policies, methods and results', in S. Estrin (ed.), *Privatization in Central and Eastern Europe,* London: Longman, pp. 218–51.

Hare, P. (1989) 'The economics of shortage in the centrally planned economies', in C. Davis and W. Charemza (eds), *Models of Disequilibrium and Shortage in Centrally Planned Economies,* London and New York: Chapman Hall, pp. 49–81.

Hare, P. and Hughes, G. (1991) 'Competitiveness and industrial restructuring in Czechoslovakia, Hungary and Poland', *European Economy,* Special Edition 2, pp. 83–110.

Hare, P. and Oakey, R. (1993) *The Diffusion of New Process Technologies in Hungary: Eastern European Innovation in Perspective,* London: Pinter.

Islam, S. (1993) 'Conclusion: problems of planning a market economy', in S. Islam and M. Mandelbaum (eds), *Making Markets: Economic Transformation in Eastern Europe and the Post-Soviet States,* New York: Council on Foreign Relations, pp. 182–215.

Kaser, M. C. (1994) 'From Market Back to Market Via Central Planning', in I. T. Berend (ed.), *Transition to a Market Economy at the End of the Twentieth Century,* Munich: Sudosteuropa Gesellschaft, pp. 153–65.

Kolankiewicz, G. and Lewis, P. G. (1988) *Poland: Politics, Economics and Society,* London: Pinter.

Kornai, J. (1980) *The Economics of Shortage,* Amsterdam: North-Holland.

Landau, Z. and Tomaszewski, T. (1985) *The Polish Economy in the Twentieth Century,* London: Croom Helm.

Lavigne, M. (1995) *The Economics of Transition: From Socialist Economy to Market Economy,* London: Macmillan.

Lee, W. R. and Swain, N. (1994) 'The new technology that failed: information technology and computing in the GDR and Hungary', in V. Prucha (ed.), *The System of Centrally Planned Economies in Central-Eastern and South-Eastern Europe after World War II and the Causes of its Decay,* Prague: University of Economics, pp. 272–310.

Litván, G. et al. (eds) (1996) *The Hungarian Revolution of 1956: Reform, Revolt and Repression 1953–1963,* London: Longman.

Lomax, B. (1976) *Hungary 1956,* London: Allison and Busby.

Myant, M. (1982) *Poland: a Crisis for Socialism,* London: Lawrence and Wishart.

Myant, M. (1989a) *The Czechoslovak Economy, 1948–88,* Cambridge: Cambridge University Press.

Myant, M. (1989b) 'Poland – the Permanent Crisis', in R. A. Clarke (ed.), *Poland: the Economy in the 1980s,* London: Longman, pp. 1–28.

Myant, M. (1993) *Transforming Socialist Economies: The Case of Poland and Czechoslovakia,* Aldershot: Edward Elgar.

Newberry, D. (1990) 'Tax reform, trade liberalisation and industrial restructuring in Hungary', *European Economy,* No. 43, pp. 67–95.

Nötel, R. (1986) 'International finance and monetary reforms', in M. C. Kaser and E. A. Radice (eds), *The Economic History of Eastern Europe 1919–1975, Volume II: Interwar Policy, the War and Reconstruction,* Oxford: Clarendon Press, pp. 520–63.

Observer, Supplement, 8 September 1996.

Radice, E. A.(1986) 'The collapse of German hegemony and its economic consequences', in M. C. Kaser and E. A. Radice (eds), *The Economic History of Eastern Europe 1919–1975,*

Volume II: Interwar Policy, the War and Reconstruction, Oxford: Clarendon Press, pp. 495–519.
Sik, O. (1967) *Plan and Market under Socialism*, Prague: Czechoslovak Academy of Sciences.
Sobell, V. (1984) *The Red Market*, Aldershot: Gower.
Spulber, N. (1957) *The Economics of Communist Europe*, London: Chapman and Hall.
Swain, G. and Swain, N. (1993) *Eastern Europe since 1945*, Basingstoke: Macmillan.
Swain, N. (1981) 'The evolution of Hungary's agricultural system since 1967', in P. G. Hare, H. K. Radice and N. Swain, *Hungary: a Decade of Economic Reform*, London: George Allen and Unwin.
Swain, N. (1992) *Hungary: the Rise and Fall of Feasible Socialism*, London: Verso.
Takla, L. (1994) 'The relationship between privatization and the reform of the banking sector: the case of the Czech Republic and Slovakia', in S. Estrin (ed.), *Privatization in Central and Eastern Europe*, London: Longman, pp. 154–75.
Transition, publication of the Open Media Research Institute: Prague.
Wightman, G. and Rutland, P. (1991) 'Czechoslovakia', in S. White (ed.), *Handbook of Reconstruction in Eastern Europe and the Soviet Union*, London: Longman, pp. 29–58.
Winiecki, J. (1988) *The Distorted World of Soviet-type Economies*, London: Routledge.

Index

Abert J. G. 106
abolition of state monopolies
  in Scandinavia 164
Active Manpower Policy xiv, 152, 168
active industrial policies 12
Adams W. J. 10, 49
Aerospatiale 65
agricultural labour force 7, 28, 38
  in Belgium and Netherlands 105
  in Spain 131
  in Scandinavia 161
  in Sweden 156
agriculture
  contraction of 64, 78, 78
  sectoral share of employment 39, 63, 85, 155
  sectoral share of value added 63, 85, 155
Air France 66
Alentejo 133, 135, 145
Algeria 51
Allen K. 83
Amatori F. 76
American investment
  in Europe 105
Angola 134
Antall government 193
Antonelli C. 93
Antwerp 108
apprenticeship training
  in Britain 9
  in Germany 9, 40, 41
Armstrong P. 27, 30, 58
Argentina 77
Asturias 140
Atkinson A. B. 3, 20
Atkinson A. F. 9
Austria xii, 77, 191
Austria-Hungary 178
Austro-Hungarian Empire 178
autarky 126
Autunno caldo 80, 97

Baer W. 138
Baklanoff E. 130, 134
balance of payments 11, 51, 61, 79, 88
  of Czechoslovakia 185
  of Netherlands 110, 117
  of Portugal 130, 136
  of Scandinavian countries 153, 157
  of Spain 129, 136
  of Sweden 164
    regional 95
Balthazar H. 108
Baltic countries 161
  ports 187
  shipyards 189
Bamford J. 98
BIS (Bank for International Settlements) 51, 93
Bank of England 14
Bank of France 72n
Bank of Italy 79, 82, 83, 88, 91
Bank of Spain 14
banks
  lending to Poland 187
  links with industry 41
  restructuring in Eastern Europe 201
bankruptcy
  in the Czech Republic and Poland 201
Barcelona 141
bargaining
  and high inflation 10
  behaviour 37
  centralized 113
  in tight labour markets 29
  models of 39
  power 92
  restraint 39
  system in Germany 40
  see also trade unions
Barker K. 69
Barral J. 64
Barro R. 35, 70
Bartoldy K. 201, 206n
Basque country 126, 128, 140, 145
Batstone E. 9
Baudhuin F. 109
Bean C. 9, 14, 15, 17, 18, 69, 70
Belgium xiii, 72, 87, 102, 106, 120
  and coal industry 102, 104
  growth in 103–4
  in the 1930s 107, 108
  politicization of public services 106
  sectoral employment 105
  traditional industries 105
  world depression 103
Bell B. 19
Benelux xii, 102, 115
  Customs Union and trade 110
Berend I. T. 200, 201, 204
Berghahn V. R. 38
Berlin Wall 29
Berlin riots 183
Berlusconi 94
Beuchtemann C. F. 38
Bishop M. 18

Bismans F. 110, 111
Bleyer M. I. 200
Boekestijn A. J. 115
Bohemia 178
Boltho A. 35, 37, 202
bond privatization 200
Bouvier J. 50, 64
Boyer M. 145
Brescia 97
Bretton Woods 11, 42, 83, 88, 152
  collapse of 30, 43
Britain xvii, 102
  and post-war reconstruction 11
  and taxation 13
  and tax policy 17
  and macroeconomic policy 10, 17
  sectoral shares of employment and value added 63
British Airways 17
British economy 1
  post-war growth of 20
British Gas 17
British labour force skills 18
British Leyland 8
British Rail 17
British Steel 17
British Telecoms 17
Britton A. 14
Broadberry S. 8, 9, 18
Brown W. A. 12
Bruce P. 141
Bruno G. 97
Brus W. 180, 181, 182, 183, 185, 186, 189, 205n
Brussels 142, 145, 174,
budget deficits 37, 67, 85, 88, 91, 93, 164, 168, 193, 205
budgetary consolidation xv
Bulgaria 179
Bull A.C. 97
Bundesbank 37, 89
  and inflation 31, 34, 40, 44,
  and monetary policy 30, 43
  and Lombard rate 34,
  and Deutschmark Ostmark conversion 35
business elites
  in Italy 84
business structure
  in Sweden 159
Buyst E. 118

Cable J. R. 41
Caetano Marcelo 134, 135
Caetanista model 135
Calabria 95
Calmfors L. 39,
Camu A. 109, 111
Cantabria 140
capital flight 79, 80
capital-output ratio 112, 113
Carlin W. 35, 37, 42
Caron F. 49
Carré J. J. 53, 57, 58, 59
CASMEZ (*Cassa per il Mezzogiorno*) 76, 96
Cassiers I. 107, 109
Castronovo V. 96
cartels
  in Germany 38,
Catalonia 126, 128,
  foreign investment in 145
catch-up xiii, xiv, xv, 5, 15, 27, 28, 30, 53, 55, 60, 71, 126
  and convergence 53, 145
  of Eastern Europe 203
  of Iberia 142
  of Scandinavia 150
  potential 132
  residual 87
Cavaco A. S. 138, 141, 142, 144
central planning 180, 182,
  fundamental features 202
  reforms of 184–6
Centre for Coupon Privatization 199
CGE 65
Ciampi 94
Ciocca P. 79
civil war
  in Spain 125, 126, 128
Chandler A. D. 38
Chevallier T. 58
DC (Christian Democratic Party of Italy) 75, 76, 82, 84, 91, 93
closed shop 15
co-determination 39
Cohen D. 187
Cohen J.C. 58
Cold War 173
COMECON (Council for Mutual Economic Assistance) 181, 184, 186, 189
Comintern (Communist International) 182
CAP (Common Agricultural Policy) 43, 64
Common external tariff 56
Common Market 49, 56, 80
  see also EEC/EC/EU
Communism
  national forms 183
Communist Party
  in France 49
  in Italy 75, 87, 89, 90
  in Poland 190
  orthodoxy xv
competitiveness 5
  in Britain 3
Concorde 65
Conservatives 15, 20
Conservative governments 13

Corbino 76
Corner P. 97
Corkill D. 139, 144
corporatism 108, 171
corporative capitalism 172
Council of Ministers 172
  and Scandinavia 172
  and Eastern European economies 44
Crafts N. F. R. 2, 7, 9, 11, 15, 17, 111
Craxi government 91
Credit Agricole 64
Credit Lyonnais 66
Currency convertibility
  in Poland 193
  of Forint 194
currency reform
  in Germany 28
currency snake 61
currency union 44
Czech Republic xii, xiii, 177, 191
Czechoslovakia xiii, 177, 179, 183
  agriculture and industry 178
  and North Vietnamese workers 204
  and reparations 180
  communist seizure of 181
  population movements 180
  Prague Spring 185, 188
  revising plan targets 184
  Soviet invasion of 1968 185
  splits 1991 195
  trade patterns 181

D'adda C. 85
Daems H. 105
Daly A. 40
Dancet G. 109, 115
Daneo C. 75
Darby J. 16
Dassault 65
De Brabander G. 111
De Cecco M. 76, 82, 92
De Gasperi 75
defensive investment 111
deindustrialization
  in Germany 38–9
De Gaulle 48
de Jong H. 112
Delors J. 62
Deleeck T. 115
Denison E. F. 52
Denmark xii, xiii, 7, 70, 72, 148, 175n
  and budgetary consolidation 154
  economic structure 154
  foreign establishments in 159
  internationalization of 158
  employment and value added 155
  shifts to the right 154
  trade partners 157

Department of Trade and Industry (DTI) 3
Dercksen W. J. 112
deregulation
  financial 151
  in Scandinavia 164
  of banking and capital markets 67, 165
  of product markets 18
  of the labour market 45
Deutschmark 90, 91
  and reunification 34
  appreciation 30, 31
  revaluation 44
  vis a vis Ostmark 35
  DM zone 90
devaluation 34, 44
  in Belgium, Netherlands and Britain 109
  in Denmark 164
  of Belgian Franc 118
  of Czech Koruna
  of French Franc 51, 62
  of Italian Lira 85, 90
  of Hungarian Forint
  of Swedish Krona 154, 164
De Vita P. 96
Dini Lambertino 94
disinflation 90
disintegration xvii
displaced worker effect 70
distributional conflict 30
Dowrick S. 27, 114
Driehaus W. 113
Driffil J. 39
Dubois P. 53, 57, 59, 72n
Dunning J. 8
Dupriez L. H. 109
Dutch
  see Netherlands

Eastern Europe xii, 143, 144, 145, 177
  and Sweden 157
East Germany
  see Germany
EC/EU (European Community/European Union) xiii, 10, 43, 48, 112, 124, 139, 141, 142, 145, 149, 158, 170, 174, 175, 193, 194, 195, 200
Eck J. F. 48
ENA (*École Nationale d'Administration*) 72n
ECE (Economic Commission for Europe) 50, 55, 81, 93, 182, 187, 190, 191, 194, 203, 204
ECSC (European Coal and Steel Community) 48, 76, 83, 115
economic miracle
  in Italy 78, 97
  in Spain 124, 132, 139
economic nationalism 124, 125

economic performance
  British 2–10
  West German 25–37
economic planning 84
  in France 49–52,
  in Spain 124, 131–2, 139
economic rationality xii
economic reforms
  in Eastern Europe 184, 185–6, 111
  in Hungary 190–1
Edwards J. 41
EEC (European Economic Community) 43, 48, 56, 57, 80, 89, 114, 138
EEWP (Enterprise Economic Work Partnerships) 191, 206n
EFTA (European Free Trade Association) xii, 127, 129
Einaudi 76
electricity industry 13, 17
Emilia
employment
  in manufacturing 63, 155, 160
  in public sector 161
Employee Share Ownership Plans 198
EMS (European Monetary System) 14
EMU (European Monetary Union) xv, 60, 71
  and flexible labour markets 71
Englander A. S. 120
ENI 82
  and energy resources 83
Erhard Ludwig
  and Christian Democrats 30
  and liberalization 28
  and ordo-liberals 38
ERM (Exchange Rate Mechanism) 14, 26, 43, 85, 90, 91, 144, 145
  and German reunification 34
  and higher unemployment 43
  and lower inflation 43
  see also European Monetary System
Esteban J. 126
Estrin S. 52
Eurodollar market 88
European Commission 143
enterprise managers 202
exchange rates xiii, xv, 71
  appreciation 31
  fixed 11, 30, 31, 92, 152, 154
  flexibility xv
  floating 11, 30, 42, 61
  multiple 128
  nominal and effective 42, 43, 71, 90, 94
  of pengo 181
  real 43
  stable 42 , 43, 107
  target 14
  volatility 43
Expansion Laws (1959)
  in Belgium 115
Exports
  Italy's share and composition 80, 81, 82, 87, 92, 93
  Netherlands' share of 113
export-led growth 29
export markets
  West Germany and UK compared 32–3
Extremadura 145

factor inputs 1, 202
Falklands War 14
Fascism 124
Federal Republic 85
Federal Reserve 89
Fernandez R. 10
Fiat 83, 96
Fifth Plan
  in France 52
Fifth Republic 51, 61
  Grande Époque of 51, 52
Figyelõ I. 196
Finland 161, 165, 175n
Finsider 83, 96
financial crises in Scandinavia 151, 165
financial intermediation 111
financial system 8
fine tuning 11
First Plan
  in France 50
fiscal transfers
  from West to East Germany 205
fiscalization 89
Fischer K. 41
Five Year Plan
  in Portugal 127
  in Eastern Europe 182–3
Flanagan R. 29
Flanders 115
Fontenaiche P. 58
Food prices
  in Poland 187–8
Foreign Direct Investment (FDI)
  and privatization 198, 199
  in Belgium and the Netherlands 105, 114
  in Czech Republic 194
  in Denmark 158
  in France 58
  in Hungary 194
  in Norway 158
  in Portugal 130–1, 139
  in Spain 132–3, 139
  in Sweden 157–8
foreign exchange
  markets 62, 89
  reserves 108
  shortages 108
Fortress Europe 44
Ford-Volkswagen plant
  Setúbal 138

Fourth Plan
in France 51
Fourth Republic 51, 142
France xii, xiii, xiv, 6, 7, 27, 43, 44, 48, 51, 54, 58, 78, 85, 87, 91, 102, 142, 159, 160, 193
and autarky 56–7
and *grands projets* 65
capital stock of 49, 54, 55
sectoral shares of employment and value added 63
Franc 44, 51
Franc zone 54, 57, 60
see also devaluation
Franc fort 59, 62
Franco xii, 124, 125, 126, 140
and nationalist forces 126
death of 145
ignorance of economics 128
regime 127
Francoism 142
Franks J. 41
Freeman C. 204
Freeman R. 45
French business 50
expectations 51
French
exports and GDP 56–7
interest differentials with Germany 62
motor vehicle industry 66
policy objectives 48
telephone system 66
Frognier A. P. 106

Gales B. P. A. 106
Gallagher T. 130
Gelb A. 200
general elections
in Portugal 144
in Spain 144
German business
structure 41
compared to UK and US
ownership 41
German industry
after the war 27
and Allied bombing 27
and cartels and profit pooling 38
German long termism 42
German property
expropriation in Eastern Europe 180–1
German reunification
and Chancellor Kohl 34
and convergence 35, 36
and employment 33
and ERM 43
and European Economy 34
and inflationary consequences 34, 37
and interest rates 91
and Italian unification 35
and taxpayers 45
and the Deutschmark 34
and wage bargaining 34, 37
and wage parity 35
and West Germany 34
costs of 34, 37
impact on East Germany 34, 35
macroeconomic consequences of 34
Germany 3, 4, 5, 6, 7, 9, 19, 25, 31, 38, 44, 48, 50, 56, 64, 68, 72, 77, 78, 80, 87, 91, 92, 107, 110, 145, 159, 160
and reunification of 25, 33–7
and supply side rigidities 31
and supply side performance 32
and trade with Europe 37
current account surplus 32
East xiii, 19, 25, 29, 34, 35, 38, 42, 44, 205
West xii, xiii, 25, 27, 29, 34, 35, 38, 44, 54, 65
sectoral shares of employment and value added 63
Giavazzi F, 89, 90
Gierek 187
Giersch H. 31, 32
Gillingham J. 110
Gilot A. 115
Gini coefficient 3, 20
Ginsborg P. 93
Giordani 76
Golden Age xiii, xv, 3, 4, 7, 9, 14, 15, 16, 17, 25, 27, 31, 45, 53, 59, 132, 170
Gomulka (Polish Premier) 183, 187
Gomulka S. 190, 196, 197
González Felipe 138, 139, 141, 142, 144
Gooch A. 139, 141, 145
Goodman A. 19
Gorbachev reformism 191
Grandes Écoles 72
Great Depression 53, 165, 178
Greece xii
Green D. 13
Greenhalgh C. 14
Griffiths R. T. 106, 117
Grimond J. 69
Groningen gas field 105, 113
Groote P. 107, 110
growth
accounting 8, 52
and Benelux countries 103–4
and economic efficiency 1
and technological progress 53
and the residual 53
British 1–8
coalition 71
deceleration 59
extensive xiii
in Scandinavia 149–51

growth *continued*
  inequality adjusted 20
  intensive xiv,
  of France 52, 59
  outcomes 13
  performance 7, 13
  proximate sources of 1, 7, 8, 17–8
  trend rates of 13
  through inflation 89
  West German 26, 27, 31–3, 40, 45
Growth rates
  in Eastern Europe 177–8

Hague summit 43
Hammond R. 130
Hare P. 198, 202, 204
Harrison J. 126, 128, 129, 131, 132, 139
Hartog J. 119
Hayward J. 61, 65
Heath government 11
Hellwig 32
Henrekson M. 167
Hindley B. 13
Hodne F. 158, 160, 169
Hogg R. L. 107, 108
Holbik K. 76, 80
Holland xiii, 69
  see also Netherlands
Holmes M. 14
Holmes P. 52
Honeywell-Bull 65
Hooper J. 139
household savings 111
  liquid assets 51
Hudson M. 125, 133, 137, 140
Hughes G. 204
Human capital
  and expenditure on training 18
  formation 18, 21, 40, 120
  in Eastern Europe 202
  in Scandinavia 150
  transferred from East to West Germany 28
Hungarhotels sale 198
Hungary xii, xiii, 177, 179, 183
  agriculture and industry 178
  and the Axis powers
  and payment of reparations 181
  and quasi-markets 186
  and 1956 revolution 183
  New Economic Mechanism 185, 188

Iberia xii, 125–45, 157
Iceland 174, 175n
ideological division
  in Belgium and the Netherlands 106
IG Metall 31
IMF (International Monetary Fund) 55, 88, 89, 129
incomes policy
  in Britain 12
  in Germany 30
  solidaristic xiii
income inequalities 1
  in Britain 3
  in Germany 45
  and growth performance 19
  and the tax system 19
indicative planning 49
  see also economic planning
industrial capital
  in Italy 75
Industrial Development and Reorganization Law
  in Portugal 127
industrial districts
  in Italy 97
industrial policy 65, 84, 112
Industrial Reconstruction Programme 1984
  in Spain 140
industrial relations
  in Britain 8, 9, 11, 14, 17, 21
  in Belgium 115
  in Germany 39
Industrial Relations Act 1972 11
Industrial Training Boards 15
industrial transformation
  in Scandinavia 149
Industrial unions
  in Germany 39
  innovative activity 4
industrialization 126, 134
  forced 178
  in Slovakia 195
industry 11, 33, 77, 78, 109, 112, 114, 131, 135, 137, 138, 139, 148, 154, 155, 171, 178, 180, 182, 183, 185, 188, 201, 202, 205
  British 9
  coal industry 33, 102, 104, 115, 193,
  Czechoslovakian 178
  East German 34, 35
  electricity 13, 17, 84
  French 50, 54, 58, 64, 65, 66
  German 27, 28, 38, 40, 41
  Hungarian 178
  links with banks 41
  motor vehicle 66
  nationalized 10, 17, 18
  Portuguese 127
  sectoral share of employment 63, 85, 155
  sectoral share of value added 63, 85, 155
  state owned 82, 83, 96
  steel 75, 76
  water 17
inflation xiii, xiv, xv,
  in Belgium and Netherlands 116, 117, 118
  in Britain 2, 3, 10, 14, 15, 60

inflation *continued*
  comparative 60, 61
  global 58
  hyperinflation in Hungary 181
  imported 43
  in Czech Republic 178, 194
  in France 50, 51, 60, 61, 62, 72n
  in Germany 26, 27, 30, 31, 34, 40, 60
  in Italy 60, 80, 87–90, 91, 92
  in Poland and Hungary 178, 191
  in Portugal 135
  in Scandinavia 152–3, 164
  in Spain 128, 129, 137, 139, 143
  of asset prices in Sweden 168
  targets 14
inflationary expectations 61, 85, 89, 91
INI (*Instituto Nacional de Industría*) 127, 141
INSEE 50, 64
insider-outsider model 70, 87
interest rates xv, 14, 34, 61, 62, 89, 91, 117, 118, 153, 154, 162, 164, 173
international business
  and Scandinavia 157–60
international capital movements 102, 106
international debt
  and Eastern Europe 187
  in Hungary 190
  in Poland 188
  via Western credits
international trade 55
  and Scandinavia 156–7
international financial system 62
Investment Privatization Funds 199
Ireland xii, 61
  and convergence 143
IRI (*Istituto per la Ricostruzione Industriale*) 76, 82, 83, 127
Iron curtain 179
Islam S. 193
ISTAT 78, 79, 81, 92, 98n
Italy xii, xiii, 51, 54, 60, 61, 64, 72, 142
  and emigration 78–9
  and state ownership 76
  and unemployment 87
  exit from ERM 85
  performance in the 1970s 85
  sectoral shares of employment and value added 63, 78, 85
  'Third Italy' 65
  turns left 84

Jackman R. 19
James H. 38
Japan 6, 25, 40, 54, 56, 59, 68, 72, 93, 140, 157, 196
Jasinski P. 190, 196, 197
Job contracts
  short-term 141, 144
Johansen H. C. 149, 169
Johnson P. 19
joint stock companies
  in Germany, the UK and the US 41

Kaplan J. J. 83
Kaser M. C. 203
Katz L. 46
Katzenstein P. J. 31, 33, 106
Kay J. 18
Keesing F. A. G. 107
Kennedy P. 144
Kennedy Round
  of GATT 56
Kervyn de Lettenhove A. 114
Keynes J.M. 163
Keynesian
  economic orthodoxy 10
  era 12, 14
  policies 29
Keynesianism
  in Scandinavia 163, 164, 166
Khruschev
  and catching the West 184
Kindleberger C. P. 109
Klaus Vaclav 194
Klodt H. 33
Knudsen T. 171
Koedijk K. 18, 19
Kolankiewicz G. 189, 190
Konsolidacni Banka 201
Korean War 51
Kormendi R. C. 10
Kornai J. 202
Korpi W. 112
kredittsosialisme 163
Kremers J. 18, 19, 116
Krengel R. 27
Kurgan-van Hentenryk F. 109

Labour administration 11
Labour government xiv
Labour market
  deregulation 45
  female participation rates 45, 79, 87, 118
  in France 68–71
  in Italy 87
  in Netherlands 113, 119
  in Scandinavia 168–70
  male participation rates 169
  rigidity 68–9, 71, 88, 143, 170
labour costs 88, 109, 112, 113, 117
  unit labour costs
    in Czech Republic and Slovakia 201
    in Germany 30
    in Italy 79, 94
    in Spain 141
    in Portugal 141

Lains P. 141, 142
Lamfalussy A. 111
Lancaster K. 39
Land reform
  in Czechoslovakia 180
  in Hungary 180–1
  in Poland 180
Landau Z. 179, 180, 184, 185
large firms
  impact on employment and tax in Sweden 160
Larsson M. 168
Latin America 125
Lavigne M. 177
Lawson boom 17
Layard R. 18, 19
Lee W. R. 204
Leite A. P. N. 138
Leonard J. 118
Levine R. 53
Lewis J. 136
Lewis P. G. 189, 190
liberalization 28, 91, 95, 115, 134, 143
  economic xiii,
  financial xiii, 67
  in Scandinavia 165
  of capital markets 151, 164
  of capital movements 91
  of trade and payments xiii, 5, 29, 56, 76, 80
  political 129
Lieberman S. 125, 137
Lindahl E. 166
Lira
  and the ERM 44
  appreciation 91
  depreciation/devaluation 85, 90
  within the ERM 91, 93
Lisbon Spring 134
Litván G. 205n
Lomax B. 205n
Lombard M. 61
Lombardy 95
London 67
Lundberg E. 166
Lutfalla M. 51
Lutz V. 49, 52
Luxembourg 72n, 102, 106
Lynch F. 50

Maastricht Treaty 62, 93, 142
  and Danish referendum 93, 172
Maastricht criteria 37, 67, 94, 139
Machado D. 130
Machines-Bull 65
Mackenzie L. 129
macroeconomic instability 52
macroeconomic policy 14, 17, 21, 61, 107, 139, 163
  in Germany 25, 30, 32
  objectives and constraints 10–11,
  snapshots of 11,
  stabilization 28
macro-indicators
  Italy 77, 86
Maddison A. 7, 8, 25, 48, 52, 53, 57, 60, 72, 77, 98n, 103, 132
Madrid 145
Malinvaud E. 53, 59
Maizels A. 81
management failure 8–9
managers
  educational background 8, 18
manufacturing 6, 35, 37, 38, 40
  activity 97
  and employment 105, 113, 160
  and investment 50
  British 6, 7, 15, 17, 32, 40
  employment share 38, 39
  exports 54
  in Denmark 154
  in France 7
  in Italy 75, 76, 79, 80, 81, 85, 86, 92, 96
  in Japan 7
  in Slovakia 200
  in Spain 129, 134, 139
  in Sweden 156
  in US 7
  in West Germany 32, 33, 39, 40, 41, 42
    manufacturing profit share 31,
    manufacturing profit rate 36
    manufacturing capital stock 36
  see also productivity
Marglin S. A. 29
market discipline 15,
Marshall Aid 27, 110, 125
  and Spain 125, 128
  in Belgium 109
  in France and the UK 49
  in Italy 75
  in Netherlands 109
  in Scandinavia 149
  rejected by Czechoslovakia 181
  rejected by Hungary 182
Marshall Plan 28
Martins F. 125
Martins J. 69, 133
Mason G. 40
Mata E. 130
Mattei 76
Mattioli 76
Mayer C. 35, 37, 41
Mayhew K. 18
mechanization
  in agriculture 63, 64, 133

MTFS (Medium Term Financial Strategy) 14
Mediterranean basin 125
Meguire P. C. 10
Mendershausen H. 38
Menichella 76
Metcalf D. 15
Mezzogiorno 25, 35, 95–6
Michalet C. A. 58
Micossi S. 89
microeconomic policy
  snapshots of 12
  changes in 15
Middleton R. 15
migration 78, 87, 133, 135
  of business and loss of tax revenue 159
Milward A. S. 81, 11, 115
miners' dispute 1973 11
mining industry 13
Ministry of Finance 58
Mistral J. 56
Mitterrand
  experiment xv, 61
Mittelstädt A. 120
mixed economy
  in Sweden 163
modernization xiii
Moncloa pacts 137
monetary integration
  cost of 62
monetary policy xv, 30, 31, 32, 43, 44, 51, 60, 71, 90, 118, 193
  and real interest rates 61, 117
  and stable exchange rates 107
  tight 71
monetary union 72, 106
  in EC 43
  in Germany 44
Montedison 96
Moravia 178, 179
Morris D. 13
Mortara A. 76
Moscow 181
Mozambique 134
multinationals 106, 114
Myant M. 179, 181, 184, 185, 186, 187, 189, 191, 194, 195, 199, 201, 203, 205n
Myhrman J. 157
Myrdal G. 166

Nagy Imre 183
NAIRU
  and the EU 70
  in Britain and Germany 19
  in Germany 29
  and wage differentials 19
Nardozzi G. 91
national champions 9, 12, 21, 65, 84, 115
National Curriculum 15
National debt
  in Scandinavia 153
  see also Public debt
National Investment funds 197
National Property Fund
  in Czech republic 199
  in Slovakia 199
nationalized industry
  and investment 10, 17
  and employment 18
  and productivity 18
nationalization
  in Czechoslovakia 181
  in Eastern Europe 179
  in France 65
  in Hungary 182
  in Poland
  problems of 12–3
Naples
  and Alfa Sud 96
NATO xiv, 173, 175n, 193, 195
Naylon J. 127, 132
Nazi Germany 178
Nestlé 199
Netherlands xiii, 56, 87, 102, 106, 120, 158
  and war damage 110
  and world depression 103
  Central Bank 117
  growth in 103–4
  sectoral employment share 105
  see also Holland
neutrality
  of Sweden 166, 173
neo-liberal agenda 139, 141
neo-liberalism 163
negative value added 205
Net Material Product 177
Neumann M. 32
New Course 183
New Industrial Policy 134, 136
New Right xv
Newbery D. M. 13, 18,
Newberry D. 196
Nguyen D-T 27, 114
Nickell S. 19
Norway xii, xiii, 148, 193
  and financial crisis 165
  and the EC/EU 172
  North Sea oil and gas 151, 153, 155
  dualistic structure 155
  low energy costs 164
  major economic activities 155–6
  sectoral shares of employment and value added 155
  trading partners 157
Nordic Council 174
Nordic Ministry Board 174
Nordic Nuclear Free Zone 175n

Nötel R. 180
Novara 97
NUM (National Union of Mineworkers) 13
Nuti D. 97
Nunes A. 130
NVQs (National Vocational Qualifications) 15

Oakey R. 204
OECD (Organization for Economic Co-operation and Development) xii, xiii, 2, 3, 5, 10, 16, 17, 31, 39, 48, 53, 56, 57, 58, 59, 60, 63, 68, 69, 86, 87, 93, 94, 97, 98n, 105, 127, 139, 156, 160, 161, 162, 170, 173, 187, 193, 194, 195, 204
OEEC (Organization for European Economic Co-operation) 56, 76, 80, 127, 129
Ohlin B. 166
oil and natural gas
  in Norway 151, 153, 155
oil price increases 58, 136, 141, 152
oil shocks 87, 88, 92, 116, 117, 118, 151, 153, 204
  and Eastern Europe 181
Olsson U. 157, 159
O'Mahony M. 5, 7, 9, 18, 32, 40
OPEC 153
open sector difficulties 116
opening of the economy 55, 56
  and FDI 58
  and the supply side 58
openness
  in Denmark 156
  in Netherlands and Belgium 104
  in Norway 156
  in Portugal 138
  in Sweden 156
Opus Dei 129
organized crime 96
Osti G. L. 82
Oulton N. 4, 17
Owen G. 18

Paci P. 97
Pacific Rim xvi
parental leave 169–70
Paris 67
participation rates in labour force
  in the EU 68
  in Scandinavia 168–9
  male participation rates 169
  women's 45, 79, 87, 118
Pasture P. T. 111
Patat J. P. 51
Peasant Party
  in Poland 193
  and Socialist Party coalition 198
peasantry in Spain 126
Pedersen T. 158, 159
Pechiney 65
Peronist Argentina 126
Petit P. 49, 117
peseta
  in ERM 143
Peugeot-Citroën PSA 66
Philips 106
Philip-Morris 199
Pilsen riots 183
Pitcher A. M. 130, 135
Podbielski G. 79, 84
Poland xiii, xv, 177, 183
  martial law 189, 191
  reparations problems 179–80
  revising plan targets 184
  servicing of debt 189
  shifts westward 179
  war devastation 179
Pollitt M. G. 18
Popular front 75
population
  growth in Belgium and Netherlands 103, 118
  size in Scandinavia 148
Portugal xii, xiii, 124, 125, 127, 130
  democratization 136
  divesting itself of Empire 138
  national plans 134
  retaining colonies 135
Portuguese
  balance of payments 130, 138
  economic space 125
  industry 127
post-war boom xiii
post-war consensus 14, 95
post-war reconstruction
  in Britain 11
  in Germany 27
  in Belgium and the Netherlands 108–9
post-war recovery
  in Eastern Europe 178, 179–82
  of France 49
  of Italy 75
  of Scandinavia 149
post-war stagnation
  in Spain 128
pound
  and the ERM 44
Prais S. 9, 40, 72n
Pratten C. F. 9
Preston P. 127
Price H. B. 49
Price S. 10, 14
private sector growth 196
privatization 15, 37, 66, 95, 120, 141, 143
  and sleaze 199–200
  in Eastern Europe 195–200
  in Scandinavia 164
  methods of 196–7

productivity xiii, xv, 1, 37
comparative levels 54, 156
gap xiii, 6, 7, 9, 18, 40
gains xv, 72, 89, 94, 107
growth / rising 13, 15, 17, 21, 55, 80, 149
in agriculture 63, 64, 79
in Belgium and Netherlands 104, 107, 111, 112, 114, 119
in industry 64, 79
in manufacturing 6, 17, 18, 34, 38
in Scandinavia 150, 162
in services 98n
in UK 8,
of labour 7, 53, 77, 87, 132, 204
of capital 204
performance in West Germany and UK 32–3, 40
and privatizations 17
profit
rates xv
share 31
profitability
in Germany 36, 37
protectionism xv, 108, 126, 134
protective devices 82
Prussia 178
PSBR targets 14,
PSD (Portuguese Social Democrats) 138
PSI (Italian Socialist Party) 84, 91, 93
PSOE (Spanish Socialist Party) 138
public debt 37
in Belgium 102, 118, 119, 120
in Italy 85, 94
public finance
in Belgium 107
in France 67–8
in Spain 144
public sector employment
in Scandinavia 161–2
public spending
in Scandinavia 161
public v. private sector
in Scandinavia 160–3

qualifications
in Britain and Germany 5,
vocational 18

R&D spending
in Britain 5
Radice E. A. 180
Ranci P. 92
Ranieri R. 76, 81, 83
Reagonomics 164
real wages
in Eastern Europe 183
in Poland 193
recessions
and the Iberian economies 136, 141, 142
in Britain 14,
in Germany 25, 35, 37
in Europe 44
in Poland 193
in Sweden 162
referenda
in Denmark 93, 172
in Norway and Sweden 173–4
Redondo N. 139
Rees R. 18
regional convergence 35
regional
backwardness 35
growth in Europe 7
regional problems
in Belgium 120
in Iberia 145
of East Germany 35
regulation
in the labour market 70
regulatory regime
RPI – X 18
Rehn-Meidner commitments 166
re-training
in Sweden and Norway 151
reunification
see German reunification
Rey G. M. 79, 98, 98n
Rhône-Poulenc 65
Richardson R. 13
Robinson P. 18
Rodó L. L. 129
Rodrik D. 10
Rollo F. 134
Romero F. 77
Rossi N. 77, 98n
Rothstein B. 171
Rotterdam 113
Rowthorn R. 39
Rubio M. R. 129
Rudcenko S. 125, 133, 137, 140
Russia xiii, 178
and Sweden 157
Ruthenia 178
Rutland P. 191

Sachs J. 55
Sala-i-Martin X. 35
Salazar xii, 124, 125, 126, 134, 142
and contained industrialization 136
and industrial development 127, 131
Salituro B. 85
Salmon K. 140
Sanders D. 10, 14
Saraceno P. 76, 96
Sassoon D. 88

St Gobain 65
Scandinavia xii, xiii, 25, 45, 69, 106, 148
 and financial crises 149, 151
 and oil price shocks 151
 and patterns of energy use 152
Scandinavian model 149
Schleiminger G. 83
Schor J. B. 30
Sejersted F. 155, 163, 171
Sen A. K. 20
services 34. 38, 64, 87, 95, 96, 98n, 113, 116, 143, 156, 161, 165, 167, 171, 177n, 182
 financial 66
 marketed 6, 7
 non-marketed 5
 politicization of public 106
 sectoral share of employment 39, 63, 66, 78, 85, 105, 155
 sectoral share of value added 63, 85, 155
 share of total output 66
 traded and non-traded 66
Seville 141
Sforzi F. 97
shareholding
 in Germany, the UK and the US 41
Sheahan J. 49
Shell 106
shipping and shipbuilding
 in Norway 155
shock therapy 178, 193, 205
Shonfield A. 41, 52, 84
shop-stewards 9, 15
Sicily 96
Sicsic P. 50, 72n
Sik O. 185
Singh A. 8
Single Market 44
Single Currency 94
Sinigaglia 76
size distribution
 of establishments 64
 of enterprises 160
Sjögren H. 168
skill
 formation 1, 19
 marketable 40
 of labour force 15, 18
Slovakia xii, 177, 179, 191, 195
slowdown xv, 18
 in Belgium and the Netherlands 116
 in Britain 16
 in France 58, 62, 64
 in Iberia 124, 143
 in Scandinavia 150, 167
 in Eastern Europe 189, 203
Sluyterman K. E. 106
Small co-operatives 191
small firms 128
 in Third Italy 97, 99n
SMEs (Small and Medium-sized Enterprises)
 in Denmark 159
 in Germany 41
 in Norway 155
SMIG/SMIC 69
Sneessens H. R. 116
Soares Mario
 and democratisation 136
Sobell V. 185
Social Contract 11, 15
Social Democracy
 in Sweden 163, 164, 166
Social Democratic Party
 and Keynesianism 30
 in Sweden 165, 170
social partnership xiv
social programming 115
socialist failure 202
soft budget constraints 202
Solchaga C. 140
Solidarity
 in Poland 189, 190, 205n
Soskice D. 9, 32, 37, 40, 42
South Asia 157
Soviet bloc 55
Soviet Union 189
Soviet hegemony 184
Spain xii, xiii, 124, 125, 126
 and Eisenhower administration 129
 and two speed Europe 144
 attitudes to industrialization 127
 democratization 136
 'Prussians of the South' 144
 transition to industrial economy 131
 Year of Spain 141
Spaventa L. 88, 89, 90
Spulber N. 178
stabilization package 51
 Plan of 1959 128
stagflation 58
Stalin
 death of 183
Stalinist
 model xii, 180, 183, 184
 system 179
state involvement
 in Portuguese economy 127
 in Scandinavia 148, 165–6
state owned industry
 and political influence 82
 and private firms 83
 in the Mezzogiorno 96
 role in infrastructure 83
State Property Agency
 in Hungary 198
Stevenson A. 83
Steedman H. 5, 9, 40, 41
Stockholm School 166

stop-go policies
  and Britain 11
  in France 51
  in Italy 88
Stout D. K. 13
subsidies to construction
  country comparisons 168
Suárez Adolfo
  and democratization 136
sunset and sunrise industries 33
supervisory boards
  composition of 41
supply of labour
  in West Germany 28, 29
supply side policies 9, 66, 109
Swain G. 190, 205n
Swain N. 181, 182, 183, 184, 185, 186, 187, 204, 205n, 206n
Sweden xii, xiii, 7, 19, 56, 148, 193
  and financial crisis 154, 165
  and return of left 154
  major economic activities 156
  trading partners 157
Swedish model xii, 149
  end of 165–8
  definitions of 165–71
Switzerland 3, 7, 78, 79
Symonds J. 14

Takla L. 199
Tanzi V. 10
tax policy
  in Sweden 170
taxation 13, 15, 19, 66, 95
tariff barriers 56, 80, 110, 132
technobureaucracy 49, 71
technological progress
  and growth 53
technology
  diffusion of xiii, 10
  transfer 6
Templeman D. C. 88, 89
Thatcher 1, 14,
  experiment 1, 15, 19
Thatcherism 1, 14, 15, 66, 164
Thatcherite xiii
Theeuwes J. 119
'Third Italy' 96–8
  and political elites 98
Thompson-Brandt 65
Tinbergen J. 110
Tomaszewski T. 179, 180, 184, 185
Topp N. H. 175n
TFP (Total Factor Productivity)
  and privatization 17
  growth of 18, 21, 52, 55, 77
  in Britain and Europe 5–8, 16
  in Eastern Europe 203
  in Scandinavia 150
tourism 133
Tracy M. 63, 64
trade barriers
  and Benelux 102
trade offs
  and policy objectives 21
trade unions 89
  and rigidity 69
  and restraint 88
  bargaining power 14
  density 69, 72n
  in the public sector 72n
  in Czech Republic 194
  membership 15
  militancy 11, 19, 80
  reforms 14
  veto 14
trade unionism
  decentralized 9
  multiple 15
transition
  to market economy xiv, 191
  process in Iberia 137–8, 139, 145
Trau F. 89
Treaty of Paris 71
Treaty of Rome xiii, 56, 64, 71, 79, 129
Trianon Peace Treaty 178
Trigilia C. 95, 96

UK xiii, 6, 8, 18, 19, 20, 27, 39, 41, 44, 45, 49, 51, 54, 56, 60, 61, 64, 68, 69, 85, 102, 158, 159, 160, 172, 196
  skewness of growth rate 17
  and Denmark 157
Ullastres A. 129
unemployment xiii, xv, 205
  in Belgium and the Netherlands 102, 109, 111, 117, 118, 119, 120
  in Britain 2, 3, 10, 11, 14, 15, 19
  in Czech Republic 194
  in Denmark 151–2
  in France 58, 59, 61, 62, 68
  in Germany xiv, 25, 29, 37, 45
  in Hungary 194
  in Iberia 137, 144
  in Italy 76, 77, 79, 85, 86 87, 94, 96, 98n
  in Norway 151–2
  in Poland and Hungary 191
  in Portugal 136
  in Spain 138
  in Sweden 151–2, 162, 168
unemployment benefit 11
Unilever 106
unionization 97
unions
  see trade unions
United Nations 125, 128
United States 4, 6, 7

UNRRA (United Nations Relief and Rehabilitation Administration) 75, 180
Urbanization 78, 79, 84
US xiii, xvi, 25, 27, 39, 41, 42, 49, 53, 54, 55, 56, 59, 64, 68, 91, 116, 118, 128, 132, 159, 203
  aid to Portugal 125
  aid to Spain 129
  decline of dominance 30
  dominance in high tech 65
  forces 108
  hegemony 71
  in Europe 173
  occupation 38, 40
USSR xii, xiii, 172, 179, 189, 203. 205n

Valerio N. 130
van Ark B. 63, 112
Van Audenrode M. 118
van Bochove C. A. 110
van de Klundert T. 27, 29
Van den Broeke C. 115
Van Den Bulcke D. 106
Van den Houte P. 114
van der Eng P. 110
Van der Wee H. 114
Van Meershaeghe M. A. G. 114
Van Meerten M. A. 107, 109, 111
Van Rijckeghem W. 111, 114
van Shaik A. 27, 29, 108
van Sorge 110
van Waterschoot D. 115
Van Zanden 108, 112, 117
Venturini A. 87, 92
Verspagen B. 53
Veugelers R. 114
Vichy regime 49
Vickers J. 10, 18
Vietnam 51
Vietnam War 152
Vignuzzi 76
Visegrad countries xii, xiii
Visegrad Four 201
  economic indicators 192, 205
vocational training 18, 40, 168
Volkswagen 144
Volkswagen Skoda 199
voucher privatization 197, 199
Vuchelen J. 106

wage
  accord 110, 112
  explosions and inflationary pressure 30
  moderation 119, 120, 140
wage indexation
  in Belgium 107, 118
  in Italy 91, 98n
  in the Netherlands 113
  in Czech Republic 194
wage policy
  and egalitarianism 167
  solidaristic 166, 167, 170
wage supplementation fund 92
Wagner K. 5, 8, 9, 18, 32, 40
Wallonia 115
Warner A. 55
Warta J. 56
Webb S. 19
Weimar Republic 37, 38
  and union fragmentation 39
welfare capitalism 164
Wells S. J. 39
Wellink A. H. E. M. 118
Werner Plan 43
West Germany
  see Germany
Western Europe 25, 48, 53, 55, 77, 79, 80, 89, 124, 126, 134, 153, 154, 157, 170, 173, 179, 203
Wightman G. 191
Williams A. 136
Winiecki J. 204
Workers' Statute 88, 97, 140
Wolf M. 94
World Bank 129, 190
World War I
  aftermath of 178
Wrenn-Lewis S. 16
Wyplosz C. 50, 72n

Yarrow G. 10
YTS (Youth Training Scheme) 15
youth unemployment 15, 87
Yugoslavia 161, 179, 202

Zamagni V. 75
Zeitlin J. 98

www.ingramcontent.com/pod-product-compliance
Ingram Content Group UK Ltd.
Pitfield, Milton Keynes, MK11 3LW, UK
UKHW020426250726
13967UKWH00007B/2832

9 780333 653258